EVOLUTIONARY NATURALISM

EVOLUTIONARY NATURALISM

Selected essays

Michael Ruse

London and New York

First published 1995
by Routledge
11 New Fetter Lane, London EC4P 4EE

Simultaneously published in the USA and Canada
by Routledge
29 West 35th Street, New York NY 10001

© 1995 Michael Ruse

Typeset in Linotron Garamond by
Intype, London

Printed and bound in Great Britain by
Biddles Ltd, Guildford and King's Lynn

British Library Cataloguing in Publication Data
A catalogue record for this book is available from the British Library.

Library of Congress Cataloging in Publication Data
Ruse, Michael
Evolutionary naturalism: selected essays/Michael Ruse.
p.   cm.
Includes bibliographical references (p.   ) and index.
1. Evolution.   2. Evolution (Biology)   3. Ethics. Evolutionary
I. Title
B818.R87 1994
146'.7—dc 20   94–18435

ISBN 0–415–08997–2

A tous mes amis français,
en particulier
Jean Gayon et Jacques Michaux

CONTENTS

CONTENTS

Part III Evolutionary ethics

ACKNOWLEDGEMENTS

As always, my debts are numerous, especially since this is a collection produced over a number of years. David Hull has been my chief philosophical friend and critic, Robert J. Richards plays the same role for history, and Edward O. Wilson in biology completes the triumvirate. A major influence on my thinking about naturalism has come through my friendship with the theologian Philip Hefner. And I simply must say that Richard Stoneman of Routledge has been my ideal of the academic book editor.

Elliott Sober, with whom I have discussed (and differed about) naturalism over a number of years, kindly read my Introduction. He feels, perhaps with justification, that I underestimate the extent to which Marx certainly saw himself engaged as a naturalistic philosopher. I still feel, nevertheless, that the deep neo-Hegelian strain in Marx's philosophy, that which is the largest single factor behind the special place given to our own species, owes more to the Western religious tradition than it does to science.

The paper on punctuated equilibria was given, in a very incomplete form, at a conference in Naples, in the summer of 1993. Philip Kitcher gave me some useful suggestions for its improvement, and it is entirely his fault that it is now the length that it is. In a somewhat different way, I owe an even greater debt to my support staff at Guelph, specifically my secretary Linda Jenkins and my research assistant Moira Howes. The latter did a huge amount of work on the punctuated equilibria paper.

Finally, let me explain that a major reason for my dedication was that I was able to complete this collection while on leave, attached to the Laboratory of Vertebrate Palaeontology at the University of Montpellier in the South of France. As a philosopher of biology, one of the wonderful things in my life has been the way in which my subject has widened from the narrow concerns of a small group of North Americans, to something which is truly global. For me, intellectually and socially, this has been pure gain.

I have imposed a uniform style on the articles and brought the references together in one bibliography. Articles 2 and 3 have been augmented somewhat, Article 5 first appeared in French, and Article 9 has been written especially for this volume. The other articles have been left otherwise untouched. I am obliged to the original publishers for permission to reproduce. 'Ought philosophers consider scientific discovery? A Darwinian case-study', from T. Nickles (ed.) *Scientific Discovery: Case Studies*, Dordrecht: Reidel, 1980, 131–49; 'Are pictures really necessary? The case of Sewall Wright's "adaptive landscape"', from A. Fine, M. Forbes and L. Wessels (eds) *PSA 1990*, East Lansing, Mich.: Philosophy of Science Association, 1991, 63–77; 'Controversy in palaeontology: The theory of punctuated equilibria' from P. Machamer (ed.), *Scientific Controversy*, Pittsburgh: University of Pittsburgh Press, 1995; 'A threefold parallelism for our time? Progressive development in society, science, and the organic world' from M. Nitecki and D. Nitecki (eds), *History and Evolution*, Albany, NY: State University of New York University Press, 1992, 149–78; 'Scientific change is a family affair!', from J. Gayon (ed.), *Filiation*, Paris: to be published in 1995; 'The view from somewhere: A critical defence of evolutionary epistemology', from K. Hahlweg and C. A. Hooker (eds), *Issues in Evolutionary Epistemology*, Albany, NY: State University of New York University Press, 1989, 185–228; 'Evolutionary biology and cultural values: Is it irremediably corrupt?', from R. Ware and M. Matthen (eds), *Science and Values*, Alberta: University of Alberta Press, 1994; 'Evolution and ethics: The sociobiological approach', from L. Pojman (ed.), *Ethical Theory* (second edn), Belmont, Calif.: Wadsworth, 1994.

INTRODUCTION

If I say that I have taken some care with the title for the collection now before you, this pretentious-sounding claim should not be taken to mean that others do not take care with what they call their books, or that this is a new departure for me. Indeed, I am rather proud of one or two of my earlier titles. What I mean is that you should take seriously the thought that, while this is a collection of articles written independently of each other over the past decade, it is nevertheless a collection with a strong underlying connecting theme, a philosophy which I call 'evolutionary naturalism'.

I hasten to add that, although I claim this philosophy for myself, I do not want to say that I alone am an evolutionary naturalist. There are others who are treading a path similar to my own, and I have certainly learnt much from them. But as is the nature of these things, although many may be going in the same direction, it would be a mistake to think that the position of any one person was identical to that of any other. Let me therefore spend this introduction telling you exactly what I mean by and hope for my philosophy, and what various roles must be played by my articles.

I will begin with 'naturalism'. This is a term much used today. Hence be warned that, although I hope you will not think me an imposter in my usage, I am more interested in giving it a meaning for myself than in finding some generally acceptable dictionary definition. For me, 'naturalism' is something to do with nature, meaning the world of experience, and since the most powerfully successful approach that we have to this world – the only true approach that we have towards real understanding – is the method of science, I take a naturalist to be someone who would understand through the methods and results of science.

1

What does this mean exactly? I believe that the chief distinguishing feature of the world, that which makes science possible, is the fact that things do not happen in a random, higgledy-piggledy manner. Rather, they take place in a regular fashion according to 'laws', that is according to universal necessities which are, however, both empirical and contingent, in the sense that their denial is not contradictory. I appreciate that at some level this belief in the ubiquity of law is a metaphysical commitment, at least in the sense that it is not some thing that I think can be proven or disproven definitively by experience. It is rather the condition of experience, scientific experience that is. But I do not think that it is irrational or unreasonable, or even an act of faith (if by 'faith' you mean believing completely beyond or against the evidence). I believe that science works and that, inasmuch as it works, it justifies the belief in unbroken law. If science simply broke down, then that would be a time to reconsider; but since no break has occurred, that time has not yet come.

Naturalism for me, therefore, means trying to understand through empirical law. This means that you have got to appeal to experience – you cannot just think things through *a priori* – and, without wanting to make this sound altogether too much like the Thirty-nine Articles, I believe that there are certain general rules which people have discovered and perfected to ensure that the understanding through law is as reliable and solid as is possible to fallible mortals, given the scope and limits of what is known at that time. Or, not to mince words although we shall certainly have to dissect them, rules which seem to show us that we are on the right road to truth, meaning a correct understanding of the way that the world truly is.

Technically, philosophers usually refer to these rules as manifesting various 'epistemic values', meaning that they promote certain desirable attributes of science – attributes which have been found through experience to provide the most reliable and forward-looking kinds of science. Noteworthy among such values are internal consistency, coherence with other parts of science, predictive fertility simplicity and – a particular favourite of mine – what the nineteenth-century English historian and philosopher of science William Whewell referred to as a 'consilience of inductions'. By this is meant the attempt to explain as much as possible by as little as possible, especially explanation involving the unification of two or more hitherto disparate areas of understanding beneath one or a few high-level hypotheses or established laws. Coincidences tend not to happen by chance but are the mark of underlying reality.

These then are the sort of things I am talking about when I talk about 'naturalism'. I rush at once to forestall a misconception and to distinguish two things that I do not mean by the term. In thus promoting science, I do not mean to belittle art or literature or other areas of human achievement. There is nothing which moves me as much as the Bach *Passions*, with the possible exception of the late Mozart operas; and while I confess to a blind spot about poetry, all my friends will agree that I am slightly unbalanced in my enthusiasm for Dickens and Trollope. I maintain, nevertheless, that science gives us a dimension of objective understanding in a way that other areas of human achievement do not. At the same time, I think that great science has a beauty that is of a type with great artistic achievement; and, as you will learn, I believe that there is, for all of the objectivity, a deep and irreducible human element to science.

Distinguishing what I do not mean by 'naturalism', the first thing which I do not mean is 'scientism'. By this, I mean the belief that science can solve all problems, intellectual and technical: that no matter how opaque or bad things may seem, the proper application of a little scientific method will soon put things to rights. Such a claim strikes me as misconceived to the point of dangerous falsity. I believe that science can be a force for bad, just as it can be a force for good; that there is certainly no reason to think that all theoretical problems are soluble, even if in theory then not in practice; and that the future of our species, notwithstanding what I shall have to say in the course of this collection, is by no means guaranteed. And if and when things do come crashing down, science will have had a hand, directly through weapons of self-destruction, or indirectly, through ensuring that there are too many people with too little to eat.

The second thing which I do not mean by 'naturalism' is 'materialism', or at a more extreme level, 'atheism' or something like that. If materialism means that there is only one substance, I confess that I frankly do not know that this is true. I can see that there are major problems with Cartesian dualism, but I am not sure that it is much more convincing to say that thoughts are no more than the motions of molecules – although I appreciate that the motions of molecules are important here. More generally, in a world of forces and electrons and the like, I have a suspicion that materialists have to stretch their term to a point of triviality.

Again, although I have seen it stated flatly that 'Crucial to metaphysical naturalism, of course, is the view that there is no such person as the God of traditional theism' (Plantinga 1991: 30), I can only say that such a denial is not crucial to my naturalism. You would be unable to subscribe to my naturalism and to the literal truth of Noah's Flood, or indeed to any of the biblical miracles interpreted as violations of law. But St Augustine warned us against taking the Bible too literally, and you do not get much more traditional than he. And in our own time many sincere believers are repelled at the thought that Jesus of Nazareth be equated with a travelling medicine man or conjurer. Salvation does not rely on circus tricks.

As it happens, I am not desperately keen on traditional Christianity, and I do believe that my position causes some tensions with this view. But I suspect that a traditional Christian could work through these difficulties: I have friends, the depth of whose commitment could be questioned by none, who assure me that (like most non-believers) I vastly over-estimate the obstacles to faith. In any case, for me the real problems with theism lie in other directions, notably the problem of evil. With respect to the ultimate questions, I am a sceptic, meaning that I simply do not know.

Returning now to the positive side of my thinking, you may be wondering why I am bothering to advertise my position and why I think it worth your time to pick up a collection of my essays. After all, if by 'naturalist' I mean no more than a belief in law and an enthusiasm for scientific method, I am hardly to be distinguished from any scientist, except that when it comes to science itself they seem to want to do it and I simply seem to want to talk about it! What makes me distinctive is the fact that I am a philosopher and proud of it. I want to take science right into my discipline. This is the force of naturalism for me, and the reason why you should read on.

Again, though, I must rush to avoid a misconception. In speaking of my pride in philosophy, I am not just boasting like a school-boy. I mean that I think there are problems of philosophy worthwhile in their own right. I do not think that these are problems that can be reduced away into other disciplines. My aim, therefore, is not to push philosophy into one or more of the already existing sciences. I take pleasure in the fact that many of today's philosophers tend to take science far more seriously than we did a generation ago; but the move simply to make one's philosophy a part of biology or physics or whatever strikes me as misguided. We have our own problems, and they are not those of the biologist or the physicist. In any case, it is a mug's game to try to better the scientists in their own fields. You can never win, and you will certainly get no respect, from philosophers or from scientists.

For me, the philosopher as naturalist has two paths to tread. On the one hand, there is the question of science itself. Self-reflectively, one must ask about the nature of the thing in which one is putting so much trust. On the other hand, there are the great problems of philosophy, to which one wants to apply the approach of the naturalist. Since these divide under the general headings of epistemology and ethics – 'What can one know?', 'What should one do?' – it is perhaps best to think of three separate (although much interconnected) journeys facing the naturalist, a triad which is reflected in the divisions of this collection.

The tasks of my essays, therefore, are to show the precise ways in which I set about my programme. But let me say a few more words and, as I conclude this Introduction, show why I do not simply describe myself as a 'naturalist' but as an *evolutionary naturalist*. Beginning with the first task, my aim is to understand science itself – a crucial part of my programme if I am to use science to turn to philosophy. As a naturalist, what I do is look at examples of science (past and present) and at its practitioners, to see what hypotheses about the nature of science itself such examples generate, confirm, support, falsify, and whatever. In other words, what I do is treat science and its history as my subject matter, just as (for example) a zoologist treats animals as his or her subject matter. I am not interested in buffaloes, but in what scientists have said about buffaloes. The hairy beasts of the plain do not excite me, but what has been said about these beasts, and why and by whom, does.

As a naturalist, I can make judgements of value. Where people have identified something as good science, that is where I find my marks of what makes for good science, and where they have not, that is where I do not. Nevertheless, in the language of the philosophers, I do agree that whereas the traditional philosopher of science tends to be *prescriptive*, I tend to be *descriptive*. Take the Popperian claim that real science is 'falsifiable', meaning that it lays itself open to check and refutation. For Karl Popper, this is an *a priori* principle of rationality. For me, it is at best something to be discovered (or not) in the realm of what people have come to cherish as the real success stories of science.

Because I am an empiricist and thus aiming first at description, I cannot simply take the whole of science as my domain; however much I may hope that what I have to say will apply throughout science. I, like all scientists, have to work on limited problems. I have to look at particular episodes in the history of science, or in its present. And by 'look', I mean 'look in detail', for it is pointless just to skim across the surface. It is this, then, that you will find in the first part of my collection: case studies, aimed at teasing out significant aspects of science itself. Ever an optimist, I hope that these studies will excite you in their own right; but whether they do or not, I am quite unapologetic about their detail, for this is what serious naturalism is all about. It is not a short cut past hard work.

My chosen area of science is evolutionary biology. At this point, I do not recommend it because it is a science superior to all others. Indeed, you will glean from later essays in my collection that evolutionary biology has troubles of its own, especially when one starts to talk about 'greater' and 'lesser' sciences. But, appreciating that in theory and to a great extent in practice, any other branch of science would have done, all I will say now is that I find evolutionary biology very interesting and that (perhaps because it is not the grandest of sciences) it does help me to draw out some points which I think important. An importance which will grow as we move to later sections of the collection, quite apart from claims I shall then make about the significance of evolutionary biology itself.

But there is one admission that I must make. I am keenly aware of the fact that, as I have admitted above, there is something self-reflective in what I am about. I am going to look at evolutionary theory to see if things like Popper's criterion of falsifiability are important to good science. (Actually, this is one example I will not take up in the forthcoming essays; but I could have done and have done so elsewhere.) Yet, as a naturalist, what am I going to conclude about the nature of science, unless I use some criterion like falsifiability itself? Is this not to get me hopelessly doomed to life on a never-ending circle?

All I can say is that although what I am up to is circular, I do not think that it is viciously circular. I have admitted already that I am not in the business of supplying ultimate metaphysical justifications. Rather, I am a pragmatist who thinks that the proof of the pudding is in the eating, or (to switch metaphors) nothing succeeds like success. If science seems to be falsifiable then that feeds back into the way I try to draw my conclusions, and so we go on trying to build a coherent picture. If things break down, then we have to rethink and try some alternative strategy. We have one of those well-known epistemological situations where you have to build your boat while you are already floating it. I do not take this as a weakness of my philosophy, but to its credit that it recognizes it, appreciating that the circularity is something in itself of great philosophical interest.

And before you think I am brushing over a major problem – behaving like Mr Micawber in thinking that acknowledging a difficulty is the same as solving it – remember that it was naturalism which led so many of us today to think that Popperian falsifiability is in fact rather less than the powerful tool than is claimed in *The Logic of Scientific Discovery*. Precisely because, in his *The Structure of Scientific Revolutions*, Thomas Kuhn gave example after example drawn from the history of science to show that scientists simply do not give up their theories in the face of counter-evidence, at least not in any easy fashion, falsifiability fell from favour. So there is certainly something in what I say about being able to move forward critically, despite circularities.

The second task for the philosophical naturalist takes us into the realm of epistemology. For me, it is here that evolutionary theory really comes into its own, not just as one source among many for discovering and developing philosophical claims, but as something which is (for all of its problems) of supreme importance. I really think it matters that we humans are – along with a lot of other organisms, from oak trees to AIDS – the end product of a slow natural process of evolution. In particular, I think it matters for what we know and can know that we are no more (and no less) than the result of blind forces rather than the intentional creation of a Good God, lovingly made in His image, on the Sixth Day. Or rather than the secular equivalent, which it seems to me is the hidden assumption of most non-naturalistic philosophies, including – especially including – Marxism.

This, then, is one of the main reasons why I think of myself as an *evolutionary* naturalist, or specifically in the present context as an 'evolutionary epistemologist'. I realize that in some of the more respectable philosophical circles – even those who do not rear back from naturalism – this is to put you with the lowest of the low. There is a feeling that much which passes under the name of 'evolutionary epistemology' is not just mistaken philosophy but is somehow rather seedy. The quality of argumentation is poor and the claims for success are out of proportion to the effort which has been invested.

As much of a snob as the next person, I have to admit to feeling some considerable discomfort with the movement with which I associate – especially since I am acutely aware that the criticisms have considerable merit and that some of my own earlier work has done little to improve matters. But, apart from a counter-emotion which takes pleasure in being one against many, I take comfort from the fact that we do today have a really good theory of evolution and a keen grasp of the important mechanism fuelling change – by this I mean Darwinism and its mechanism of natural selection, leading to the overwhelming significance of organic adaptation. I take comfort also from the fact that, naysayers notwithstanding, increasingly this theory is being applied in fruitful ways to the understanding of human nature.

Hence, without in any sense denying that a full naturalistic attack on epistemology will require the aid of psychology and sociology and all the other sciences which talk about human beings, I quell my elitist yearnings and try to play my role in showing how the proper application of an evolutionary approach to humankind can throw much light on key questions of epistemology. I doubt that traditional epistemologists will be satisfied with the answers; but that could be because they have the wrong questions rather than that I, and others who think as I do, have the wrong answers.

Parenthetically, given what I have just said about evolution and its mechanisms, I am keenly aware that many today severely criticize Darwinism and the central role that it gives to natural selection. To some extent, in my essays I shall defend the biological science on which I rely; but my main defence is that I have much to say (according to some, too much to say) on these topics elsewhere. In the course of the essays, however, I shall have other things to say about why many, especially my fellow philosophers, do not eagerly embrace what seems to me to be blindingly obvious. I should also say that I do fully expect to see ongoing revisions in the science on which my philosophy rests. That is the nature – and strength – of science. Inasmuch as mine is a truly naturalistic philosophy, I shall take such revision, and the consequent effects on my philosophical conclusions, as a sign of success rather than failure.

Third and finally, the philosopher as naturalist must move beyond the values inherent in science and turn to the broader question of moral and social values. And let me take an almost lugubrious pleasure in telling you that in the opinion of the average philosopher – a point where, almost uniquely, Anglo-Saxon philosophers come together with their continental counterparts – if evolutionary epistemology is thought seedy, 'evolutionary ethics' is considered positively unclean.

This was a view to which I myself long subscribed. I now think that I, like virtually every other philosopher, was completely mistaken; even though I would add, somewhat ungenerously, that those who did take seriously evolution and ethics (a group incidentally which contained many distinguished biologists) tended to be no less mistaken. Fortunately, thanks to recent advances in the science, we can now see that it is only by taking an evolutionary approach to human nature that we can hope to solve some of the most pressing questions of traditional ethics. This is a line of hope which extends also to the many pressing social questions facing us in this rapidly changing world of science and technology. We may not solve them – remember that I am no enthusiast for scientism – but without an evolutionary based ethics, we will not solve them.

Part of me would like to be able to say that I worked this all out on my own. Part of me, especially that part which is a professional scholar, rushes with dread from claims for complete originality. People like Mary Baker Eddy thought they were being original. Let me therefore say that, apart from those of my contemporaries whom I shall acknowledge as having had an immediate influence, I take pride in the fact that my evolutionary ethics is something which stands firmly in the traditions of the past. Here, as always, evolution gives us absolutely irreplaceable insights; but it is silly to pretend that nobody before Darwin knew anything about ethics. Biologists draw on their predecessors. Philosophers likewise draw on their predecessors.

Enough of my talking about what I am going to do. I want you to read on, and find out for yourself what I really do do. When you have finished, I hope you will end by agreeing with me that although I am trying to do different things in the essays of this collection, they are truly bound together by a shared philosophy: evolutionary naturalism.

Part I
CASE STUDIES

INTRODUCTION

The three papers in this section deal with three items from the history of evolutionary biology – items separated by roughly fifty-year intervals, from Darwin to the time when genetics was brought into evolutionary thought in the earlier parts of this century, and from this second time to the present day, when evolutionary studies thrive as perhaps never before. I begin with the genesis of the mechanism of natural selection, taking as my theme the different routes pursued by the two co-discoverers, Charles Darwin and Alfred Russel Wallace; I move next to the thought of the American population geneticist Sewall Wright, and the significance of his picture of an adaptive landscape; and I end with the recent palaeontological theory of 'punctuated equilibria', trying to assess the extent to which, and reasons why, it has proven controversial.

But, as stated in my Introduction, I am not interested in history just for its own sake. I want to explore and test philosophical ideas. Most immediately, I am concerned with the issues of discovery, display and dispute. Uniting this section, however, is my attempt to find a theory of scientific knowledge which captures what I believe all three of my case studies show, namely that science has both an objective side, something which tells us about a real world 'out there', and a subjective side, a reflection of the culture in which the science is formed.

The first essay, on Darwin and Wallace, was written some ten years before the others, a fact which it does show, somewhat. I do not offer it as a testament to my earlier immaturity or to the development since, but to show how someone who took very seriously both the spinning and the fabric of science, could be led to a position which wanted to bridge or to break the objective/subjective divide. I do note, however, that although I did not then have a formal or articulated general system that I was endorsing, I was sensitive to the nature and use of metaphor in science. I can certainly attest that this was one of the main things which made me sympathetic, in the years shortly after, to the 'internal realist' position of the American philosopher Hilary Putnam, which is the epistemology against which I try to place my discussion in the second essay, and which underlies my thinking at the end of the third.

I appreciate that, from a conceptual viewpoint, 'placing' is about the best I can hope for at this point. I am certainly not 'proving' my favoured philosophy. But it could be that Thomas Kuhn in his influential *Structure of Scientific Revolutions* is right, and that for most scientists most of the time, the reality is 'normal science', which means working away at problems set within an accepted overall background or 'paradigm'. As a philosophical naturalist perhaps I should be happy that I now have *my* paradigm, internal realism, and that it is thus open to me to do normal science precisely because I have an overall position, which I am using more than I am justifying.

1

OUGHT PHILOSOPHERS CONSIDER SCIENTIFIC DISCOVERY?

A Darwinian case study

My concern in this paper will be with Darwin's discovery of his theory of evolution, particularly the part centred on its mechanisms. What I want to know is whether knowledge of Darwin's route to discovery tells us something about the finished theory, say as it is found in the first edition of *The Origin of Species* (1859). Do we, as philosophers, need to know how Darwin got his theory in order to understand his theory? I take it that there is a school of philosophical thought, 'logical empiricism', that would argue that essentially a scientist's route to discovery is irrelevant to his or her finished product. A scientific theory or hypothesis is in some sense intended to be a reflection of reality. Hence, that a scientist may have got his ideas after years of painstaking fitting of the data to possible ideas, like Kepler, or in a flash through mystical contemplation of his navel, is of absolutely no concern.[1] Even if Archimedes had never taken a bath in his life, his principle would still have been the same.

I assume that it is this kind of philosophy of scientific discovery (i.e. that there can be no significant philosophy of scientific discovery) that underlies Carl Hempel's quick dismissal of discovery in his (excellent) little textbook, *Philosophy of Natural Science* (1966). A scientist may hit on an idea by the craziest of means, like Kekulé finding the benzine ring through dreaming of a snake swallowing its tail, but the 'real' science has no place for this. Were a herpetologist to complain that benzine cannot be circular because snakes do not swallow their tails, his worries would be dismissed as inappropriate. A similar philosophy seems to be held by Karl Popper, who has the singular distinction of having written a book called *The Logic of Scientific Discovery*

15

(1959), which is not about scientific discovery at all. In a more recent paper, Popper states: '[T]o me the idea of turning for enlightenment concerning the aims of science, and its possible progress, to sociology or to psychology (or ... to the history of science) is surprising and disappointing' (1970: 57). And someone like Mario Bunge (1968) seems almost to want us to forget discovery as soon as possible, so that we might not illegitimately read into our theory things which helped us to get to the theory – otherwise we shall start worrying about whether the benzine ring is cold blooded and whether bath salts are necessary for a true application of Archimedes' Principle![2]

I shall argue that this belittling view of scientific discovery is wrong: philosophically castrating in fact. Let us turn at once to history.

DARWIN'S ROUTE TO DISCOVERY

Charles Darwin published his *Origin of Species* late in 1859. For reasons which are not entirely clear, Darwin had been sitting on his idea for twenty years – it had in fact been fifteen years since he had completed a 230-page draft of his theory[3] – and even when he did publish it, it was only because he had been sent a paper by the young naturalist, Alfred Russel Wallace (Darwin and Wallace 1858), which contained evolutionary speculations uncannily like his own. As is well known, Darwin argued that evolution is chiefly a function of 'natural selection', the differential survival and reproduction of the more adapted over the less adapted, and that this in turn is fuelled by the 'struggle for existence', where animals and plants compete with each other and the environment for limited resources. Then, having produced his mechanism, Darwin applied it to many different areas of biology – geographical distribution (biogeography), instinct, embryology, and others (see Figure 1.1).

The crucial move to natural selection as an evolutionary mechanism was made by Darwin in the autumn of 1838: late September to early October, to be more precise. However, controversy exists over precisely how Darwin moved to natural selection. In his *Autobiography* (1969), Darwin claimed that the work of animal and plant breeders using artificial selection gave him the notion of natural selection, and then reading Malthus' *Principle of Population* (1826), with its description of the struggle for existence – a function

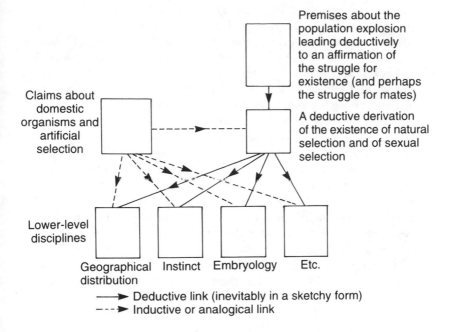

Figure 1.1 The structure of Darwin's theory in the *Origin*. From Ruse 1975b

of geometric population growth potential always outstripping food and space arithmetic growth potential – showed him how to apply selection as a mechanism for evolution. And this route to discovery is confirmed by several other recollections by Darwin of his momentous discovery.

But this account of discovery does not mesh very easily with entries Darwin made in notebooks around the time of the discovery. The importance of Malthus is reinforced, but the key role played by the artificial/natural selection analogy is put in doubt. From comments Darwin made right up to the time that he read Malthus, he seems to have had some doubts about the power of artificial selection and the consequent analogy to natural selection. 'It certainly appears in domesticated animals that the amount of variation is soon reached – as in pigeons no new races' (Darwin 1960: D175). And indeed, some scholars have concluded on the basis of this and like passages that Darwin did not really use the analogy from the domestic world in his discovery of natural selection (see Herbert 1971 and Limoges 1970). Others, however, are loath to make a liar out of Darwin. My own position, which I shall state but not really argue for here, is that although Darwin was not as certain of the value of the analogy before Malthus as he became afterwards (and thought that he had been before), the analogy did indeed play an important part in Darwin's discovery. (I do argue my case in Ruse 1975a and 1979a.)

I argue this claim chiefly on the basis of what Darwin read in the months before he read Malthus. We know that in the summer of 1838 Darwin read influential pamphlets on animal breeding, in which the principles of selection were clearly stated, and the analogy was even drawn between the artificial and natural worlds! 'A severe winter, or a scarcity of food, by destroying the weak and the unhealthy, has all the good effects of the most skilful selection' (Sebright 1809: 16). We know also that Darwin reacted enthusiastically to this reading and that at that point he did some speculating about the effects of continued selection – how it would lead to new species. So for these and related reasons, I believe and shall assume that the analogy from the domestic world – specifically including the analogy from artificial selection – was important to Darwin in his discovery of natural selection.[4]

THE CASE AGAINST THE IMPORTANCE OF THE PATH OF DISCOVERY

But where does all this take us? Darwin got his mechanism of natural selection, first from the analogy of artificial selection, and then from reading Malthus' quasi-mathematical speculations about humans in his *Principles* (1826) (speculations, somewhat ironically given the use Darwin was to make of them, directed towards showing the futility of attempting any real progress or change). Does any of this matter when it comes to considering Darwin's theory, or should we concern ourselves solely with the justifications Darwin offered: whether he relied on real laws, the precise nature of the links between his premises and conclusions, and so forth?

Considering matters first at a general level, and recognizing that initial suggestions will probably require some refinement, it should in theory be possible to decide empirically some of the pertinent questions about scientific discovery – at least in a one-way negative manner somewhat akin to the Popperian falsification of scientific hypotheses. Suppose one has a scientist A, who gets to theory T by route of discovery R. If one now has another scientist B, who also gets to theory T, but *not* by route of discovery R, one can certainly conclude that R was not necessary for getting to T, and therefore can hardly be that essential for understanding T: it is not going to be embedded in T in any significant way. This line of argument is one-way however, because if A gets to T via R, and B, not on R, does not get to T, there is always the logical possibility of a third scientist C who gets to T but not on route R.

Now, as I have just said, this is an empirical line of argument. If one has a situation with the right kinds of scientist, one can stop one's *a priori* theorizing and check. And the beautiful thing about the Darwinian case is that one does have just such a situation with the right kinds of scientist: Wallace came to natural selection as well as, but quite independently of, Darwin.

> Most or perhaps all the variations from the typical form of a species must have some definite effect, however slight, on the habits or capacities of the individuals.... [Consequently, if] any species should produce a variety having slightly increased powers of preserving existence, that variety must inevitably in time acquire a superiority in numbers.
>
> (Darwin and Wallace 1858: 273)

And if this keeps happening long enough, the process 'must in the end, produce its full legitimate results' (ibid.: 275). What is of crucial importance to us here is that although Wallace was as dependent on Malthus as Darwin for getting to the mechanism, *he did not use the artificial selection analogy.* Indeed, like everyone but Darwin, Wallace looked upon the domestic world as one of the rightful pillars of the case *against* evolutionism! Domestic change is limited; therefore, any analogy is that natural change is limited.

In other words, even if one could legitimately follow Lakatos (1970) in creating history to fit one's philosophical theses, it would seem that in the Darwin–Wallace episode, one could not have more definitive support of the irrelevance of a scientist's route to discovery for understanding that which he discovers. Two men discovered the identical principle of natural selection. For one, the analogy from the domestic world in general and artificial selection in particular was crucial. For the other, the analogy played no role at all; it played an *anti*-role, for he looked upon it as a problem

19

to be surmounted. Obviously therefore, when it comes to understanding a completed theory, discovery is irrelevant.

SUBJECTIVE AND OBJECTIVE ELEMENTS IN SCIENCE

And yet I am not sure that this is all that there is to be said, even about the Darwin case. In order to articulate my objections, let me introduce the terms 'objective' and 'subjective', although I am a little hesitant about so doing: too often the terms have meant all things to all people and have been applied indiscriminantly in the most inappropriate of situations. But understanding 'objective' to mean something public, 'out there', with existence independent of the observer, and understanding 'subjective' to mean something which in a very real sense depends on the human mind, which has no reality away from the individual, what I would argue is that science has both objective and subjective elements.[5] More precisely, scientific theorizing contains elements which reflect objective reality, and elements which are more subjective in nature. Moreover, I would claim that while the Darwin case certainly shows that science inasmuch as it is objective (i.e. talks about objective things) is independent of discovery, the Darwin case also shows that science inasmuch as it is subjective is dependent on discovery. Furthermore, I am not sure that one can or would want to eliminate the subjective element.

Clearly the Darwin case does point to the fact that independent of Darwin or Wallace there exists a process in organic nature of differential survival and reproduction. This is going on – some animals survive to reproduce, whereas others do not. In so far as a scientist like Darwin or Wallace grasps this fact, his science is objective, because it is reflecting something independent of the observer. And as we have seen, this objective element stands in its own right, independently of how anyone comes to grasp it.

But what about the subjective element? Here I am on somewhat shakier ground, if only because, as previously argued, the fact that two scientists taking different routes arrive at different ends does not logically preclude the existence of a third who takes yet another route and ends where the first (or the second) also ends. However, I think that (in theory) some sort of case can be made for the position I am proposing. Even if I cannot make my case logically watertight, I can at least try to make it factually convincing (i.e. if not deductively certain, at least inductively probable). If a scientist builds some element into his theory which there is reason to believe is directly connected with his route to discovery, which for various independent reasons one would think unlikely to be there without that route, which last suspicion is reinforced by the fact that another scientist taking a different route does not put the element into his version of the theory and, moreover, gives evidence that that is the very thing he would *not* want to do, then one has grounds both for thinking the element in some way subjective and linked with the way of discovery.

Perhaps the kind of case I am trying to establish can best at given plausibility by turning once again to the Darwin–Wallace episode. I offer the following three suggestions as instances of the importance of a scientist's route to discovery.

DARWIN'S LANGUAGE

First, take the question of language. Both Darwin and Wallace referred to the struggle for existence, by that name. This was natural enough because the term occurs in Malthus' *Principle of Population* (1826),[6] of key importance to both Darwin and Wallace, and had also been picked up and used by others who were influential on Darwin and Wallace. In particular, the term occurs in the work which probably had more influence than any other on the two evolutionists: Charles Lyell's *Principles of Geology* (1830–3). On the other hand, only Darwin referred to the process of differential survival and reproduction as 'natural selection'. Darwin claimed that he got the term from breeders, who used it to refer to the natural process of some organisms dying off through the environmental conditions. Breeders were certainly aware of this phenomenon, and Darwin was aware that they were aware, although I have not yet come across a written use of the term.

But this is as it may be. What is of importance to us here is the fact that Darwin obviously got the term in some way from the breeders' use of the term 'selection' to denote their process of picking the organisms they wanted (what we now call 'artificial selection' to distinguish it from natural selection).[7] What I would suggest is that this term 'natural selection' is a subjective element in Darwin's theory, in the sense of subjective that I have characterized. Moreover, I would suggest that without the analogy from the domestic world, Darwin would never have got it or used it,

21

and that the term itself has a status which makes it an integral part of Darwin's theory (i.e. it is not just a symbol but is philosophically interesting and important, as was Darwin's application of natural selection to the fossil record).

That the term is subjective seems fairly obvious. The differential reproduction is public and exists independently of observing theorizers. What we humans call the process is another matter. It could have been called almost anything – 'Twelfth night, or what you will'. Darwin himself suggested that it might have better been called 'natural preservation'. Herbert Spencer suggested, and Darwin later accepted, 'the survival of the fittest' (Darwin and Seward 1903, Vol. 1: 269). Wallace in his paper did not really call the process anything: he just described it.

But would the term have been used without the analogy, and without the prior use of 'selection' by breeders? It seems highly improbable that it would have been, or, to strengthen the claim a little, that if the breeders had used some other term, that term would have been used without the analogy. Logically, monkeys might type Shakespeare; actually, they are not very likely to do so. Take again the (natural!) control experiment of Wallace. He proves that one did not need the analogy to get at the process of selection. But he also suggests strongly that without faith in the analogy, one would be most unlikely to use the term 'selection' to describe the process. As has been mentioned, Wallace followed everyone but Darwin in thinking that if any analogies can be drawn from the domestic world, they *disprove* selection. Wallace wanted as little as possible to do with man's selective power. Consequently, we have the paradoxical situation that whereas Darwin emphasized the analogy, a major theme of Wallace's paper is that there is no significant similarity between the domestic and the natural worlds. Stated Wallace:

> It will be observed that this argument [denying evolution on the basis of the domestic world] rests entirely on the assumption, that *varieties* occurring in a state of nature are in all respects analogous to or even identical with those of domestic animals, and are governed by the same laws as regards their permanence or further variation. But it is the object of the present paper to show that this assumption is altogether false.
>
> (Darwin and Wallace 1858: 269)

In short, Wallace was not looking to the domestic world for

guidance, and for him to have adopted the term 'natural selection' would have meant his going against his whole strategy. For all real purposes, therefore, it would seem that Wallace could not have got or employed the term; only one thinking as Darwin thought could have done so. Significantly, it was Wallace who urged Spencer's alternative on Darwin.

At this point, I suspect some readers may be getting impatient. I am labouring to produce a molehill. Let us concede that the use of the term 'natural selection' is subjective. Let us concede that although terms are subjective, a theory must have them. Let us even concede that Darwin could not have got his term 'natural selection' without his route to discovery, and that therefore if we philosophers are to understand Darwin's use of the term, we must make reference to the context of his discovery. So what? The important things Darwin does in the *Origin* are identifying and describing the process of natural selection, and offering evidence for its power, like the evidence of the fossil record and of geographical distribution. None of this required Darwin's route of discovery: the actual words he used are irrelevant. A rose by any other name would smell as sweet.

Obviously there is truth in this objection; but, I contend, not the whole truth. In looking at a theory, particularly as philosophers, we want to consider what is important or essential about the theory. But what is to be counted as important? What is to be counted as essential? One thing which must be included presumably, however one decides, is the elegance of the theory – its simplicity. Another is the extent to which the theory fits with our metaphysical preconceptions: does it violate accepted beliefs about causality? And yet another is the hard evidence for the theory: what makes it plausible? I would suggest that, judged by precisely these criteria, the particular terms used can be important, and that Darwin's term 'natural selection' is a paradigmatic illustration. After the *Origin* was published, the term 'natural selection' was as much a matter of controversy as anything else, like the hard evidence (Ruse 1979a). For instance, some complained that by the use of 'selection' Darwin had unwittingly introduced a theistic concept into his theory – one cannot talk about selection without implying a selector, or rather, a Selector. Others, conversely, agreed with this point, but found no cause for complaint! They felt much happier with Darwin's theory precisely because it necessarily involved God. But whether one deals with supporters or critics,

23

important questions about the acceptability of Darwin's theory revolved about his use of words. It seems clear that the term 'natural selection', coming as it did uniquely from artificial selection, brought with it a certain 'flavour' of artificial selection. People could not think about natural selection any more without thinking about the origin of its name, and this influenced the way they reacted to natural selection itself.[8]

I might add that some of the questions raised by the term 'natural selection', or at least by the implications of the use of the term, remain with us today. For instance, had Darwin not used 'natural selection' but the more neutral 'natural preservation', he would not then have made the dreadful mistake of allowing Wallace to persuade him to adopt Spencer's 'survival of the fittest' as an alternative. And then we would not have people like Karl Popper still arguing today that evolutionary theory is either second-rate science or disguised metaphysics, because its central notion reduces to the empty tautology that those that survive are those that survive. In short, if we are at all sensitive to the actual historical fate of Darwin's theory – why people accepted or rejected it – we must allow that his use of language was important.

My claims therefore in this section are: Darwin's use of the term 'natural selection' was subjective in the sense specified. It came uniquely from the use of the term 'selection' in the domestic world, that is, although its origin was not logically necessary, as a matter of fact it was highly unlikely to come in any other way. Historically the use of the term was important in reactions to Darwin's theory, because it is clear that people could not use the term without in some way thinking of its origins. To us as philosophers, trying to understand Darwin's theory, because apparently people cannot use the term without bringing in origins and because this affects their reactions to Darwin's theorizing, necessarily we must concern ourselves with Darwin's route to discovery.

ARTIFICIAL SELECTION AS JUSTIFICATION AND HEURISTIC GUIDE

The second way in which Darwin's route to discovery was reflected crucially in his theory centres on the use to which he put the domestic/natural analogy in constructing his theory. Readers of the *Origin* will know that Darwin does not just present the struggle for existence and natural selection right at the beginning. Rather, he begins with a detailed discussion of the domestic world and of breeders' successes with artificial selection. Then, having talked about everything from pigeons to sheep, from strawberries to cabbages, Darwin broadens his gaze to the animal and vegetable kingdoms in the wild.

Now, although a number of commentators have been rather inclined to depreciate Darwin's reasoning powers, as he himself admitted, the *Origin* is one long argument from beginning to end. In the first chapter, Darwin was not simply wasting time as he summoned up courage to get to the controversial notion of natural selection. Rather Darwin was doing two things (Ruse 1973b; 1975b). First, he was preparing the way for the *justification* of his overall theory: because artificial selection is so effective in the domestic world, analogously, we should expect it to be effective in the natural world. And later in the *Origin*, Darwin returned repeatedly to this analogy. For instance, in his discussion of embryology, Darwin justified his claim that the differences between embryos and adults is a function of the differences in selective forces, by reference to the domestic world. Second, Darwin was discussing artificial selection as a *heuristic* guide to natural selection. Even if one did not think the analogy offered support, it certainly helped the reader (in Darwin's opinion) to understand what natural selection is all about (see Figure 1.1, p. 17).

Had Darwin not arrived at natural selection by means of artificial selection, I doubt he would have put the analogy to either of these uses in the *Origin*. One could, I suppose, argue that even if (like Wallace) Darwin had come to natural selection despite artificial selection, he could then later have decided that artificial selection offers support for natural selection and thus have introduced it as justification. This, I take it, was what Wallace's position grew to be (with reservations to be noted), and it is certainly true that it was after he discovered natural selection that Darwin made his most extensive study of the domestic world in his search for evidence for his theory.[9] On the other hand, it seems improbable that Darwin would have sought information from the breeders had he not first thought the analogy of value, and certainly he would have made the justificatory use of it that he did in the *Origin*. Even more strongly, had Darwin himself not been led to natural selection via artificial selection, he would hardly have offered it in its heuristic guise. For Wallace, it was anything but!

Hence, here as before, it seems plausible to suggest that Darwin's route of discovery influenced the theory he produced.

I take it that also as before we are dealing with a subjective element in Darwin's theory. What someone finds heuristically valuable does not seem to have the independence of the observer in the way that the brute fact of differential reproduction does. Indeed, it might be felt that everything is so subjective and personal at this point, that although Darwin certainly introduced the analogy into the *Origin*, it was not really part of his theory proper – certainly not inasmuch as it was intended to have a heuristic value. However, I am not sure that this reply is really fair: at least, the reply seems to presuppose an *a priori* view of what constitutes the essence of a theory that one is imposing upon history. Darwin's aim in the *Origin* was to persuade the reader to accept evolution and to accept natural selection as its chief mechanism: that was his 'theory', and the artificial selection discussion/analogy played a key role. Moreover, like the term 'natural selection', artificial selection figured mightily in the controversy in the years after 1859. For instance, although T. H. Huxley was Darwin's most vocal supporter, he could never fully endorse the power of natural selection, because he thought that artificial selection proves the limitations of natural selection (Hull 1973; Ruse 1979a)! Hence I conclude that unless one prescribes that only formal deductive systems are the 'real' parts of theories, one has no right to exclude artificial selection (and even with such a prescription one has no right).

THE NATURAL/SEXUAL SELECTION DICHOTOMY

We come to the third and final way in which Darwin's path to natural selection through artificial selection is reflected in the theory of the *Origin*. Although it was always his major mechanism, natural selection was never Darwin's sole putative mechanism of evolutionary change. Darwin was, for example, always a Lamarckian, in the sense of believing in the inheritance of acquired characteristics.[10] But Darwin's major secondary mechanism was *sexual selection*: even in his earliest drafts of his theory, Darwin mentioned this kind of selection (Darwin and Wallace 1958); in the *Origin* (1859) he spelt it out clearly, albeit without developing it; and then in his seminal work on our species, *The Descent of Man* (1871), Darwin discussed sexual selection in great detail, both as it applies through the animal world and as it applies to *Homo sapiens*. I argue that not only was artificial selection crucial in Darwin's getting to this kind of selection, but it was essential for the place that Darwin gave it in his theorizing. In other words, without understanding Darwin's route to discovery, we cannot understand the structure of Darwin's argument. Moreover, I claim that while sexual selection is not itself subjective, Darwin's treating it as an independent kind of selection is.

First, there is the historical question of how Darwin got to sexual selection. There are hints of sexual selection in the evolutionary meanderings of Darwin's grandfather, Erasmus Darwin, as well as in the writings of others that Darwin read (for example, Sebright 1809). However, study of what Darwin produced makes it overwhelmingly certain that the key to discovery for Darwin, as well as the conviction that the discovery was important, lay in the analogy from the domestic world and the breeder's power of selection (Ghiselin 1969). Breeders select for two things: attributes of animals and plants that are useful to us, like shaggy sheep coats and fleshy root crops, and attributes that are pleasurable to us, like fancy pigeon tails and vicious bull-dogs. It was this division that gave rise to the natural/sexual selection dichotomy. Furthermore, the division that breeders make in the pleasurable attributes was exactly reflected in a division that Darwin always made in sexual selection. Breeders select (*qua* pleasure) for pugnaciousness, as when they breed vicious fighting cocks, and for beauty, as when they breed beautiful birds. For Darwin, in the natural world, these translated into sexual selection through male combat and sexual selection through female choice. We can see therefore that the analogy from artificial selection played a powerful role for Darwin when he came to introduce and justify sexual selection in the *Origin* and in later works. But did he have to have the analogy or metaphor? And what was the status of the natural/sexual selection dichotomy?

Take first the question of the necessity of the analogy from the domestic world. Wallace certainly never discovered sexual selection. Moreover, when he was introduced to the notion, although initially he accepted both forms, before long he became very hostile to sexual selection through female choice. He thought the notion unduly anthropomorphic, imputing human standards of beauty to animals. Instead, Wallace argued that the brightness of males and drabness of females is a function of the need for females, vulnerable as they protect their young, to camouflage themselves, rather than a function of males being chosen by females. In other words, sexual dimorphisms of this kind should be seen as a matter of dowdy females rather than flashy males (Vorzimmer 1970: 200).

Of course, one might argue that the fact that Wallace had trouble with sexual selection does not exactly prove the necessity of the artificial selection analogy – and this is true. But it is really hard to see how one would come to make the natural/sexual selection division without the analogy, let alone endorse it. There is no other basis than the analogy to make the division, or to separate male combat from female choice. For instance, Darwin talks about sexual selection being less fierce than natural selection, for it does not involve death, but natural selection, as Darwin recognized, does not always involve death either. The key to natural selection, as with sexual selection, is reproduction – survival is incidental. A plant less able to reproduce in the desert than another is selected against, even if both survive. Similarly, the natural/sexual dichotomy is not really based on the relationship of the competitors. Sexual selection can occur only between members of the same species, but Darwin explicitly allows that one can have natural selection between members of the same species also. Nor is the dichotomy based on the animal/plant dichotomy. Sexual selection is restricted to animals, but one has natural selection in that kingdom too.

Similar remarks apply to the division between the kinds of sexual selection. In recent years, particularly with the advent of sociobiology, sexual selection has enjoyed something of a renaissance (Campbell 1972; Ruse 1979b). But the male combat/female choice division is not really maintained. One prominent sociobiologist, for instance, divides sexual selective strategies into the 'domestic bliss' strategy and the 'he man' strategy (Dawkins 1976); but these cut across Darwin's divisions. The 'he man' strategy requires that the female try to mate with the male with the most attractive characteristics: these attractive characteristics include both strength and beauty.

I argue therefore that one cannot grasp Darwin's natural/sexual selection division without recognizing his route to discovery through artificial selection. In one asks what the rationale behind the distinction really is, and as philosophers we surely ought to, we must make mention of the way in which Darwin discovered his mechanisms. Note that I am not saying that Darwin's division of selection into two kinds was wrong. He made good use of it, even though selection through female choice did get surrounded by controversy. I would, however, suggest that the division is artificial or subjective in the sense discussed earlier. In a typically perceptive passage, William Whewell points out that the difference between a natural and an artificial classification lies in the fact that the former alone can be delimited in two different, logically independent ways: 'And the Maxim by which all Systems professing to be natural must be tested in this: that the *arrangement obtained from one set of characters coincides with the arrangement obtained from another set*' (1840, Vol. 1: 521. Whewell's italics). This very point applies to the case we are discussing. The natural/sexual selection distinction is artificial simply because its only justification is the analogy from human selection. (For more on this question of artificial/natural classification see Ruse 1969 and 1973a.)

CONCLUSION

In three different ways I have tried to suggest that Darwin's route to discovery through the domestic world significantly and uniquely influenced the theory presented in the *Origin*. I have allowed, however, that this influence was at the level I have called 'subjective', and that Wallace's work shows that there was another side, an 'objective' side, to Darwin's theory that lay beyond the route to discovery. I suspect that some of my readers, even if they grant what I have argued so far, will nevertheless feel less than impressed. They will argue that, by my own admission, the 'real' or 'true' part of a theory is understandable without knowledge of discovery. In the case at point, the essential theory of the *Origin* is independent of the precise way that Darwin got to his mechanisms. I have tried to explain why I would not accept this criticism: I believe it to be insensitive to the historical reality of science. But in conclusion, let me hint why I believe that knowledge of a scientist's passage of discovery might be even more crucial to understanding a completed theory than I have so far argued.

As many modern commentators have noted (for instance, Laudan 1977), scientists do not simply set out to give a faithful reflection of reality – any old reality. Rather, they set out with problems that they want to solve. These problems and the strictures that scientists set on themselves in solving the problems – the regulative principles – crucially influence the finished product.

Take once again the Darwinian case. First, there is the question of why one should want such a theory as that of the *Origin*, at all. Wherein lies its interest? This may seem like a very odd question indeed, particularly to those of us trained in the logical empiricist tradition. Obviously Darwin's theory is interesting: the plethora of stuff written on it in the past hundred years amply attests to this fact. And in any case, surely there is something logically absurd about asking whether a theory is interesting: at least, inasmuch as one wants to understand the theory philosophically. What one should ask is whether it is true.

However, it we look at history, and *only* if we look at history, we see that the question is not so very odd, nor is it insignificant. The origins of organisms had to be seen as a major problem for Darwin to want to solve it, or for anyone – supporter or critic – to take his suggestions seriously. It was not by chance that the *Origin* appeared midway in the nineteenth century or that it appeared in Britain, at that time certainly not the world leader in science (Ruse 1979a). A theory like Darwin's was not going to be important until there was all the unexplained and curious information on geographical distributions, the fossil record, embryology, and so forth; nor would it have been so important had not the British had this rabid desire to mesh their science with their evangelically inspired biblical speculations. I suspect that most French people still do not accept Darwin; but to such rational souls – Catholic or atheist – the whole matter is really not very important. They are not stunted by the claustrophobic effects of Wesley's Protestant Christianity, and hence to them a theory like Darwin's which challenges these effects does not have an *a priori* morbid fascination. Of course, if you like, this whole question of the importance or interest of Darwin's theory is still subjective, in a way that the objective matter of the theory's truth or falsity is not. But this is a fact I find quite insignificant. There is no point in having a pretty face if no one is going to fall in love with you.

Second, there is the question of the solution of the problem, once it is seen as significant. Darwin bound himself by at least two methodological dicta, or, following the neo-Kantians, what I would call 'regulative principles': norms of what constitute good science, or even more strictly norms to which a scientist's work must adhere if it is to be called 'science' at all (Ruse 1979c).

On the one hand, in so far as possible, Darwin felt he had to be 'Newtonian', where the model for this was the astronomy of the 1830s (Ruse 1975c). This led Darwin to put his central arguments to natural selection in the deductive form as found in Malthus. Also it was for this reason that the *Origin* is strikingly structured in a fan-like form, with the core of selection explaining in so many different areas: biogeography, palaeontology, embryology, and so forth (refer back to Figure 1.1, p. 17). This 'consilience of inductions' was what J. F. W. Herschel and William Whewell found so admirable about Newton's theory (as well as the wave-theory of light).

On the other hand, Darwin tried to be 'teleological'. Darwin is often portrayed as taking God, particularly Paley's divine clockmaker, out of biology; and this is true (Ruse 1975d). All British pre-Darwinians thought that the most distinctive feature about the organic world is the way it shows functions, organization, and ends: the adaptations of the kangaroo are *as if* they were designed because, in the opinion of virtually all, they *were* designed ('irrefragable evidence of creative forethought': Owen 1834: 348)! Darwin certainly did not follow the herd in thinking that 'as if' implies 'was'. Nevertheless, he agreed fully that the manifestation of organization and ends – 'teleology' – characterizes the organic world, and consequently he deliberately sought a mechanism to explain it. Even after he became an evolutionist, Darwin went on seeking until he found the mechanism of natural selection, which he thought could explain organic teleology. In the *Origin* therefore, Darwin felt quite free, not to say obligated, to use the terms and categories of the Paleyites, like 'adaptation', and 'function'. The concern with ends was no less an obsession for Darwin than it was for his opponents, although the latter did not think that Darwin had done a good enough job.

Both in his Newtonianism and his teleology, Darwin let his way of discovery influence the theory he produced. It may be argued that any theory has to be axiomatic as Newton's theory was and as Darwin's theory tried to be. This is a moot point. However, not every theory is or tries to be as consilient as Darwin's. Similarly, it would be hard to maintain that a biological theory *has* to be teleological, even though much might be lost if it were not. One could, as one does in physics, stay just at the level of material causation and refuse to ask questions about ends. To ask for the function of the heart would be illegitimate: all one could ask is physiological questions about embryological development, and so forth (Ruse 1973a; 1977).

In these two modes of Newtonianism and teleology therefore, I would suggest that Darwin incorporated subjective elements into his theory of organic origins, and that these elements were a direct function of his route to discovery. Since these elements were so pervasive and significant in his theory, given also what has been argued previously, I conclude that the attempt to understand Darwin's theory philosophically, without full consideration of the context of discovery, is hopelessly doomed to failure.[11]

NOTES

1 As part of their not-so-subtle denigration of scientific discovery, logical empiricists (e.g. Hempel 1966) are usually quick to point out that Kepler had some pretty wild neo-Pythagorean ideas about the mystical significance of mathematics.

2 Honesty compels me to confess that this attitude towards scientific discovery pervades the minor logical empiricist writings: for example, Ruse (1973a).

3 Darwin wrote a thirty-five-page sketch of his theory in 1842 and a 230 page essay in 1844. These are reprinted in Darwin and Wallace (1958). Even in the sketch all the essential ideas appear.

4 Even if I attribute too much to the analogy from the domestic world in Darwin's actually grasping the rudiments of differential reproduction in September/October 1838, what I shall argue will not thereby fail. My concern, as will become clear, is with Darwin's *theory*. As pointed out (note 3), the theory of the *Origin* first appeared in outline in the sketch of 1842. Hence what I shall have to say really depends crucially on all work up to that point. But between 1839 and 1842 Darwin continued to read extensively in the writings of breeders, definitely by then taking seriously the domestic/wild analogy. Hence it is indubitable that inasmuch as Darwin had a conceptual argument (a theory) the analogy could and did play a vital role.

5 I am presupposing that the reader, like myself, has a fairly robust sense of reality and is prepared to accept without too much question that chairs, tables and trees really do exist, whether or not we are around. 'The tree is an oak' I take to be about objective fact, 'I prefer mahogany to oak' I take to be more in the subjective realm.

6 Actually, Malthus speaks of struggles for existence.

7 Note the use of the term 'selection' in the passage from Sebright (1809) quoted above.

8 Obviously, I am here getting fairly close to the view of metaphor proposed by Max Black (1962) and accepted by Mary Hesse (1966). People viewed natural selection through the 'lens' of artificial selection, and at least as a matter of contingent fact people's understanding of natural selection could not have been the same as it was without the artificial selection metaphor. An extremist might perhaps argue that, *logically*, without the metaphor the understanding could not have been

the same. I am hesitant to go quite that far, although it might be argued that even if logically one could have got the term 'natural selection' without the metaphor, the thoughts it would conjure up would not be the same.

9 In line with the point made in note 4, what I mean here is that after Darwin had discovered differential reproduction in 1838 and before he wrote down his theory in 1842, he made his most extensive study.

10 Lamarck's main force of evolutionary change was a kind of teleological drive up the chain of being. This was never part of Darwin's theory.

11 [Note added in 1984] As you will learn from the essays following, that 'fairly robust sense of reality', to which I referred confidently in footnote 5 above, has proven through time to be not quite as robust as I then thought. The reader will realize, however, that none of the points I make in this essay are at all affected. I would still claim that 'The tree is an oak' is objective, that 'I prefer mahogany to oak' is subjective, and that science is a blend of the two.

2

ARE PICTURES REALLY NECESSARY?

The case of Sewall Wright's 'adaptive landscapes'

Biologists are remarkably visual people. I have before me a flyer from a major publisher, promoting the new edition of an (apparently) highly successful college text in cell biology, co-authored by (among others) the Nobel laureate, David Baltimore (Darnell, Lodish and Baltimore 1990). The 1,105 pages include no less than 1,050 illustrations; the people asked to publicize the book harp on the virtues of the pictures ('I appreciate the use of data and actual micrographs. The artwork, and especially the use of color, is outstanding.'[1]); and instructors adopting the book as a text get a free set of overhead transparencies, with the opportunity to buy more.

Nor is this love of the pictorial confined to the pedagogical. If you look at the papers that biologists produce, and even more at their books, you find them chock-a-block full of photographs and drawings, of graphs and figures, of maps and of stylized tables. Moreover, thanks to advances in technology – photography, computers, printing – the use of pictures of one sort or another is, if anything, increasing rather than otherwise. Bursting with vibrant coloured photographs, some publications seem to owe as much to Walt Disney as they do to Charles Darwin.

Biological illustration has been around for a long time – plenty of time for the philosophers, whose self-appointed task is the understanding of science, to react to it, delving into its nature and significance. So let us ask about what they have to say – and the answer, I am afraid, is 'remarkably little'. To the best of my knowledge, the classics of logical empiricism never raise the general question of scientific illustration, and the same seems to be true of non-classics of that era devoted explicitly to problems of biology.[2]

Moreover, one suspects that the silence was, if anything, actively hostile. People did not talk about biological illustration, because they did not judge it to be part of 'real science'. This enterprise produces statements or propositions, ideally embedded in a formal system. It may be *about* the real world, but it is not in any sense *of* the real world, in being a copy or mirror-image. Like Plato in the *Republic* and (many years later) Pierre Duhem (1914), who contrasted the admirable French mind of pure reason with the grubby English fondness for concrete models, philosophers recognized that regretfully human weakness demanded the visual. But it was judged at best a prop. And in the discussion of physical models, about the closest that the logical empiricists ever did get to the visual, one was warned constantly of the dangers of illicitly identifying aspects of the artifactual with aspects of reality (see, for instance, Braithwaite 1953, Hempel 1965 and Bunge 1968; although see also Achinstein 1968).

I am a philosophical naturalist, thinking that one's philosophy must be informed and in accord with the methodological dictates of science. I believe that one must be true to the real nature of science, not to an idealized preconception. I am, therefore, made most uncomfortable by this tension between the reality and the theory. I say this with even more discomfort because, admittedly in a very minor way, I myself have been responsible for the tension (especially in Ruse 1973a). The aim of this discussion here, therefore, is to start to make amends. At the very least, so voluminous an item as biological illustration demands philosophical attention, whatever one's ultimate conclusion.

As a philosophical naturalist, my scientific-type inquiry is focused on science itself.[3] As the biologist studies organisms, so I study what the biologist thinks and produces about organisms. Hence my starting point here has to be with actual examples of biological illustration or diagram. I shall, indeed, look at but one example; though I hope that its great importance in the history of science will justify such selectivity, even to the point of allowing me to draw some general conclusions. From among the many candidates – Richard Owen's vertebrate archetype, Charles Darwin's tree of life (not to mention Ernst Haeckel's), the chromosome maps of T. H. Morgan and Co., the million exemplifications of the double helix – I chose the adaptive landscapes of the great population geneticist Sewall Wright. And the question I ask is:

What was/is the status and role of 'adaptive landscapes' within evolutionary biology?

I start by looking at the landscapes themselves, asking about their nature and history. Then I go on to inquire into their significance. Next come some thoughts about the quality of the science in which they are embedded. My discussion concludes with a few comments of a more general nature. One example cannot justify a whole theory of (scientific) knowledge, but it can set us in a certain direction. Technically speaking, my concern is with the first actual public presentation of an illustration of an adaptive landscape by Sewall Wright. Since he and others repeated the performance many, many times, unless confusion would ensue I shall refer indifferently to the class of such illustrations.

ADAPTIVE LANDSCAPES

Sewall Wright's first job after leaving graduate school (Harvard) was with the US Department of Agriculture. In 1926 he was appointed to the faculty at Chicago, and it was about this time that he wrote the major paper in evolutionary theory (Wright 1931), on which his reputation (justly) rests. His biographer, Will Provine (1986), suggests that the motivation might have been Wright's desire to prove himself as a real academic; but as it happens the paper was not published until 1931. By then, especially in response to dialogue with R. A. Fisher, there had been some modifications to the text, although one understands that they were not drastic.

Much of the text of this paper is given over to complex mathematics – at least by biological standards, especially by biological standards of the day. Wright concerned himself primarily with the fate of genes in populations, under given conditions of selection, mutation, and so forth, and he was interested in the consequences of population sizes being genuinely finite and thus subject to random factors in breeding (errors of sampling). He was able to show that if population numbers (or rather 'effective' population numbers, taking into account such things as sex ratios) are large enough, and the forces are strong enough, then selection and similar factors determine the fates of genes. For instance, a favoured gene or gene combination will establish itself in a population. However, what Wright was also able to show is that if population numbers are small (judged against the other factors), then genes will 'drift' either to total elimination or total fixation – despite counter-forces of selection and the like. Chance becomes a real phenomenon for change.

To illustrate the mathematical points, Wright gave graphs showing possible effects, and these together with the formal conclusions were used to launch Wright's own particular theory of evolutionary change: the 'shifting balance' theory (Figure 2.1). Wright argued that very small populations would suffer from significant drift and rapidly go extinct. However, conversely, large populations under fairly uniform selective pressures would not truly be candidates for any significant change, good or bad, or at least that they could incorporate only change of a *very* slow and stately change (see Figure 2.1, especially his figures 18 and 20).

For significant change, within realistic timespans, one needs a more dynamic mechanism. This is provided by the breaking of a species into sub-populations of a size-order where drift could be effective, but not of a size so small that drift could be too effective! Every now and then, such a sub-population would, by chance, come up with a highly adaptive gene complex, and then this combination could take over the species, either by direct selective elimination of rivals or by interbreeding.

In formulating this theory, we know that Wright drew heavily on his knowledge of animal breeding. This point is not of great importance to us here. What is of importance is the fact that, presumably like his knowledge of animal breeding, Wright's theory transcended his formalisms. It was based on them, but was not identical. It was more inclusive (more falsifiable, in Popper's terminology). There was nothing in the formalisms about species subdividing, about new adaptive complexes being hit upon, about insufficient time for selection in large groups, and so on. This was added. Significantly, Wright and Fisher agreed on the mathematics, but because Fisher added different non-formal elements, he came up with a very different theory of change. (Most importantly, Fisher (1930) believed that selection in large groups *did* hold the key to evolution. I will be returning to this point at the end of this discussion.)

Wright's paper, a long paper, appeared in the journal *Genetics*. The next year (1932) he had a wonderful opportunity to promote his theory, because he was asked (by E. M. East, his doctoral supervisor) to participate in a forum (with Fisher and with the third great theorist, J. B. S. Haldane) at the Sixth International Congress of Genetics, at Cornell. Normally, Wright was as given

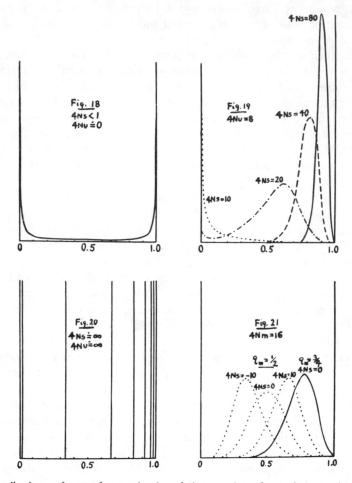

Distributions of gene frequencies in relation to size of population, selection, mutation and state of subdivision. Figure 18. Small population, random fixation or loss of genes $(y = Cq^{-1}(1-q)^{-1}$. Figure 19. Intermediate size of population, random variation of gene frequencies about modal values due to opposing mutation and selection $(y = Ce^{4Nsqq-1}(1-q)^{4Nu-1}$. Figure 20. Large population, gene frequencies in equilibrium between mutation and selection $(q = 1-u/s$, etc.). Figure 21. Subdivisions of large population, random variation of gene frequencies about modal values due to immigration and selection. $(y = Ce^{4Nsqq4Nmq_m-1}(1-q)^{4Nm(1-q_m)-1}$.

Figure 2.1 These four figures illustrate the various fates of a gene in a population. Note (his) Fig. 18, where the gene either gets fixed or gets lost entirely. N is effective population size, s is selection coefficient, u and v are mutation rates, m immigration rate. From Wright 1931

to long mathematical demonstrations in lectures as he was in print, but here he was forced to keep his presentation very short – and urged to keep it simple. To do this, he dropped the mathematics entirely, presented his shifting balance theory in words (as he had done in his long paper) and backed up his thinking with a new metaphor, which he presented pictorially: the *adaptive* landscape.

Wright wrote, and illustrated, as follows:

> If the entire field of possible gene combinations be graded with respect to adaptive value under a particular set of conditions, what would be its nature? Figure 1 [Figure 2.2 in this essay] shows the combinations in the cases of 2 to 5 paired allelomorphs. In the last case, each of the 32 homozygous combinations is at one remove from 5 others, at two removes from 10, etc. It would require 5 dimensions to represent these relations symmetrically; a sixth dimension is

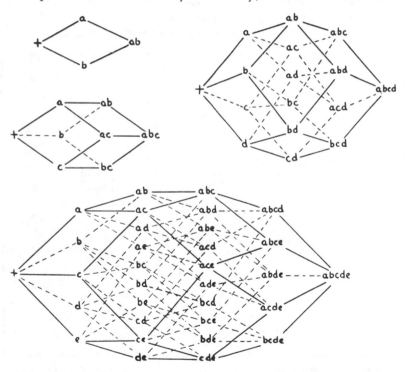

Figure 2.2 The combinations of from 2 to 5 paired allelomorphs. From Wright 1932

needed to represent level of adaptive value. The 32 combinations here compare with 10^{1000} in a species with 1000 loci ch represented by 10 allelomorphs, and the 5 dimensions required for adequate representation compare with 9000. The two dimensions of Figure 2 [Figure 2.3] are a very inadequate representation of such a field. The contour lines are intended to represent the scale of adaptive value.

One possibility is that a particular combination gives maximum adaptation and that the adaptiveness of the other combinations falls off more or less regularly according to the number of removes. A species whose individuals are clustered about some combination other than highest would move up the steepest gradient toward the peak, having reached which it would remain unchanged except for the rare occurrence of new favorable mutations.

But even in the two factor case (Figure 1) [Figure 2.2] it is possible that there may be two peaks, and the chance that this may be the case greatly increases with each additional

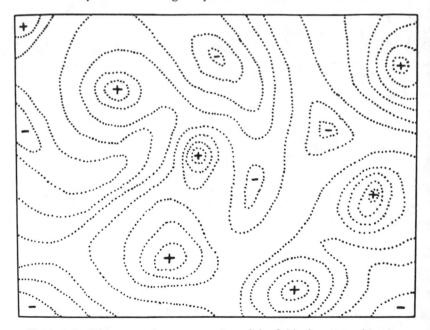

Figure 2.3 Diagrammatic representation of the field of gene combinations in two dimensions instead of many thousands. Dotted lines represent contours with respect to adaptiveness. From Wright 1932

locus. With something like 10^{1000} possibilities (Figure 2) [Figure 2.3] it may be taken as certain that there will be an enormous number of widely separated harmonious combinations. The chance that a random combination is as adaptive as those characteristic of the species may be as low as 10^{-100} and still leave room for 10^{800} separate peaks, each surrounded by 10^{100} more or less similar combinations. In a rugged field of this character, selection will easily carry the species to the nearest peak, but there may be innumerable other peaks which are surrounded by 'valleys.' The problem of evolution as I see it is that of a mechanism by which the species may continually find its way from lower to higher peaks in such a field. In order that this may occur, there must be some trial and error mechanism on a grand scale by which the species may explore the region surrounding the small portion of the field which it occupies. To evolve, the species must not be under strict control of natural selection. Is there such a trial and error mechanism?

(Wright 1932: 162–4)

Next Wright presented (without the mathematical backing) versions of the graphs of gene distribution that had been given in the large paper (my Figure 2.4, his Figure 3). He showed visually how drift and other phenomena can occur, given the right specified conditions. Then, using the landscape metaphor, Wright showed how the various options might or might not lead to change, and – as before – he opted for a position that involved a break into small groups, drift, and then reasonably rapid adaptive change in one direction (my Figure 2.5, his Figure 4).

Finally (Figure 4F) [Figure 2.5], let us consider the case of a large species which is subdivided into many small local races, each breeding largely within itself but occasionally crossbreeding. The field of gene combinations occupied by each of these local races shifts continually in a nonadaptive fashion (except in so far as there are local differences in the conditions of selection). The rate of movement may be enormously greater than in the preceding case since the condition for such movement is that the reciprocal of the population number be of the order of the proportion of crossbreeding instead of the mutation rate. With many local races, each spreading over a considerable field and moving relatively

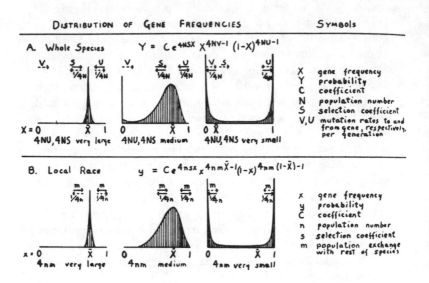

Figure 2.4 Random variability of a gene frequency under various specified conditions. From Wright 1932

rapidly in the more general field about the controlling peak, the chances are good that one at least will come under the influence of another peak. If a higher peak this race will expand in numbers and by crossbreeding with the others will pull the whole species toward the new position. The average adaptedness of the species thus advances under intergroup selection, an enormously more effective process than intragroup selection. The conclusion is that subdivision of a species into local races provides the most effective mechanism for trial and error in the field of gene combinations.

(Wright 1932: 168)

HOW IMPORTANT WERE THE ILLUSTRATIONS?

Let us start with the basic historical facts. Wright's talk was a great success.[4] People grasped what he had to say and they responded warmly to his claims – at least, this seems to have been true of his American audience. Moreover, word seems to have got out and Wright was flooded with reprint requests. Most important was the fact that among Wright's listeners at Cornell were active and

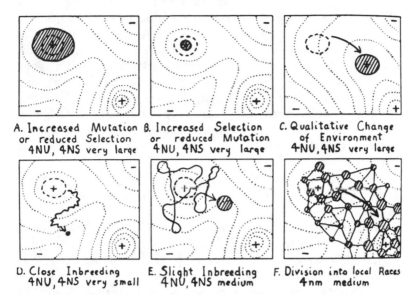

A. Increased Mutation B. Increased Selection C. Qualitative Change
or reduced Selection   or reduced Mutation   of Environment
4NU, 4NS very large   4NU, 4NS very large   4NU, 4NS very large

D. Close Inbreeding   E. Slight Inbreeding   F. Division into local Races
4NU, 4NS very small   4NU, 4NS medium   4nm medium

Figure 2.5 Field of gene combinations occupied by a population within
the general field of possible combinations. Type of history under specified
conditions indicated by relation to initial field (heavy broken contour)
and arrow. From Wright 1932

ambitious young evolutionists, simply desperate for a good theory
around which to structure their empirical research.

One of these people was the Russian-born Theodosius Dobzhansky, then working in Morgan's laboratory at Cal Tech. In his
own words, 'he simply fell in love with Wright', or at least with
the ideas (Provine 1986: 328). Thus, when in 1936 Dobzhansky
was invited to give the Jesup lectures at Columbia, Wright's shifting balance theory had pride of place, and in the published version
next year – *Genetics and the Origin of Species* – Wrightian adaptive
landscapes got full treatment. Indeed, it is not too much to say that
the metaphor was offered as the crucial key to the understanding of
evolution.

Dobzhansky's book had immense influence. It has fair claim to
having been the most important work in evolutionary theory since
the *Origin*. And with the influence has gone the Wrightian landscape, reproduced again and again in work after work (not the
least of which were Wright's own writings, which were using
the original illustrations right down to the 1980s). In America,

all the major evolutionists used the notion of a landscape. The metaphor itself found its way across the Atlantic; though, to be quite candid, people in Britain were not as keen on it, especially inasmuch as it was tied to non-adaptive drift. (More on this point later.) Indeed, in America most people used the actual illustrations, and even with those that did not, the idea can usually be found lurking in the background. In his *Systematics and the Origin of Species*, Ernst Mayr displayed his lifelong churlishness towards genetics. But although the actual illustrations are absent, the idea is there.

Most interestingly, those evolutionists who could not use Wright's landscapes directly adapted them to their own ends. As a palaeontologist, G. G. Simpson (1944) could not work at the genetic level, nor could he think in terms of individual populations of a species. So he hypothesized landscapes of phenetic or morphological difference, and he supposed taxa of higher categories working their ways across the landscapes, down valleys and up peaks. Wright, incidentally, approved of this extension (Figures 2.6 and 2.7).

Actually, by 1951 (when Dobzhansky published the third edition of GOS), he too had started thinking in terms of multiple species rather than populations with a single species. What is as interesting as this point is the fact that as evolutionists in America (Dobzhansky particularly) became more selectionist in the 1940s (thanks to empirical findings about chromosome polymorphisms), so Wright's picture was retained and reinterpreted. By 1951, in the third (very selectionist) edition of GOS, the picture was at its height.

> Every organism may be conceived as possessing a certain combination of organs or traits, and of genes which condition the development of these traits. Different organisms possess some genes in common with others and some genes which are different. The number of conceivable combinations of genes present in different organisms is, of course, immense. The actually existing combinations amount to only an infinitesimal fraction of the potentially possible, or at least conceivable, ones. All these combinations may be thought of as forming a multi-dimensional space within which every existing or possible organism may be said to have its place.
>
> The existing and the possible combinations may now be

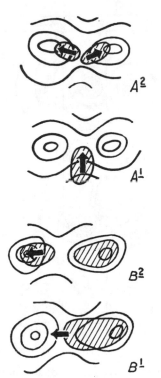

Figure 2.6 Two patterns of phyletic dichotomy; shown on selection contours. Shaded areas represent evolving populations. A, dichotomy with population advancing and splitting to occupy two different adaptive peaks, both branches progressive; B, dichotomy with marginal, preadaptive variants of ancestral population moving away to occupy adjacent adaptive peak; ancestral group conservative, continuing on same peak, descendant branch progressive. From Simpson 1944: 91

graded with respect to their fitness to survive in the environments that exist in the world. Some of the conceivable combinations, indeed a vast majority of them, are discordant and unfit for survival in any environment. Others are suitable for occupation of certain habitats and ecological niches. Related gene combinations are, on the whole, similar in adaptive value. The field of gene combinations may, then, be visualized most simply in a form of a topographical map, in which the 'contours' symbolize the adaptive values of various combinations (Fig. 1) [Figure 2.8]. Groups of related combinations

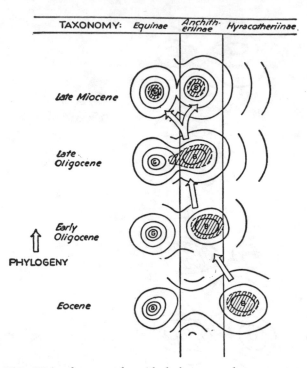

Figure 2.7 Major features of equid phylogeny and taxonomy represented as the movement of populations on a dynamic selection landscape. From Simpson 1944: 92

of genes, which make the organisms that possess them able to occupy certain ecological niches, are then represented by the 'adaptive peaks' situated in different parts of the field (plus signs in Fig. 1) [Figure 2.8]. The unfavorable combinations of genes which make their carriers unfit to live in any existing environment are represented by the 'adaptive valleys' which lie between the peaks (minus signs in Fig. 1) [Figure 2.8].

(Dobzhansky 1951: 8–9)

Diminished now are the drift aspects, and emphasized are the adaptationist aspects.

So much for history. Wright's idea of an adaptive landscape – where by 'idea' I mean at the general level the metaphor, but at a specific level actual pictures, and usually the original pictures of

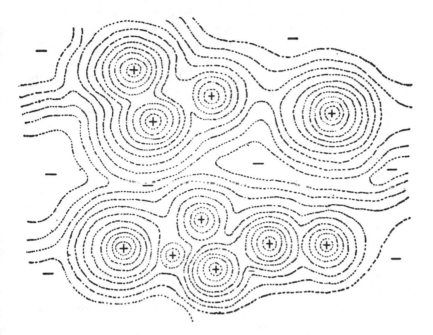

Figure 2.8 The 'adaptive peaks' and 'adaptive valleys' in the field of gene combinations. The contour lines symbolize the adaptive value (Darwinian fitness) of the genotypes. (After Wright). From Dobzhansky 1951: 9

Wright himself – became a commonplace in evolutionary thought. Moreover, note that – identify metaphor and picture if you will – I am not talking about any old adaptive landscape. I am talking about landscapes precisely of the kind as are exemplified by the pictures. Or rather, of *representations* of landscapes as are exemplified by the pictures.

But, speaking now at a philosophical level: Were the landscapes *really* part of evolutionary thought? Or, rephrasing the question, since Dobzhansky is generally taken as one of the founders of the 'synthetic' theory of evolution, also known as 'neo-Darwinism': was Wright's metaphor in general, and his pictures in particular, *really* part of the synthetic theory of evolution, of neo-Darwinism? The answer, of course, depends on what you mean by *'really* part of'. The pictures were around in a big way, so they are clearly candidates for inclusion in a manner that, for instance (to take an object entirely at random), the head of King Charles I was not.

The decision for inclusion must therefore depend on how one construes inclusion itself. Let us run through some possible senses.

At the most basic level, the pictures obviously are part of evolutionary thought. Evolutionists thought about them a great deal and put them into their publications. There is an end to the matter. The pictures were in, and King Charles' head, which went unmentioned, was not. I realize, of course, that many philosophers – all of those of the older cast of mind – will find this answer profoundly unsatisfying. They will claim that the question is not whether people did think about them (we know that they did) but whether they *had* to think about them. Were the pictures an integrally necessary part of the science? Putting matters another way: The pictures were part of evolutionary thought. But were they part of evolutionary *theory*?

Let me say right out that, as a naturalist, I do not find the basic-level answer quite so trivial as all that. While I see a place for philosophy being prescriptive, it should also be descriptive. The illustrations occupied a lot of space – mental space and printed space. An adequate philosophy of science must recognize this fact. But I will accept that this conclusion leaves open the possibility that in some sense the pictures were not absolutely necessary. As established thus far, the science in some fashion could have gone on without them. The process might not have been so fast, but presumably that is the price one pays for conceptual purity – assuming, as I am sure traditional philosophers would assume, that pictures are impure. I add parenthetically that I am not sure how easy, or indeed possible, teaching might have been without the pictures, without the very metaphor. However, for sake of argument, I adopt here the traditional academic stance that teaching does not occupy the first-class mind anyway.

Returning to the question of the status of the pictures: the argument for their necessity can be made a notch stronger. Not only were the pictures part of evolutionary thought, the scientists involved could *not* have done their work without the pictures. I speak now at the empirical level of psychological or intellectual ability. Wright's mathematics was simply too hard for the average evolutionist. It was certainly too hard for that very non-average evolutionist Theodosius Dobzhansky. He admitted again and again that he could not follow Wright's calculations.[5] And he was not alone. G. L. Stebbins, another who heard Wright at Cornell, and later to provide the botanical arm to the synthetic theory, likewise was quite incapable of thinking mathematically.

But they could understand the pictures! And so, as a matter of empirical fact, this was the level at which these men worked. They seized on the notion of an adaptive landscape and they experimented and theorized around it. Dobzhansky, for instance, studied natural populations of Drosophila, looking for evidence that they have drifted apart in a non-adaptive fashion (Lewontin *et al.* 1981). At first he did think he had evidence for his hypothesis; then he found evidence against it. What is important is that, as noted above, in both cases it was at the picture level that he was thinking, because quite frankly he could do no other. In this sense, therefore, history supports the philosophical claim that the pictures were necessary. The science would not have been done without them.

'The science would not have been done without them'? Here the traditionalist philosopher will again enter an objection. The important point surely is whether the science *could* not have been done without the pictures. A philosophical analysis tries to strain out the fallibility of the individual and to aim for the ideal. Remember that Popper (1972) refers to science as 'knowledge without a knower', meaning not that science exists independently of individuals – although sometimes his metaphysical speculations about World 3 seem to imply just this – but that the idiosyncrasies, including the intellectual weaknesses, of individual scientists have no place in real science. In this spirit the claim will be that, although the pictures were undoubtedly needed for the real scientists involved, in theory they were dispensable. Moreover, the claim will probably be that the ideal, that which is in some sense preferable, would do away with the pictures. In a perfect world, the pictures could and would go.

I know this kind of claim will be made, because in the past I would have been one to make it. Now, as a naturalist, I find myself very uncomfortable with it. Somehow I feel that even a philosopher should acknowledge the realities of human nature. Of course, there is always the danger of subjectivity or relativism here. No one would (or should) want to argue that the only adequate philosophical analysis is one which embraces everyone who has ever thought scientifically, right down to the most lazy, inadequate undergraduate. But however one makes the cut, in talking about Dobzhansky and Mayr and Simpson and Stebbins, we are talking about the top evolutionists, the men who made the subject. So let me say simply that I find unconvincing the flat *a priori* dictum that the abilities of the scientists involved must necessarily (obviously?) be excluded from any adequate philosophical analysis. To the contrary, my feeling now is that the philosopher should start with the empirical necessity of the pictures and base his or her analysis on that.

However, again for the sake of argument, let us grant the traditionalist the point. Let us be swayed by some such claim as: 'The history of recent evolutionary theory shows that, although the pictures were needed in the earliest days, over time with increased formalism, their use has declined, thus showing that the ideal is a science without pictures.' As a matter of fact, I do not know if this claim is empirically true, but it is certainly the kind of claim that will be or has been made. So let us go along with it.

Still the traditionalist has problems. It must still be conceded that the pictures were important, and may indeed now still be important, if not always in the future. And by 'important' here I do not just mean 'helpful'. We have seen that the formalisms themselves did not express Wright's theory fully. The formalisms alone were shared by Fisher who had an altogether different theory. The adaptive landscape idea went beyond the formalisms, expressing the notion that drift could generate variation in isolated populations, and that selection could then act to bring about rapid change. Moreover, let me point out that this, more than anything, was the *theory*, so the traditionalist cannot wriggle out of the claim that the adaptive landscape idea was (and may still be) part of Wright's basic science.

WRIGHT'S TWO (1931 AND 1932) PAPERS

The response no doubt will be that although Wright's theory clearly did go beyond the formalisms (because at that stage it was 'immature'?), the claim for the necessity of the pictures can be jettisoned. After all, in the main 1931 paper there were no pictures or even the metaphor. Everything that needed to be said, could be said and was indeed said, in words, literally.

In reply to this I will say three things. First, I simply do not know whether or not Wright had the landscape metaphor in mind when he first thought up his theory. We know that it predated publication of the 1931 paper, because it is used in an earlier letter to Fisher (see Figure 2.9). Wright may have had it all along. I do know that the young Wright (and the old Wright, for that matter) was an Henri Bergson enthusiast, and something very much like the adaptive landscape metaphor occurs in *Creative Evolution* (published in 1912). It could well be that Wright was thinking seriously about landscapes even before he began his formalisms. The case for the necessity of the landscapes in the 1932 form of the theory does not depend on this, but I think the critic should tread warily before making sweeping claims about what *must* have been the case, historically. (Towards the end of this paper, I will have more to say about the historical underpinnings of Wright's thought.)

Second, I would challenge the claim that the 1932 version of Wright's theory was simply the 1931 version, without the mathematics. The pictures do indeed add some factual claims – most importantly, that there are going to be some adaptive peaks for organisms to occupy, so long as one drifts far enough. The 1931 version really does not say much about why drift will eventually pay off. I have quoted the relevant passages and they are very vague. Indeed, Wright has already said that one small group drifting will probably go extinct. In the 1932 version, the pictures make it clear that there are all sorts of good opportunities waiting for drifters. Wright could have drawn a peak with a plain all

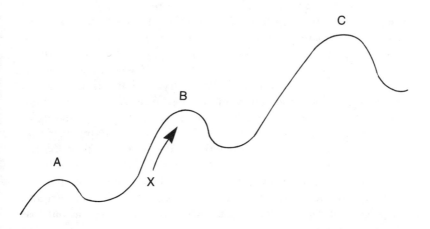

Figure 2.9 Two-dimensional fitness surface. Redrawn from a letter from Wright to Fisher, 3 February 1931. From Provine 1986: 272

around it, or with all kinds of (by definition) inhospitable seas or uncrossable rivers or chasms. But he does not, and it is certainly part of the plausibility of his theory that every peak seems to have other relatively accessible peaks in the vicinity.

Third, before it is immediately objected that one could have expressed all of Wright's new (post 1931) claims in words, let me point out that he did not. Moreover, let me point out also that (as people like Mary Hesse (1966) have pointed out generally about metaphorical thinking) there is a heuristic element to adaptive landscapes which escapes a simple list of factual claims that a scientist might make at a particular time (specifically Wright in 1932). Like all metaphors, they are 'open-ended' in a way that the strictly literal is not.

In this context, consider Dobzhansky's own 1951 rendering of the landscape (Figure 2.8). He has peaks clustering together in a way quite absent from Wright. Although, interestingly, he does not acknowledge the fact (that is, he does not write it down in words), he is adding a distinctively new element to the theory – that adaptations are not random and that what works well in one way might have similar (although somewhat different) mechanisms also working well. The point is similar to someone noting the virtues of both gasoline and diesel motors, and noting also what a big gap there is between them and a steam engine or a jet engine.

There is therefore a forward-rolling aspect to Wright's picture. It stimulates you to push ahead with more claims. Just as in real life peaks tend to be clustered (the Alps, the Rockies), so Dobzhansky was stimulated to think of adaptive clustering. In doing this, I suspect that Dobzhansky was following what was already assumed by Simpson (see Figures 2.6 and 2.7 which make significant the spacing of the peaks). Relatedly, as I mentioned earlier, Dobzhansky like Simpson went beyond Wright's thinking about the landscape working *within* a species, to the landscape telling of relationships *between* species. For Wright, it was populations on the road to speciation climbing the peaks. For Dobzhansky, the peaks were occupied by different species. It is in this significant sense, how Dobzhansky pushed beyond Wright's own picture, centring on the heuristic value, that I would deny that Wright's adaptive landscape could, even in theory, be dropped without loss of content.[6]

But what about the final claim of the critic, at least in this line of argument? My original thesis was about the status of pictures in science. However, by my own admission, I have moved freely back and forth between metaphor and illustration, basically counting them as one and the same – or, rather, I have in the specific instance of Wright's adaptive landscapes. Yet there is a difference: the one is a physical picture on a printed page; the other is not. My original claim was about the former, not the latter. Even if we concede the necessity of the latter, it does not follow that the former was necessary. Perhaps the population geneticists did need the metaphor. They did not necessarily need the pictures. Wright could have talked about an adaptive landscape and that would have been enough – for him, for Dobzhansky, and for all the others.

At this point, I give up. 'You win!' Though why anybody should insist on keeping the pictures out, unless their computer could not handle graphics, altogether beats me. However, the victory strikes me as being pretty thin. The case that Wright had an uneliminable (without loss of content) pictorial metaphor at the heart of his (post-1931) theory is unchanged. And that, quite frankly, is good enough for me. Moreover, in line with a point made earlier, I remind you that the identity is not between a picture and an adaptive landscape *per se*. It is between a picture and a particular representation of an adaptive landscape, namely the kind of representation one finds in the picture! I suppose one could describe all this in words; but somewhere, it seems to me, we would have to have an image at play, even if it were only a mental image.

BUT IS IT GOOD SCIENCE?

We cannot yet turn positively to explore the implications of our findings for more general questions about scientific knowledge. There is another line of argument which will tempt the traditional philosopher of science. It will be granted now that at least some science, at some level, incorporates pictures. But the complaint will now be that the *best* science does not. All science, even relatively good science, would be better were there no illustrations. Top quality science is just a formal system.

I confess that my general reaction to this line of inquiry is to query precisely whose criterion of value is being invoked here. Why is the best science non-pictorial? It seems to me that by just about any standard of excellence you might normally raise, the work of Wright and his successors like Dobzhansky rates highly. If anything, it defines the criteria rather than is measured by them. But since I have staked my position so firmly on one single case, perhaps the critics can come back on the basis of this case. Good though Wright's work may have been, there are reasons to think it might have been better without the adaptive landscape idea.

Interestingly, almost paradoxically, Provine (1986) seems to incline this way. He characterizes the general reading of adaptive landscapes as 'unintelligible' (313) and concludes his discussion of the notion on a very negative note: 'I would emphasize in conclusion that Wright's shifting balance theory of evolution in no material way depends upon the usefulness of his fitness surfaces as heuristic devices' (Provine 1986: 317). He is very much of the school that as evolutionary science has matured, the need for and value of the surfaces has dropped away. (Since I am about to criticize Provine's position quite strongly, I want to enter more than the conventional disclaimer. Without Provine's brilliant work on the history of population genetics in general and on Sewall Wright in particular, it would be quite impossible for philosophers such as myself to work with any degree of sophistication on the meta-theory of this area of evolutionary biology.)

How might the critic argue the negative point? Most obviously, I suppose, by pointing out that the heuristics of the landscape are all very well, but if they lead one on false trails, their virtues are of dubious status. Take the question of other peaks surrounding any specified peak. Perhaps these represent niches which do truly exist. Perhaps they do not. One has no right to assume, as the metaphor forces on one, that they are always there. In fact, they are probably not.

In response, I would agree that perhaps Wright's picture does suggest false trails. But, with respect, 'So what?' No one wants to say that scientific hypotheses – exciting scientific hypotheses – always work or are always true (although sometimes philosophers have a yearning towards this last option). The point is that the theory is fertile and, with respect to something like available niches, can be tested and rejected or revised if necessary. In fact, as comments I have made already clearly imply, one can certainly redraw Wright's landscapes if one finds that niches are not readily available. And if no niches at all are available, then the whole theory must be rejected, not just the pictures. I am not now saying that the empirical evidence is irrelevant to the worth of a theory.

I am assuming what is true: that Wright's work led to a mass of successful empirical research.

I might add in this context that, although treatment of metaphor usually labels implications cleanly as good, bad or neutral heuristics, in real life (as our example shows) it is often not so easy to decide whether or not implications are such a very good or bad thing. Take the presumed stability of Wright's landscape. Although the possibility of change is certainly mentioned, generally – as with landscapes as opposed to water-beds – the terrain is supposed to be fairly solid. This suggests that organisms will scale ever-higher peaks, and that in the long run there will be progress.

However, although many today – like George Williams (1966) and Stephen Jay Gould (1989) – would consider this the consequence of a negative heuristic, others are not so sure. I am certain that Wright himself endorsed progress. (Look at Figure 2.9, p. 51 taken from a letter to Fisher.) Not only is the botanist G. L. Stebbins a progressionist, he has used Wright's ideas to make precisely such a case (Stebbins 1969). And active today, someone like E. O. Wilson (1975) is an organic progressionist and would, no doubt, find any supporting implications of Wright's metaphor most comforting. He does indeed talk of the 'peaks' of social evolution (occupied by the colonial organisms, the social insects, the higher mammals and humans) and of our own species having 'reversed the downward trend' (where sociality is getting ever looser). We are on the way up to the highest point of all.

The critic might now argue in a slightly different way. Wright himself admits that in his diagrams he is collapsing down a huge amount of information into two dimensions (three if you consider the axis from eye to page). But is this legitimate? One is taking drift from many dimensions and confining it to two dimensions. One of the things that Wright always prided himself on was his recognition of the fact that genes in combination might well have very different effects from genes taken singly. What right therefore have we to assume that the many drifting genes will combine to behave like one drifting gene (or, rather, a line of such genes)?

There is an important point here, one which shows that although Wright himself may have been sensitive to gene interaction, critics like Ernst Mayr (1959) were not simply revealing their personal prejudices when they accused the population geneticists of undue reductionistic thinking, in treating their subjects as beans in a bag. However, note that if there is a problem here – that the collapse of dimensions is too dramatic – it is one which affects all levels of theory and not just the illustrations. Again, therefore, I suggest that Wright's theory should simply be put to the test, and a check made to see if genes do wander in the way that he suggested.

In fact, as I have intimated, a decade after Wright published, Dobzhansky and others found strong evidence that selection is far more powerful and effective than Wright and others had suspected. (I am not now referring to molecular genes which, by their very nature, evolve at levels below the power of selection.) The shifting balance theory required modification. But I am not sure that such modification required or requires rejection of the very notion of an adaptive landscape. One can rework the landscape to show that factors other than drift are significant. This, indeed, was precisely the move of Simpson and Dobzhansky.

None of this is to deny, in line with some of the points made by Provine, that even as it stood, there was some confusion in Wright's thought about selection and adaptation – a confusion reflected in the pictures. Like many around 1930, Wright was torn between adaptationism and non-adaptationism. As one who revered Darwin, he thought that selection was important; but all the (American) naturalists around him were saying that it was not. Hence, in one respect, Wright wanted selection to be important between (members) of groups, and his pictures rather imply this. In another respect, Wright doubted that there is much adaptive difference between group members, even when the groups are as large as species or more, and he rather implies that drift proves this also!

However, it seems to me that the correct analysis here is that Wright was trying to have his cake and eat it too. The problems and any weaknesses do not come from the pictures as such. Moreover, as the case for adaptation was strengthened, Wright could and did more firmly opt for his first alternative – and even deny that he ever held the second alternative. The presence or absence of the pictures was irrelevant. (Actually, this is not quite true. If selection is completely unimportant, then the adaptive landscape becomes an uninteresting plain. It is clear that Wright always thought that at some level selection is important. He was unsure about the level. What this means is not that the landscape is irrelevant, but more that there is confusion about the status of the groups that hover around the peaks. Are they sub-groups or are they full-blown species? As we have seen, people went both ways on this.)

INDIVIDUALS VERSUS GROUPS

Let me go at the problem one more time, making the case against Wright's work in a way that I think would be favoured by Provine. There is at least some confusion in Wright's theorizing (paralleling a similar confusion of Fisher's) over whether he is talking about individuals or about groups. Sometimes the theme seems to be that of the fate of a gene (or a string of alleles) in a population. Sometimes the theme seems to be that of the fate of a group, and of the gene ratios varying within that group. In fact, strictly speaking, Wright's early analyses were couched more in terms of the former and later (after the mid-1930s) in terms of the latter – presumably in line with Dobzhansky and others – but Wright tended to slip back and forth. More significantly, sometimes he spoke of his landscapes in terms of the former and sometimes the latter.

Now, in a sense, you might think this is not desperately important. As Provine notes, most biologists simply think the group treatment is the integral of the individual and so (biologically) not much rests on the distinction. But as Provine rightly notes also, in respects the group perspective does set major questions for landscape metaphor. What are the co-ordinates of the (two-dimensional) map? Does one have two sets of gene ratios? If so, what about the (possibly) many hundreds of other ratios? Moreover, how now does one interpret the map? Points are presumably groups. At the least, this is going to require some fairly drastic redrawing.

In fact, as Provine points out, when Wright moved his mathematics to a group level, the theory became highly abstract – calculating the adaptive value of a population ($\bar{W}$) 'for more than one locus with two alleles was practically impossible' (305–6). To be honest, I am not sure whether this point counts against the landscape metaphor, or for it. Does this mean that we can push on only because of our picture – mathematics fails – or that we should not dare to move because the mathematics fails? I cannot see why the first option is necessarily incorrect. (Of course, this is to talk of long ago. Today, with much more mathematical talent in biology, not to mention computers, we are in a much stronger situation.)

Provine stresses that Dobzhansky could never follow Wright's mathematical extensions, but we virtually knew that anyway. He could not follow the mathematics at the individual level. It is true that, even assuming the legitimacy of an extension, the landscape in its original individual based form remains important; indeed, its mathematical base seems even more crucial. What then of the individual perspective? Provine refers to the diagrams understood at this level as 'unintelligible' – hardly the mark of the best quality science. What are the grounds for this drastic assessment? Let me quote Provine in full:

> The first and most important thing to notice about Wright's first published version of his fitness 'surface' is that his construction does not in fact produce a continuous surface at all. Each axis is simply a gene combination; there are no gradations along the axis. There is no indication of what the units along the axis might be or where along the axis the gene combination should be placed. No intelligible surface can be generated by this procedure. By no stretch of the imagination can Wright's famous diagrams of the 1932 paper be constructed by his method of utilizing gene combinations. The diagrams represent a nicely continuous surface of selective value of individual genotypic combinations; the method Wright used to generate this surface actually yields an unintelligible result. Thus the famous diagrams of Wright's 1932 paper, certainly the most popular of all graphic representations of evolutionary biology in the twentieth century, are meaningless in any precise sense.
>
> (Provine 1986: 310)

Is this conclusion well taken? One thing that Provine highlights is the fact that, strictly speaking, we do not have a continuous surface, but a set of discrete points. However, if the points are vanishingly small and jammed in together tightly enough – both conditions that Wright meets – then like the printed version of a photograph, also made of many small discrete points, we have an effectively continuous surface.

A more important point that Provine highlights is that we certainly have no typical linear dimensions along the axes, as one would with a regular map. But even this does not strike me as critically fatal. We never did have a conventional map, although I do concede that probably many read Wright as if we did. We are not thinking quantitatively but more qualitatively (in the third dimension we are quantitative). But maps of this kind are not unknown – those of the world, for instance, which blow up areas with a certain quality and drastically reduce areas without such a quality. One cannot measure regular distances on such a map, but it is still a map in the sense of showing what leads where.

Actually, for all the concessions I am prepared to make, I am not sure that Provine reads the maps altogether accurately. Each axis is *not* a gene combination. Each point is such a gene combination. Therefore one might perhaps construe the axes as measured in 'unit gene changes' or some such thing. Even though I am not altogether certain what it would mean to say that each gene change was equal, at least one would have properly ordered sequences along the axes. Although our problem here is somewhat compounded by the fact that apparently Wright accepted Provine's criticism – 'When I spoke with Wright about the problem, he thought it over for several days, and suggested that the only way he could see to save something of his original version of the individual fitness surface was to use continuously varying phenotypic characters as the axes of the surface' (311) – it could just be that Wright's response translates back to a rough equivalence to the suggestion I have just made.

All in all, then, I conclude that the criticisms of Provine or fellow conservatively minded analysts are not well taken. Wright's work was not perfect, in the sense of being absolutely true or totally without conceptual blemish. But this is a far cry from saying it was not first-rate science. Fortunately scientific theories are like human beings: they are complex entities, with lives of their own, and the best are the best, not because they never do anything wrong, but because they do so many things right.

PUTTING WRIGHT IN CONTEXT

What have I proven? I have certainly not proved that every scientific theory has to have pictures, or that every scientific picture is essential. By my own admission, I have been dealing with a picture of a special kind, namely one which expresses a metaphor. Nor am I claiming here that every scientific theory contains metaphors, although as a matter of fact this is a claim I would be prepared to defend. I am not even claiming that every scientific metaphor gives rise, actually or potentially, to a picture. Indeed, this seems to me to be a false claim. Only in a very limited way do such important biological metaphors as natural selection or the struggle for existence give rise to pictures, and these are usually misleading. (Most struggle is not a literal struggle.)

Nevertheless, some scientific metaphors are pictorial; Wright's landscapes prove this. Especially, the landscapes are crucial when you think (with Dobzhansky) of species and their adaptive relations to each other. And those metaphors or pictures are in an important sense (any sense which is important) essential parts of the science; Wright's landscapes prove this. Moreover, the science containing these pictures can be good science; Wright's landscapes prove this also. These seem to me to be a good set of conclusions with which one could end this somewhat preliminary foray into the philosophical significance of biological illustration. But, on the admirable principle that one should never end a discussion on a safe and reasonable note, let me now push on out into treacherous depths, making a few comments about what my discussion implies for broader questions concerning scientific knowledge, and indeed knowledge generally.

I shall not pause here to consider in detail the implications of my findings for discussions about the nature of scientific theories. Clearly, the old idea (beloved by the logical empiricists) of a scientific theory as a formal axiom system – a hypothetico-deductive system – is inadequate. At a minimum, it needs a major supplement. A popular alternative today to the traditional view is the so-called 'semantic' view of theories, where one thinks less of all-embracing systems and more of families of limited models, which might or might not be applicable in certain situations. I am not convinced that a naturalist necessarily must abandon ideal pictures or the belief that somehow the hypothetico-deductive picture functions as an ideal. Nevertheless, as a naturalist, I do find this alternative position attractive because it does seem to me to describe truly the way that much science actually functions, and this applies particularly to evolutionary biology. But, even if one embraces the semantic view, let us not forget that this view is itself generally presented in no less a linguistic and formal manner than the standard view. So it too has got to be extended to encompass metaphors and pictures. Perhaps the extension can be done more readily on the semantic view than on the traditional view. I am open to argument.

My real concern now, however, is with the light that my analysis and findings throw on knowledge itself – our relationship to the external world, especially as mediated through science (which I will flatly and provocatively say is our highest form of knowledge). And as I turn to this, first let me go again to history, and let me say more about the context in which Wright's picture appeared. I have said that it is quite probable that he got his picture under the immediate stimulus of a kindred metaphor of Bergson. But this is only part of the story. Wright was looking for, or primed for, such a metaphor, for his whole approach to evolution came from and was shaped by a particular tradition. Wright was (as, I have said) unambiguously Darwinian, thinking natural selection a significant factor in evolutionary change. Far more so, however, was he a follower of Herbert Spencer, Darwin's contemporary and fellow Englishman and evolutionist.

This will seem amazing, for Spencer's reputation today is as low as Darwin's is high. But in his time Spencer was *the* authority, and nowhere more so than in America. Significant for us is the line of influence to Wright, through his first biology teacher. This was the woman who introduced him to evolutionary thought, Wilhelmine Key, a student of C. O. Whitman, one of the most ardent of American biological Spencerians. Even more significant is the yet stronger connection through Wright's graduate school experience at Harvard, for his teacher there was L. J. Henderson, author of *The Fitness of the Environment*.

Many today think that Spencer's main contribution to evolutionary thought was a stern version of 'Social Darwinism', a particularly vicious form of *laissez-faire* economics, where the rich succeed and the weakest go to the wall. Far more influential, however, was Spencer's 'dynamic equilibrium', a kind of progressive force upwards, from simplicity to complexity, from the valueless to the valued, marked by stages of equilibrium or balance which eventually prove unstable (or are dislodged) forcing a shift up to a new plateau (Pittenger 1993). This view was adopted in its entirety by Henderson and passed straight on to his pupil, who obviously translated it directly into populational genetical terms and who visualized it exactly in his landscape metaphor.[7]

Parenthetically, once the Spencerian background is made public, one can see precisely why (a matter of puzzlement to many) Wright called his theory the shifting *balance* theory. It is a balance or equilibrium between forces promoting genetic homogeneity and genetic heterogeneity – in themselves very Spencerian notions. It also explains why, despite his thinking having become far more selectionist in the 1940s, Wright always maintained his theory was unchanged. With respect to the crucial Spencerian notion of balance, it always was. What changed was the much less significant (for Wright) item of the forces promoting such balance.

Completing the historical background and locating fully the setting of Wright's diagram/metaphor, let me make two final points. First, reconfirming what has been said already, Wright's work does not simply look backwards. It looks forward also, through the very great influence he had on his fellow evolutionists, even down to this day, where it is the shared underpinning of the thought of people who *prima facie* take very different positions. Fellow Harvard faculty members Stephen Jay Gould and Edward O. Wilson have been at ongoing loggerheads, with Wilson expressing contempt for Gould's palaeontologically inspired theory of 'punctuated equilibria' and Gould being no less critical of Wilson's 'sociobiology'. Yet Gould's punctuated equilibria theory (think of the name!) stands right in the tradition, both through direct debts to the Wrightian-inspired synthetic theory and through more indirect debts thanks to its use of the notion of stability or homeostasis, a pet idea of W. B. Cannon, a Harvard (Spencerian) buddy of Henderson. Wilson's sociobiology has been noted already as having come straight from Wrightian aspects of the synthetic theory; although, it does also owe much to another of Henderson's Harvard chums, the entomologist William Morton Wheeler. Wilson, incidentally, openly admires Spencer.

My second point, also picking up on something said earlier, is that the American tradition is not the British tradition. In that country, Charles Darwin was the icon and font of inspiration for evolutionists. And for Darwin – and especially for his ardent followers like Wright's rival, Fisher – the key metaphor had little to do with progress and balance. It was rather that of adaptation – seeing organisms as if they were artifacts, objects of design. It was this that was addressed and highlighted by British natural theology, most notably the author of Darwin's undergraduate reading, William Paley. It was this that was tackled and explained by Darwin's key mechanism of natural selection. It was this that convinced Fisher that selection, working in large groups, could be effective. And it is this that has come right down to the present and inspires and informs the work of leading British evolutionists today: William Hamilton (1964 a, b) and Geoffrey Parker (1978), to take two major examples. For them, adaptive landscapes are really very small beer.

I do not want to exaggerate. I have noted Wright's Darwinian debts, even as I have noted also that selection was ever for him a secondary mechanism to his dynamic equilibrium view. I have noted also that some British took up Wright's landscapes, although the greatest enthusiast for the landscapes and drift was Julian Huxley, a man who – for all his trumpeting of Darwinism – had a very tenuous relationship to the British tradition. He was ever a vitalist, an enthusiast for Bergson (in turn much influenced by Spencer) and (later) the very non-Darwinian Teilhard de Chardin.[8]

My point now is simply that there were/are these two traditions, and Wright (thanks in larger part to his landscapes) is a central figure in one and not the other.

INTERNAL REALISM

With Wright's work now firmly located in context, what can we or would we want to say philosophically? At one level – and this does seem fairly definite – we are being pointed towards a view of science (and knowledge in general) which takes metaphors, including visual metaphors, very seriously. They inform and structure our thinking. Yet, at the same time and just as crucially, one must accept that no one metaphor seems to be crucial. One can be a good evolutionist and yet deny (or, more likely, ignore) the Wrightian landscape.

In line with a powerful trend in modern history and sociology of science, therefore, one does seem to be pushed to some sort of 'constructivism', where science is seen as a construct resting on and emerging from the culture of its day and place. And, one might add (although not in context of my example) precisely such a philosophy has been endorsed by students of biological illustration.

> Scientists intend their pictorial representations, like their verbal expressions, to illuminate reality. Nevertheless, commentators of scientific activity should not give interpretative primacy to the issue of correspondence between representations and nature. Instead we should center our sights on interventions within a nature and society that scientists are continually helping to construct. The multiple references

built into diagrams deserve attention because they point to many of the resources mobilized in such constructions.

(Taylor and Blum 1991: 291)

However, although all this is fair enough, our example surely gives no warrant for pushing constructivism all the way to rabid subjectivism, where science is seen to be no more than a creation of society (taken as a whole or through individual members). Wrightian-inspired evolutionary biology is more than a mere fiction, where anything goes. Reality may be mediated through Wright's picture; but his picture succeeded and was used enthusiastically by others precisely because it did help to make sense of reality – both as known then and as new discoveries came in down through the years. It provided the basis for a fruitful 'paradigm' or ongoing 'research programme', to use the language of the philosophers (Kuhn 1962 and Lakatos 1970 respectively).

We seem therefore to be pushed towards a middle position, one somewhere between the extreme objectivism of the traditional philosopher of science (like the Popper of science as 'knowledge without a knower'), and the extreme subjectivism of the constructivist, who sees everything as mere psychological or sociological whim. I cannot, given what has gone before, pretend now to offer any logical argument for what this middle position must be. But, as a naturalist (and a Popperian) I am allowed to make bold conjectures, and in this spirit I nominate the ontology/epistemology of Hilary Putnam, something he labels 'internal realism'. Recognizing that there are as many versions of realism as there are realists, he writes as follows:

One of these perspectives is the perspective of metaphysical realism. On this perspective, the world consists of some fixed totality of mind-independent objects. There is exactly one true and complete description of 'the way the world is'. Truth involves some sort of correspondence relation between words or thought-signs and external things and sets of things. I shall call this perspective the *externalist* perspective, because its favourite point of view is a God's Eye point of view.

The perspective I shall defend has no unambiguous name. It is a late arrival in the history of philosophy, and even today it keeps being confused with other points of view of a quite different sort. I shall refer to it as the *internalist* perspective, because it is characteristic of this view to hold

that *what objects does the world consist of?* is a question that
it only makes sense to ask *within* a theory or description.
Many 'internalist' philosophers, though not all, hold further
that there is more than one 'true' theory or description
of the world. 'Truth', in an internalist view is some sort of
(idealized) rational acceptability – some sort of ideal coherence of our beliefs with each other and with our experiences
*as those experiences are themselves represented in our belief
system* – and not correspondence with mind-independent
'states of affairs'. There is no God's Eye point of view that
we can know or usefully imagine; there are only various
points of view of actual persons reflecting various interests
and purposes that their descriptions and theories subserve.

(Putnam 1981: 49–50)

The talk is of coherence. Yet, one is not precluded from the kind
of correspondence demanded by the semantic view of theories:

In an internalist view also, signs do not intrinsically correspond to objects, independently of how those signs are
employed and by whom. But a sign that is actually employed
in a particular way by a particular community of users can
correspond to particular objects *within the conceptual scheme
of those users*. 'Objects' do not exist independently of conceptual schemes. We cut up the world into objects when we
introduce one or another scheme of description. Since objects
and the signs are alike *internal* to the scheme of description,
it is possible to say what matches what.

(Putnam 1981: 52)

But we certainly do not and cannot have the correspondence of
the traditional objectivist, where 'snow is white' can be slapped
on to an independently existing white snow. (Philosophically
informed readers will of course, recognize the 'snow is white'
example as that which Alfred Tarski used to illustrate his correspondence theory of truth. Expectedly, this is a theory much
favoured by Popper.)

As it happens, I have argued elsewhere for internal realism,
using modern evolutionary biology as my foundation (Ruse 1986).
In other words, I have argued for the position on naturalistic
grounds, although Putnam himself seems not to be a naturalist
and denies the pertinence of evolutionary biology (see Putnam

1982). Here I am happy simply to endorse such realism, pointing merely to the fact that it does seem to be an epistemology/ ontology that welcomes my discussion of Sewall Wright's adaptive landscape picture/metaphor. One has the world as mediated through a human creation – the metaphor of a landscape – and one cannot escape from this mediation without a loss of content. Yet, at the same time, one is constrained and stimulated by the empirical discoveries one makes through the creation. There is no 'God's Eye view', but there is a lot more than mere feeling or intuition.

What I will note here, now starting to bring my discussion to a close, is that my analysis of Wright's work meshes exactly with some of the most exciting recent work on metaphor, and that (on grounds independent of my own) these thinkers have themselves been pointed towards internal realism. George Lakoff and Mark Johnson (1980) argue that metaphors are essential, uneliminable parts of our thought, themselves in some sense creating reality.

> New metaphors, like conventional metaphors, can have the power to define reality. They do this through a coherent network of entailments that highlight some features of reality and hide others. The acceptance of the metaphor, which forces us to focus *only* on those aspects of our experience that it highlights, leads us to view the entailments of the metaphor as being *true*.
>
> (Lakoff and Johnson 1980: 157)

There is a sense of correspondence. '*We understand a statement as being true in a given situation when our understanding of the statement fits our understanding of the situation closely enough for our purpose*' (179, their italics). But, in an equally crucial sense, because truth is relative to understanding, there can be no absolute, viewer-independent knowledge. We have to work from within a culture; although this certainly does not mean that all standards are jettisoned and that 'anything goes'.

> We have seen that truth is relative to understanding, which means that there is no absolute standpoint from which to obtain absolute objective truths about the world. This does not mean that there are no truths; it means only that truth is relative to our conceptual system, which is grounded in, and constantly tested by, our experiences and those of other

members of our culture in our daily interactions with other people and with our physical and cultural environments.

(193)

In later writings, Lakoff and Johnson (Lakoff 1986; Johnson 1987) tie in their 'experientialist position' to Putnam's internal realism, arguing that the two are the same thing by different names. Recognizing that we are working still in the realm of conjecture rather than proof, this does neatly parallel the way in which my discussion of Wright's work has pointed me to the same ends. And the connection is made yet stronger, giving Lakoff and Johnson's discussion particular immediacy, as one learns that a key plank in their argument for the significance of metaphor is the existence of basic 'orientational' metaphors, rooted in personal bodily experience, that structure all of our thinking.

These spatial orientations arise from the fact that we have bodies of the sort we have and that they function as they do in our physical environment. Orientational metaphors give a concept a spatial orientation; for example, HAPPY IS UP. The fact that the concept HAPPY is oriented UP leads to English expressions like 'I'm feeling *up* today'.

(Lakoff and Johnson 1980: 14)

Obviously Wright's diagram/metaphor fits right into this thinking, given its stress on 'up/down' (an example highlighted by Lakoff and Johnson) and 'balance', something just as crucial to us as upright vertebrates. Not only does it fit, it gives just what the naturalist craves, namely an unexpected explanation of the hitherto obscure. If you think for a moment, there is something very odd about Wright's picture, namely the fact that he paints a landscape with the need for genes to climb up mountains. Much more obvious would have been a landscape stressing valleys, where genes have a natural tendency (thanks to gravity) to roll *down*, unless disturbed otherwise. (Interestingly, the English evolutionary geneticist C. H. Waddington (1956), did produce pictures of this nature, in the context of a theory of gene interaction.)

Apart from the more obvious progressionist implications – something certainly seized on by the likes of Dobzhansky and Stebbins (although more recently deplored by Gould) – it seems plausible to suggest that Wright's thinking, having genes defy gravity, was an aspect of the general structural metaphorical thought of human beings, stressed by Lakoff and Johnson. Putting the matter bluntly, because we are upright mammals, we do tend to think in vertical terms, and (for all the obvious reasons) stress the upwards direction as the positive/healthy/valued orientation. Wright was no less human than the rest of us, and so his thinking came out the way that it did.

CONCLUSION

As a naturalist committed to evolutionary biology, and as one who has, as I have said, already argued elsewhere for internal realism on biological grounds, I am readily sympathetic to a philosophy which ultimately locates Wright's visual thought in his personal bodily experiences. But, I am much aware that I have long since ceased to prove anything, and am trying simply to fit my example into a pattern of philosophical thought that I find congenial. Yet the fit is neat and suggestive. Hence for this reason I commend it to you. Wright's adaptive landscapes have played a crucial role in evolutionary thought in this century. In themselves, they offer much of historical and philosophical interest. My feeling is that they point to matters and conclusions of much broader epistemological and ontological significance.

NOTES

1 R. W. Merriam, State University of New York at Stony Brook.
2 To my eternal credit, although I may not have talked about pictures, I have always acknowledged their significance by using them. This began in a minor way in my first book *The Philosophy of Biology* (1973a) and reached a peak in *Darwinism Defended* (1982).
3 I expound my naturalism as a general system in Ruse 1986, and am now writing a book on the concept of progress in evolutionary biology in which I try to show how one does a naturalist philosophy of science. Methodologically and metaphysically I owe much to my long personal and philosophical friendship with David Hull, although we differ widely on many actual issues. See Hull 1988 a and b and Ruse 1989a.
4 I have this on the authority of G. L. Stebbins who was in the audience. (Interview, May 1988.)
5 Provine (1986) deals with this point in some detail.
6 As you can see in a passage quoted above, this idea is in Wright's text but only in a restricted fashion, and it is not carried over into the map.
7 I was led to the Spencerian influence on Wright's thought by a number of letters which he wrote to his brother Quincy, around 1915. These are now in the Quincy Wright Papers, at the University of Chicago. I

am as obliged to Will Provine for telling me of them as I am shocked by Provine's refusal to see the influence of Spencer or anyone else of a philosophical mind-frame on Wright's thinking.

8 All of these points, including those in subsequent paragraphs, are dealt with in my forthcoming book, *Monad to Man: The Concept of Progress in Evolutionary Biology.*

3

CONTROVERSY IN PALAEONTOLOGY
The theory of punctuated equilibria

Evolutionary biology has always been marked by controversy and this is something especially true of the subject for the past twenty years. In this essay, I want to look specifically at one such controversy, that which arose in palaeontology about the so-called theory of 'punctuated equilibria'. Although I have written about this topic before, I want to take a more empirical, naturalistic approach than previously (Ruse 1989). The justification for my approach will be the strength of my results, so without further ado, let me get to work.

PUNCTUATED EQUILIBRIUM – CLAIMS AND COUNTER-CLAIMS

My story begins in the 1960s with two young would-be palaeontologists, Niles Eldredge and Stephen Jay Gould, in graduate school at Columbia University, New York. Students of evolution's history will know that these were the full summer days of neo-Darwinism, the 'synthetic theory' blending natural selection and Mendelian (already becoming molecular) genetics, supposedly explaining phenomena right across the biological spectrum. The key to understanding was 'adaptation', seeing organic features moulded by selection to serve life's needs, and it is important to stress, particularly in the light of what was to come, that both Eldredge and Gould felt the need to acknowledge their acceptance of this adaptationist picture.

This acceptance, on the surface at least, can be seen fully in a review paper written by Gould (1966) on problems of relative growth (allometry). Again and again, it was stressed that one must see the living world in terms of adaptive function, and that this is the key to the problems of biology that one such as he would consider: 'As a paleontologist, I acknowledge a nearly complete bias for seeking causes framed in terms of adaptation' (588). Nevertheless, let me add (for the moment, without comment) that, especially reading with the advantage of hindsight, this is a most interesting piece of work. Darwinism (meaning adaptationism) may 'rule OK', but the very essence of relative growth is that one has various bodily parts growing as functions of the growth of other parts. Overall one may have an adaptive picture, but looking at individual parts reductionistically, one often sees an adaptive compromise in one area to promote greater efficiency in another.

Move next to the early 1970s. Eldredge was on the staff at the American Museum of Natural History, already a trilobite expert. Gould was at Harvard, attached to the Museum of Comparative Zoology. A student of fossil snails, he was starting to show broader literary interests, as well as a fondness for the history of his subject. In 1971, Eldredge published a paper (in the evolutionists' leading journal, *Evolution*) on one of the most puzzling questions facing the palaeontologist. Why is it, if evolution be true, that we rarely if ever see in the fossil record the evidence of a smooth transition from one form (species, genera, and above) to another? Why do we rather see one fixed and defined form ('stasis') and then as we move through the strata an abrupt change, a jump, to another equally defined form?

Denying the usual face-saving move, supposing that one has a gradual process of 'phyletic' change, and that the gaps are due to an incomplete record, Eldredge argued rather that the record as we see it is precisely what one would expect were the synthetic theory true! Drawing attention to what he claimed (I think truly) was what students of living organisms believe to be the major form of speciation, so-called, 'allopatric speciation', where new species are the result of the isolation of small sub-populations from the main group (with an inevitable atypical genetic constitution and consequent rapid evolution), Eldredge claimed that this would give one just the step-wise record that one actually finds: 'I would suggest that the allopatric model ... rather than gradual morphological divergence, is the more correct view of the processes underlying cases of splitting already documented by numerous workers' (Eldredge 1971; 156–7).[1]

I should stress that, as becomes a junior scientist publishing in a prestigious journal, Eldredge's tone was modest and respectful: a

71

normal scientist doing normal science, to use Kuhnian language. The same tone of deference cannot be found in the next publication, co-authored by Eldredge and Gould (1972). Appearing in a volume intended to push a more biologically informed approach to palaeontology, they made every move one counsels one's graduate students to avoid. Full of rhetorical flourishes – 'the cloven hoofprint of history', 'innocent unbiased observation is a myth'; totally without shame or modesty – 'Science progresses more by the introduction of new world-views or "pictures" than by the steady accumulation of information'; sarcastically contemptuous of much that had gone before – 'we are amused by the absurdity of a claim that we should rejoice in a lack of data because of the taxonomic convenience this provided' – the authors threw down the gauntlet. Distinguishing between 'phyletic gradualism', where fossil lineages change gradually and smoothly, and 'punctuated equilibria', where changes comes in spurts, they announced boldly:

> The history of life is more adequately represented by a picture of 'punctuated equilibria' than by the notion of phyletic gradualism. The history of evolution is not one of stately unfolding, but a story of homeostatic equilibria, disturbed only 'rarely' (i.e. rather often in the fullness of time) by rapid and episodic events of speciation.
>
> (Eldredge and Gould 1972: 84)

There is small wonder that, having commissioned the piece, the editor of the volume had to be pressured to accept it. He did, and the rest (as they say), is history.

There are various questions one could ask about the piece, but what I do want to emphasize is the extent to which the authors were now actively in the business of moving out from the adaptive constraints of strict neo-Darwinism. I will ignore, although not forget entirely, the fact that the allopatric theory of speciation puts a premium on non-selective factors as a few organisms are somewhat randomly separated off from their parent species, and move on to the point that, although Eldredge and Gould did not want to argue that new species appear entirely without regard to adaptive needs, they did argue that what is immediately adaptive is not necessarily long-term adaptive. Species might appear according to the needs and opportunities of the moment (set within the context of the randomness imposed by allopatric speciation); but the overall pattern (trend) may well be pointing in other directions.

This move from adaptationism is backed by their treatment of the question of stasis. Why do we not get ongoing morphological change in evolving lines of organisms? Why is there stability – equilibrium – between spurts of rapid change? Here there was a turning to notions of 'homeostasis', where this is to be understood as meaning that there are certain in-born constraints buffering against the external world and its immediate effects. And, once again, the effects of selection were minimized. Selection may have been important in the past; but, once its work is done, stability becomes, in its own right, 'an inherent property of both individual development and the genetic structure of populations'. Moreover, 'its power is immeasurably enhanced, for the basic property of homeostatic systems, or steady states, is that they resist change by self-regulation' (114).

GAUGING THE CONTROVERSY

So much for the initial expression of the theory. It was not long before the Eldredge–Gould papers started to attract attention, first among palaeontologists and then more widely. Some liked their ideas; others did not. I will turn in a moment to reactions and counter-responses. First, however, both as a general expression of my naturalistic approach and specifically because of some questions I shall have to ask, I want to start trying to measure the effects of the punctuated equilibria hypothesis. How much attention, favourable and unfavourable, did it attract? How big a controversy was it, or was it going to be? Was it really significant, or was it all a storm in a tea-cup?

When faced with a problem like ours, there is one tool of inquiry which springs to mind, namely the *Science Citation Index*. That the *Index* is a very crude tool needs no argument here. The problems with its use are already much discussed (for instance, MacRoberts and MacRoberts 1986; Hicks and Potter 1991; and references). But, for all the failings and crudities, perhaps through its use we can say something about our controversy as a controversy. At least, we can get a start to matters, and possibly after the start we can even hope to improve matters somewhat. So, it is worth a try. (As an appendix to this paper, I present my raw data. I am not going to defend my use of the *Index* in this discussion. I will simply say that I am aware of the criticisms, and as appropriate I have tried to avoid the glaring problems.)

I have surveyed the *Index* for a quarter century (in fact, twenty-six years) from 1965 to 1990, inclusive. My aim has been to compare Eldredge and Gould against their peers and others, judging their influence, or, rather, the interest taken in their work, and specifically in the key documents of the punctuated equilibria theory. Beginning at the beginning, let us see what we can learn about the two initial periods of 1965–9 and 1970–4, that is the half-decade before the theory was presented and the half-decade when it was first presented.

First, a couple of benchmarks. By the 1960s, molecular biology was the really hot area in the life sciences, and there was nothing more important than the Jacob–Monod operon theory of the gene. This is reflected in the fact that, in the period 1965–9, François Jacob got over 3,000 references, of which about a thousand were to his classic paper (Jacob and Monod 1961a) announcing his find. I take it, incidentally, that this work was not particularly controversial, but right from the start it was considered very important. Whether it was considered 'revolutionary' probably depends on how you would use that term. In a somewhat less prestigious science, although one with obvious connections with our inquiry, geology, there had been a move forward which everyone did recognize as revolutionary (Ruse 1981). I refer to the theory of continental drift, and to its mechanism of plate tectonics. One of the major figures here, Fred Vine, who made his major discovery as a graduate student, garnered (overall) about an order of magnitude fewer references than did Jacob, and this held true also of *his* key paper (Vine and Matthews 1963).

Turning now to evolutionary biology, the dominant figure – especially in America – was undoubtedly Theodosius Dobzhansky. Overall, he got about half the references as did Jacob, and like Vine the references to his key work (*Genetics and the Origin of Species*) was about an order of magnitude less than for the molecular biologist (although one should note that the last edition of this book had appeared way back in 1951). Of younger evolutionists, the best and brightest of the new crop was surely Richard Lewontin, just now applying molecular techniques to traditional problems. Overall he was about level with Vine, although his key paper (using so-called 'gel electrophoretic' techniques: Lewontin and Hubby 1966) got fewer references than did Vine's key paper. (It did appear somewhat later, only at the beginning of our period, so there would have been a lag here. I am also including information on the other paper jointly authored by Hubby and Lewontin, and you will see that I shall continue this practice of covering certain key works where the person in whom I am interested is second author.)

If, with an eye to our discussion, we ask about people just starting to make a mark in the evolutionary field, one thinks first of George Williams, author of the stimulating critique, *Adaptation and Natural Selection*, published in 1966. He was very small beer, with only twenty-five references to his book. The same is true also of England and of its really creative thinkers, especially of William Hamilton, who had just published (what was essentially) his thesis, including the idea of kin selection – a breakthrough many would consider the most significant since the work of Ronald Fisher and Sewall Wright, if not back to Darwin (Hamilton 1964a, b). And completing our background survey, mention must be made of Edward O. Wilson, on the threefold grounds that he was a keen adaptationist, that he was establishing himself as one of the new generation of evolutionists up there with Lewontin, and that he too was to be embroiled in controversy, one which certainly entangled Gould. In our period, he got about the same number of references as Lewontin. (Wilson insists on the authorship of publications being listed alphabetically, so it is especially important to consider some key works where he was second author.)

Against this background, we find that in 1965–9, Eldredge got two references (one by Gould!) and Gould got forty references (only about half those of Hamilton and Williams), including fourteen to his *Biological Reviews* paper (his most cited publication). Although these are modest figures, I take it that they are absolutely no surprise whatsoever. After all, we have merely two young men, just out of graduate school. The surprise, perhaps, is that the figures are not more modest than they might have been. Already Gould seems set to make his mark. It is true that a review paper is a good way to boost your representation in the *Index* and should not be compared to an innovative publication (like Hamilton's). But to do the job well takes a talent of its own, and a good review – like Gould's – is far from an exercise in disinterested reporting.

Moving straight on to the five-year period 1970–4: Jacob's work is still very important, but no longer quite so innovative in such a fast-moving field as molecular biology. Vine's work is fully recognized, but still one has the feeling that geology is not a science in the same league as that of Jacob. Dobzhansky holds solid (at the beginning of our period he published his *Genetics of the Evolutionary Process*, essentially the fourth edition of his great book). Lewontin's significance is being appreciated (although his major book, *The Genetic Basis of Evolutionary Change* did not appear until the end of our period), and the same is true of Wilson (whose *Insect Societies* got immediate attention, and whose jointly authored *Theory of Island Biogeography* is getting solid attention). Note, however, that both of these men are still more in the geology category than in that of molecular biology, and the same is true of Williams and Hamilton, although they too are starting to get attention.

What of our two palaeontologists? It certainly seems fair to say that Eldredge and Gould have careers which are solidly on track. Gould in particular is attracting attention, in no small part because of his *Reviews* article, although certainly not exclusively because of it. Already their punctuated equilibria papers are being noted, and interestingly the joint paper (published a year later) is more of a hit than the strictly scientific publication of Eldredge – although the figures are small and may not be very significant. What surely is significant is that the smallness of the figures points to the fact that punctuated equilibria hardly arrived to a major crashing of symbols. Compare, for instance, the far greater effect in the earlier half-decade of the Lewontin–Hubby study. Punctuated equilibria is under way, but this is not yet really the stuff of controversy.[2]

THE CONTROVERSY BUILDS: 1975–9

Let me again pick up the story, for the next five-year period. It was this time, I suspect, that most today would remember as having seen the rise up to the high point of the punctuated equilibria debate/controversy. There were some, either in series or in parallel, who were arguing for a picture of evolution very much in line with that of our palaeontologists. One was Steven Stanley, a young palaeontologist at Johns Hopkins University, who had been the junior author of the then basic text in palaeontology (Raup and Stanley 1971). It was he who coined the term 'species selection' for the supposed process whereby the overall pattern of change (between species) might display epiphenomena quite independent of the immediate adaptive needs of individual species, either their origins or their survivals (Stanley 1975, 1979). Thus, individually, the adaptive pressure might be towards increased size, but overall the trend might show reduced size. This could happen, for instance, if there were an appropriate differential rate of extinction.

There were also identifiable and articulate critics. One of these – he who epitomized the opposition – was a young vertebrate palaeontologist, Yale educated and now teaching at the University of Michigan, Philip Gingerich (1976, 1977). Relying on incredibly detailed studies, ongoing for nearly twenty years by a Yale-sponsored group, Gingerich argued that now we do have a record of micro-evolution in action. And the message is gradualism. Punctuated equilibria is just plain false.

Expectedly, Eldredge and Gould responded to these criticisms, arguing that no one is making absolute claims – a swallow does not a summer make, nor does one case of gradualism disprove punctuated equilibria. But in any case, virtually all of the supposed cases of gradualism turn out not to be so very gradualistic on close examination. And this applies particularly to Gingerich's evidence, which is a paradigmatic case of stasis interspersed with rapid change! 'Gingerich's data for *Hyopsodus* offer the finest confirmation now available for the most important implication of punctuated equilibria' (Gould and Eldredge 1977: 132).

So far, so good. If this had been all, then I doubt that I would have been writing this paper. What made punctuated equilibria *controversial*, as opposed to simply a disagreement between professionals – that is, what added a real edge to the debate – was the fact that the major response, appearing in 1977 and written now mainly by Gould, was larded with provocative musings, ranging from the merely metaphysical to the apoplectically outrageous (Gould and Eldredge 1977). It was bad enough that, for all that evidence was being bandied about to crush critics, the reader was airily told that much of the opposition to punctuated equilibria was simply *a priori* prejudice. What really proved to be gasoline over flickering flames was the suggestion that those who accept traditional Darwinian gradualism are still stuck with nineteenth-century *laissez-faire* liberalism. Perhaps, it was suggested, there is an alternative, better philosophy. 'It may also not be irrelevant to our personal preferences that one of us learned his Marxism, literally at his daddy's knee' (Gould and Eldredge 1977; 145–6).

It is important to point out that, at the very moment that this claim was being made, there were factors external to palaeontology which would lead one to expect that this statement would have proved particularly inflammatory. Most particularly, this was the height of another controversy in evolution, that over the supposed biological basis of human thought and behaviour, epitomized by opposition to Edward O. Wilson's *Sociobiology: The New Synthesis*. Gould was one of the co-signatories to a notorious letter to the *New York Review of Books* (Allen *et al.* 1975) faulting Wilson as a genetic determinist and crypto-racist/sexist/capitalist (not so crypto, in fact). This really was a nasty dispute, especially given that Gould (and fellow signatory Lewontin) were in the same department at Harvard as Wilson. As can be imagined, any other controversy in which Gould was embroiled was going to be examined with great care, and his sociobiological opponents (especially Wilson) were not about to miss an opportunity of bedaubing Gould on grounds of his (supposed) Marxism.

There are matters here which beg us to return to the *Citation Index*, but before we do, let us finish the story of our period, first by noting that beneath the inflammatory remarks of the Gould–Eldredge response one can see clear evidence that the screw is being turned a little more tightly on adaptationism. Again there was no denial. But now more explicit was a belief that organisms have basic blueprints, *Baupläne*, and that these could constrain and cause stasis. Significant change can occur only as one switches from one *Bauplan* to another, and this could require a relaxation of selection. Close functional tracking was being questioned.

> At the higher level of evolutionary transition between basic morphological designs, gradualism has always been in trouble, though it remains the 'official' position of most Western evolutionists. Smooth intermediates between *Baupläne* are almost impossible to construct, even in thought experiments; there is certainly no evidence for them in the fossil record (curious mosaics like *Archaeopteryx* do not count).
>
> (Gould and Eldredge 1977, 147)[3]

Parenthetically, one might add that this was all very much in line with the message of a major scholarly book, *Ontogeny and Phylogeny*, just published by Gould. This was a combination history and conceptual analysis of problems of relative growth as expressed through time – in major respects a continuation of

Gould's (now ten-year-old) *Biological Reviews* survey, but one making even more explicit the ways in which constraints on and effects of growth might be expected to create problems for the strict Darwinian, that is for one who sees all organic features all of the time as direct functions of immediate adaptive needs:

> morphology is simply not the primary ingredient of many . . . adaptations. The redirection of selection towards the timing of maturation might well release the rigid selection usually imposed upon morphology. Morphology would then no longer be fine tuned to a changing environment.
>
> (Gould 1977b: 338)

The way was now prepared for an all-out assault on adaptationism, which came some two years later, in a paper co-authored by Lewontin. With brilliant use of example, metaphor and simile, the evolutionists argued that much in the organic world has but an indirect connection to adaptive necessity. *Baupläne*, constraints on growth, incidental effects, and more, are major shapers of organic form. Natural selection is all very well, but it has a limited and hobbled effect on the processes and products of life. Against the adaptationist argument, there is an alternative which has to be the choice of the unprejudiced evolutionist:

> It holds instead that the basic body plan of organisms are so integrated and so replete with constraints upon adaptation . . . that conventional styles of selective arguments can explain little of interest about them. It does not deny that change, when it occurs, may be mediated by natural selection, but it holds that constraints restrict possible paths and modes of change so strongly that the constraints themselves become much the most interesting aspect of evolution.
>
> (594)

The distaste for pure Darwinism was now explicit, and the way was prepared to push the punctuated equilibria controversy to its highest pitch. But first, let us take people's temperatures through the *Citation Index*.

GAUGING THE CONTROVERSY, 1975–9

The background facts are as one might have expected. Lewontin is now apparently a really major figure, right up there with his (just deceased) teacher Dobzhansky – just what one would have expected, as well the decline of people like Jacob. And, expectedly, the sociobiology controversy makes a major impact. Overall, Wilson explodes in recognition status, and *Sociobiology* is a significant factor. Moreover, whether as cause or effect, related work is getting more attention: that of Hamilton, for instance.

Yet, before turning to punctuated equilibria, perhaps the sociobiology controversy does help us to remember one important point. We must draw a careful distinction between a *scientific* controversy and a controversy involving *scientists*. To be perfectly candid, the sociobiology controversy was in major part the latter, with the battle being fought in the media, and with the full and happy participation of people who were not professional evolutionists. These included philosophers like myself, for instance (see Caplan 1978; Ruse 1979b. Kitcher (1985) was much admired by those who do not like human sociobiology, but it did not really appear until after the controversy had died down somewhat).[4]

Indeed, the *Index* itself rather hints at the status of the sociobiology controversy. Judging from citations of *Sociobiology: The New Synthesis*, Wilson's reputation rests almost as much on his *Insect Societies*, which was really not controversial at all. Or looking at things from another perspective, consider Wilson's *On Human Nature*, published in 1978. This really was at the heart of the human sociobiology controversy, for it was exclusively on our species, gained huge publicity, and even won a Pulitzer Prize. It was, however, explicitly marked as for the general reader, and as far as the scientific community was concerned (looking ahead also to the 1980s) was so regarded. I am not saying that there was no scientific controversy, but I am making a classificatory caution.

Against this background, what can we say about punctuated equilibria? Gould as a scientist is certainly gaining respect and appreciation in the scientific world, although note that he is certainly not up with Lewontin or Wilson, or Williams and Hamilton for that matter. The other participants – Eldredge, Stanley, Gingerich – are establishing solid careers, although they in turn lag behind Gould. If you look at the references to Vine, for comparison, one might well conclude that (by analogy) what we are seeing here is simply the fact that palaeontology is less respected or central to evolutionary thought than are other areas. But my inclination would be to argue that the still relatively junior status of the men involved was the major factor determining citation count.

If we think about punctuated equilibria in particular, there seem to be two main conclusions to be drawn. First, one does get the distinct impression that without Gould – and one presumes his rhetoric and philosophy – there would not have been much of a controversy. The solo-authored Eldredge article, for instance, got very little attention. If one looks ahead to the next decade (that is the period 1980–90), this is a conclusion which is confirmed strongly. Second, within the scientific community, it is still not that big a controversy. It is nowhere like as controversial as Wilson's *Sociobiology* (unless we make some highly counter-plausible assumptions, such as that whereas all the references to Wilson were neutral, all those to Gould and company were controversial. Even then, punctuated equilibria would not rate with sociobiology in overall visibility. In any case, as can be seen from the data, it is certainly not the case that Gould's work has been invariably controversial. Look at the *Evolution* findings!).

If we compare say the original Eldredge–Gould paper with Hamilton's seminal papers, we see that the scientific (for which I would read 'evolutionary') community does not seem to rate the palaeontologists' ideas of comparable importance with kin selection, whether or not either was thought controversial. What I do start to see, however, specifically in the case of Gould, is that people in the scientific community are showing an interest in the views which he holds challenging strict adaptationism – which views come in writings including, but extending beyond, his punctuated equilibria writings. The *Reviews* article – which I have suggested may be adaptationist but can be read, with hindsight, for rather more – receives a lot of attention, and notice how *Ontogeny and Phylogeny* is also getting noticed. It is true that the attention is not great, but keep this point in mind as we move to our next period. (Note also, in passing, that although *Ever Since Darwin* was a bestseller, it was regarded by the scientific community as a popular book, which it was. Scientists are selective about what they quote – there is no quoting of Gould simply because he is becoming famous.)

Highly pertinent here are the breakdown figures from *Paleobiology* and *Evolution*. They suggest strongly that punctuated equilibria as such has made little inroad to the evolutionary community taken as a whole. Even the few references tend to be neutral. However, more general work by Gould does tend to get some (more) attention. This does all fit with the common-sense observation that scientists are likely to be much more attracted to something they can use, rather than more general – dare I say 'philosophical' – ideas. One can use kin selection, one can use (check, test, experiment with, etc.) non-adaptation through growth, and so forth. One cannot, if one is a general evolutionist, use hierarchies and macro-theories and the like. (I take it that this impression is supported by the Eldredge and Stanley *Paleobiology/ Evolution* comparisons.)

THE CONTROVERSY BOILS OVER, 1980–4

The beginning of the new decade, 1980, saw the peak of the punctuated equilibria controversy. It really became a matter of interest in the scientific community at large and with the general public. This was thanks particularly to a symposium on the topic at the Field Museum in Chicago and a provocative report in *Science* by the journalist Roger Lewin (1980), telling us that the old way of doing evolution is past. Evolution by fits and starts is the new orthodoxy – perhaps we do indeed have a new 'paradigm', in the Kuhnian sense.

Gould himself, however, played his role, publishing (in 1980) his most extreme discussion of punctuated equilibria, declaring that neo-Darwinism is 'effectively dead' – that none of its major tenets remains standing. Moreover, he began flirting with the idea that perhaps species change can occur in one or two generations. Never an outright saltationist, he nevertheless began championing the reputation of the geneticist Richard B. Goldschmidt, a saltationist and an arch-opponent of the synthetic theorists. The case for the distinctiveness of the punctuated equilibria thesis was now pitched in these sorts of terms.

Although, we must note that even by micro-evolutionary scales the moment of extremism was short lived. The geneticists were now truly stirred to action, and the criticism started to flood in. It was one thing for a palaeontologist to presume in his own field; it was another if he presumed in neontological studies. It is to take too gentle a view of human nature to assume that none of Gould's critics at that time was indifferent to the fact that they were critiquing the man who had now, thanks especially to his popular writings, become 'Mr Evolution'. Though let me stress that the nastiness was never that of sociobiology. Perhaps the simple fact of the matter is that the fossil record, as such, does not excite human emotions in a way that occurs when the spotlight is focused upon us.

One should probably add that – and I do not now want to appear unduly cynical – Gould himself quickly realized that, apart from the shaky scientific ground on which he stood, appearing too much of a maverick was not in his own best interests. It is one thing to be provocative. It is another to be thought unsound, or just plain silly. Fame, respect and all the other goodies desired by a scientist were coming his way, without need for recklessness. There was therefore a swift move into line. We learn that Gould had never meant to be read as a radical, just as he had never meant to be read as a Marxist! He was much more interested in 'expanding' conventional Darwinian evolutionary theory, than in refuting it. At the micro-level, it may well be that natural selection is all-important. It is at the macro-level – where the palaeontologist is monarch – that we must come to appreciate the force of punctuated equilibria. Evolutionary thinking must therefore be hierarchical, with different ideas respectively appropriate for different levels.

> Terminological issues aside, the hierarchically based theory would not be Darwinism as traditionally conceived: it would be both a richer and a different theory. But it would embody, in abstract form, the essence of Darwin's argument expanded to work at each level. Each level generates variation among its individuals: evolution occurs at each level by a sorting out among individuals, with differential success of some and their progeny. The hierarchical theory would therefore present a kind of 'higher Darwinism' with the substance of a claim for reduction to organisms lost, but the domain of the abstract 'selectionist' style of argument extended.
>
> (Gould 1982: 386)

In short, the implication was drawn that it was not so much that Gould was unsound, but that those who would not go with him were unduly conservative, blinkered by the constraints of their own narrow discipline.

What of other supporters of punctuated equilibria? Always more interested than Gould in classification for its own sake, Eldredge was (like most others at the American Museum of National History) an enthusiast for the school of cladism, trying to do taxonomy on strict phylogenetic lines (Eldredge 1972). This interest had extended into work on biogeography, a pursuit which led to fruitful collaboration with others of a similar bent (Eldredge and Cracraft 1980). Not that he ceased to write on punctuated equilibria, and we can see that the scientific community appreciated his efforts. There was solid, if not outstanding, success for the co-authored *Phylogenetic Patterns and the Evolutionary Process*, published in 1980.

The same can be said of a new book by Stanley (1979).[5] What is especially noteworthy is that real efforts were now being made to find new and (hopefully) decisive pieces of empirical information. Much praised (by punctuated equilibria supporters!) was the work of a young invertebrate palaeontologist, Peter Williamson (1981, 1985), who apparently had found solid evidence of punctuated evolution among molluscs of East African lakes. The fact that Williamson was a member of Gould's department at Harvard meant that there was full opportunity to spread the word to the world at large.

GAUGING THE CONTROVERSY, 1980–4

The *Index* in this time-period strongly confirms the extent to which Gould was rising to be a public man; although note that generally there seems to be a heightened interest and activity in matters evolutionary.[6] It is not true yet that (within the scientific community, as opposed to the world at large) Gould is *the* major evolutionist. Wilson, if anybody, has the honour, but Gould alone among the palaeontologists has achieved major status. What is becoming increasingly evident, in line with what I have said already both about Gould and about Wilson, is the extent to which people are referring selectively to Gould's work. It was Gould's 1980 paper in *Paleobiology*, 'Is a new and general theory of evolution emerging?' that really got shocked gasps, and yet its scientific effect was hardly overwhelming. The direction in which people still preferred to turn was towards his earlier, more moderate (in scientific claim) punctuated equilibria work. What was quickly judged inadequate did not receive continued major attention.[7]

However, if we look at the work of Gould which did get attention, it seems to me that an interesting effect (already suspected) is really starting to emerge. People are interested in punctuated equilibria, but they are as interested – *if not more!* – in Gould's other work, where there is a more general attack on or querying of general ubiquitous adaptationism. Even back to the *Biological Reviews* paper (1966), and then up through *Ontogeny and Phylogeny*, and on to the jointly authored 'Spandrels' paper (1979), there are solid sets of references. For now, I will simply note this fact, although there are some obvious explanatory hypotheses (likewise already suspected) to which I shall turn shortly.

Looking briefly at the others involved in the punctuated equilibria controversy, I note that the *Index* does support the claim that, in general, non-palaeontological critics got in and made their points and then went on to other things. (This, at least, is what I read from the data on Stebbins and Ayala 1981, and Charlesworth 1982. A random check of the content of the references does not suggest that it is more.) For palaeontologists involved in the punctuated equilibria controversy, there is solid interest in their work, but the outstanding fact to emerge is just how much slighter the punctuated equilibria controversy remains compared to sociobiology. Nothing seems to have had the impact, one way or the other, of *Sociobiology: The New Synthesis*. This is something which is true, even if we include Gould taken as a whole, but it is even more striking if we confine ourselves to Gould and others when they are writing directly on punctuated equilibria.[8] Again, there are some obvious hypotheses here about the relative statuses of sub-areas within the evolutionary synthesis.

THE CONCLUDING YEARS, 1985–90

Of course these years were not really concluding. The story goes on. But from our viewpoint, speaking especially now of *controversy*, but also more generally, this completes the tale. Although both Eldredge and Gould have remained prolific authors, frenetic even, conceptually (and empirically) I see no significant innovations. And I think this is reflected in the fact that no one now seems inclined to argue in a heated fashion for or against punctuated equilibria. Basically, commitments have been made, and people think about other things.

For Eldredge, 'thinking about other things' means (most recently) an expansion of evolutionary mechanisms to economic factors (Eldredge and Grene 1992). Gould has continued to write on punctuated equilibria, working alone and with others (notably the South African palaeontologist Elizabeth Vrba (Gould and Vrba 1982; Vrba and Gould 1986)); but his most visible object of recent concern (especially in his latest bestselling book *Wonderful Life*) is biological progress – the idea that through the processes of evolution, most notably selection, there is an upward increase in value, from the simple to the complex, from the monad to man.

His strong objection to this thesis is readily connected to punctuated equilibria, especially inasmuch as the theory incorporates, centrally, the notion of species selection. Note, as its enthusiasts all emphasize, that this is not necessarily a causal process in quite the same way as natural selection. It is more a tally at the macrolevel of what has happened at the micro-level. Species come into being and go extinct. Even if there are adaptive forces directing the origination of species, the overall effect through extinction might be against the usual direction of origination. Most importantly, the effect through extinction might be a function of purely random effects.

But, as Gould (and others) note, randomness can frequently give the *appearance* of order. Thus trends through time – from smaller to larger, from slower to faster, from thicker to brighter – may have no real significance, certainly no real adaptive significance. However, since trends are the very stuff of progress, if these are undercut, we have no reason to think that alleged progress of life's history is more than wishful thinking (Gould 1989, 1990). As with adaptationism, and for strongly related reasons, another myth based on a misunderstanding of the true nature of evolution hits the ground.

Eager now to get to the analytical part of my discussion, believing that (*qua* controversy) things are winding down, let me move straight to the information yielded by the *Index*. The professional Gould seems to have caught up with the public Gould, and he is now the most frequently cited evolutionist – as first author, at least. But despite this, and despite the solid careers of the other punctuationists, the conclusions derived earlier still stand. Punctuated equilibria does not seem to have had the same impact as sociobiology, and the major interest in Gould's work seems to be in his general attack on pan-selectionism. Wilson's *Sociobiology* is still a more cited work in our survey.

Likewise, if we look at the actual pieces published on and around punctuated equilibria, and compare them with Gould's more general material, the same pattern as before prevails. Nobody could say, for instance, that Eldredge or Williamson dominate the field. And Gould himself has more effect away from his theory, considered directly. Twenty years after it was published, his *Reviews* paper still gets more citations than any single piece he wrote on punctuated equilibria, including the original article co-authored with Eldredge, and more generally it is his book (*Ontogeny and Phylogeny*) and his co-authored 'Spandrels' paper which receive the fullest attention. The basic punctuated equilibria papers just hold steady or decline, and the same seems true of more recent general statements.

ANALYSIS

What then can we now say about the punctuated equilibria dispute? In the light of our findings, I want to make three interrelated points, beginning first with the fact that many critics insist that the punctuated equilibria dispute was no real dispute at all. It is dismissed as a 'wrinkle' on evolutionary thought (Dawkins 1986): as 'mere hand-waving by the palaeontologists', as it was characterized by one eminent evolutionist when I asked for his opinion. I take it that this kind of sneer is not merely personal – jealousy of the less well known of the more well known – but truly does represent a strongly held judgement that, in essence, punctuated equilibria theory is no true theory, certainly no true advance. It may not be a falsity like cold fusion, but in the long haul it is little better. Its status is about on a par with supply-side economics: no relationship with reality whatsoever. And this is reflected by the lack of interest, by scientists as scientists.

Now we know that, at one level, this is simply not true – if the criticism is meant to imply that there was no dispute at all, or even that there was no *scientific* dispute at all. I accept that much of the attention came from outside the professional scientific community, and that within the community it certainly does not seem to have been that big a matter. But judging from the interest paid, both to the key pieces of advocacy and to the major critiques, there was a dispute within the evolutionary community. That cannot be denied.

At another level, if you are pointing to the subjective and personal dimension in some respect, there is surely truth in what you claim. If anything is certain, it is that the punctuated equilibria controversy would never have existed without Gould's brilliant rhetorical skills. His use of apt example or provocative metaphor; his folksy casual style, which adds rather than detracts from the fact that one is to see a very serious concern about science and its morality; his lawyer-like nose for the weakness in the other's argument – all of these things are quite without equal (Lynne and Howe 1986). Of course, Gould's skills come out most fully in his more popular writings, but they do come out through and through his professional work. The difference between Eldredge (1971) and Eldredge and Gould (1972) is simply the difference between night and day. The latter absolutely screams for attention – which is precisely what it got!

Not that I want to conclude that Gould was simply into punctuated equilibria as a literary exercise or for the personal glory. For Gould and for all the others pushing punctuated equilibria, it has always been very clear that there is much more at stake than personal glory. Again and again the advocates of the idea stress that what really concerns them is the hope of finding a significant place for palaeontology within the evolutionary family. For too long the field of evolution has been dominated by the geneticists and experimentalists. Despite the general public identification of evolution with the fossil record, among professional evolutionists palaeontologists have been despised, told when and where to jump. Now, however, with punctuated equilibria these hewers of wood and drawers of water (breakers of rock?) can play their part in the full development – the articulation and the justification – of evolutionary thought (Gould 1983).

In fact, as the dispute developed, I see the palaeontologists getting bolder in their claims. At first, the feeling seems to have been joy that one no longer has to twist and turn – invoking an incomplete fossil record – to fit palaeontology into causal thinking about evolutionism. It can indeed support it. Then confidence grew to the point where it was thought that palaeontology can contribute in places where genetics and the rest must fall silent. It is true that there was a nasty reminder of limitations when Gould was rapped sharply on the scientific knuckles over his perceived saltationism. But this was more a setback than a defeat. The claim for essential status was revised in such a way that there is no danger of overlapping and contesting the beliefs of already-established areas of evolutionary biology, except where they themselves are clearly out on a limb. Thus the strong emphasis in recent years on the hierarchical nature of evolutionary thought, and on the significance of palaeontology for understanding macro-evolution (Gould 1982, 1989, 1990; Eldredge 1985a, b; Eldredge and Salthe

1984; and much, much more). I am not saying that the desire for status is the only thing motivating Gould, Eldredge, and the others when they push ideas like these; but I do say that it is an important factor.

As we now know, the palaeontologists were successful, but only partially successful, in what they set out to do. They certainly got attention within the scientific community. But the fact is that they just did not get the attention that other areas get, sociobiology in particular. Even if we ignore the fact that, when there was a clash with genetics, it was the palaeontologists who had to step smartly back in line, the overall recognition gained by punctuated equilibria was respectable rather than stunning (as measured by references). Eldredge and Gould (1972), for instance, got less than half the recognition that Hamilton (1964a, b) got for kin selection. The simple fact is that we are still left with the feeling that we are dealing with a science of the second order (look at the data on Gould references in *Evolution*).

Positively, it is true that even if we think only of palaeontology, punctuated equilibria has certainly brought life to a rather staid area of study. But I am sure you will realize that I want to claim more than this, and here I come to my second point. I see punctuated equilibria theory as an idea through which Gould (he significantly, but I am happy to agree, not he exclusively) has been stimulated to think about life's processes, and in particular the true causes of evolutionary change. In particular, it has been a stimulus to move away from a strict Darwinian perspective. I do not want to say that this has been entirely a one-way causal process, with palaeontology the dog that wagged the tail of everything else. After all, Gould was starting to think about processes back in his essentially non-palaeontological *Reviews* paper, published well before punctuated equilibria appeared. And the earliest version of the theory, both Eldredge alone and in the joint paper, was still pretty Darwinian. So whatever is to be said, it has to be against the background acceptance that there is a complex causal web linking punctuated equilibria to broader questions about mechanisms.

However, given that Gould and the others are professional palaeontologists, given that punctuated equilibria is their theory, and especially given that palaeontology has always been a field where adaptation is not that pressing – I speak now comparatively, judging palaeontology against subjects like ecology or animal behaviour

– it seems plausible (if pressed, I would put things more strongly than this) to say that the causal chain has not been entirely the other way, from general evolutionary thought to palaeontology. The general critique on adaptationism owes something to the experiences and theorizing in palaeontology. And if this be so, then in light of what we have learnt from the *Index* – I refer specifically to the general interest in Gould's attack on strict Darwinism – we see that (indirectly perhaps, but causally significantly almost certainly) punctuated equilibria has had a wider influence on evolutionary thought.

Which is perhaps the way that one might have expected things to be. Picking up again on a point made earlier, the reason why Hamilton's work has been so significant is that he gave people models that they could use – a bright graduate student could take kin selection into the field and see if it applies to some interesting species of organism. In the other corner, however, hierarchies and jumps are all very well, but after you have finished talking about them at a conference, what can you do with them?[9] Yet this impotence does not hold true of a general critique of adaptationism, particularly when it is linked to ontogeny (embryology, genetics including the molecular variety, etc.). Such a critique offers something that impinges on the work of everyone, even offering the chance of doing something, experimentally or in the field. Hence the increased interest, reflected in the frequency of the references.

If what I say is true, we are led straight to another item of interest, which is the third and final point of this paper. This is not something which can be drawn straight from the empirical findings (especially those from the *Index*); but it is something which helps us to make sense of these findings. Whatever the major direction of the causal links, it is clear that at some level the punctuated equilibria enthusiasts, Gould particularly, managed to sound a responsive chord in the biological community. Apparently, the supposed ubiquitous adaptationism of the synthetic theory was sufficiently unstable that, within twenty years of its triumph (I date this as the centenary of the *Origin of Species* in 1959), people were listening with attention to those prepared to argue that neo-Darwinism is an impoverished view of the evolutionary process.

As it happens, my findings rather suggest that (probably) because most evolutionists are non-palaeontologists, they preferred to work from non-palaeontological writings. But, this in no way detracts from the fact that, as punctuated equilibria theory has evolved, it has become the epitome (certainly in Gould's version) of the move away from adaptationism – constraints, randomness, *Baupläne*, and so forth. It is the general position cast in stone, if I might be permitted a dreadful metaphor. It symbolizes and encourages the case for non-adaptive evolution – more accurately, for non-ubiquitous adaptive evolution.

The question which I ask now is about the meaning of all of this. Whatever other factors were involved, and I am sure there were several, might I suggest that in some way the ground was already prepared? I am emboldened to ask this question because, as we have seen, it is just not the case that the anti-adaptationist movement epitomized by punctuated equilibria has come up with stunning new findings (as in the physics case of super-conductivity) or new models (as with Hamilton) – findings and models which simply compel discussion and agreement. Much of the discussion has been rhetorical and/or philosophical in some broad sense. I ask it also since some people – English adaptationists, in particular – seem not merely to be unreceptive to the attack on adaptation, but incapable of seeing even that there is the slightest force to the attack. (If you do not know what I mean, look at Richard Dawkins' *The Blind Watchmaker*.) For them – intelligent, hard-working, good-quality evolutionists – punctuated equilibria and all that it represents is not so much false but simply time-wasting gobbledegook (see also Maynard Smith 1981).

To answer my own question, what I would suggest is that punctuated equilibria has had the success that it has had because it is in tune with a deep strain of already-existing (although perhaps for a time submerged) non adaptationism in evolutionary thought, or rather in evolutionists' thinking. The adaptationism of the synthetic theory was a veneer over rather different sympathies – at least, it was a veneer for some evolutionists, although for others (like Dawkins, or those in whose steps he follows) the adaptationism was solid oak all the way down.

In particular, I am inclined to argue (and I make no pretence now that I am doing other than taking ideas I have developed and justified elsewhere, to try to explain particular facts facing me here) that what we have are two different 'paradigms' or conceptual frameworks or *Weltanschauungen*. We have two different visions of the evolutionary process and product (Russell 1916; Ruse 1989).

Although the one may have been submerged for a while, the palaeontologists have been at the forefront of reviving it. To talk in terms of *metaphor*, one set of evolutionists (the Darwinians, the synthetic theorists) regards the organic world in terms of adaptation, which is to say as though it is *functioning* or *designed*. The other set of evolutionists, of which Gould is a prime representative, does not. They think of the organic world in terms of form, which means that there are certain basic *structures* or *blueprints* according to which organisms are *constructed*.

Historically, there has always been this dichotomy in the history of evolutionism, with people like Darwin pushing function, and people like the German *Naturphilosophen* arguing rather that transcendental laws of form are what govern the processes of transformation. (Gould himself, especially in his *Ontogeny and Phylogeny* has long stressed this point.) My argument here is that punctuated equilibria theory stands in the second transcendentalist tradition, and this (at least in part) accounts for its success. It is simply doing what many evolutionists have always been doing.

I used to think that, given Gould's oft-repressed enthusiasm for aspects of German thought (the fondness for *Baupläne* for example), one could in fact make a fairly direct link with the transcendentalists of the early nineteenth century (Ruse 1989a). Now, however, although I think that there is still much grist for this mill, I am inclined to think that we should look for immediate influences closer to home – apart from the fact that, while we may be able to take Gould back to Weimar and the world of Goethe, there is no reason to think that others would want to join him.

Today, I would point to the fact that American evolutionism has always deeply internalized non-adaptationism in a way that British evolutionism never has (Richards 1987). Asa Gray may perhaps have won the debate with Louis Agassiz, but it was the latter who influenced deeply two generations of evolutionists – they simply took his ideas and made them continuous (Winsor 1991)! More than this, *the* crucial figure dominating American evolutionism in the last century was never Charles Darwin. Beyond doubt, it was Herbert Spencer (Russett 1976; Pittenger 1993). And the crucial point to note here is that, unlike Darwin, he was ever a man with (let us say) a casual attitude towards adaptationism – an attitude he passed on to others. It was not that Spencer was against adaptation. It was rather that, for him, it was not the overriding mark of organic nature. Far more significant was the upward rise of organic life, the move from homogeneity to heterogeneity, as organisms increasingly complexify down through the course of time.

Furthermore, before you rush to tell me that what happened in the last century should never be extrapolated to this century, I would add that the evidence is mounting that Spencer's ongoing influence can be traced through his enthusiast L. J. Henderson to *his* student, none other than the eminent evolutionist Sewall Wright.[10] Spencer argued that evolution is characterized by a series of moves, from one state of balance to another. We have what he called a process of 'dynamic equilibrium', with ongoing jumps up from one stable point to another. This theory, which (like the Germanic theories on which Spencer drew) is essentially indifferent to adaptation, was made respectable by being made mathematical by Wright, at the end of the 1920s. It is true that in the 1940s, along with everybody else, Wright became more of an adaptationist, but it was never this that really excited him. What counted was the move from one state of equilibrium to another – a move from one homeostatic peak to the next.

My argument simply, then, is that punctuated equilibria stands in this American tradition. It succeeds as – because it is – non-adaptationist, because this has always been the way of American evolution. Moreover, before you dismiss this all as a fantasy, let me remind you first of the need to explain away the obvious debt to Wright – a debt which flows from the fact that Mayr's 'founder principle' (the non-selective element of which I noted) is little more than a corollary of Wright. And, let me remind you second of the gloriously Spencerian name of 'punctuated equilibria', pointing out that in making their case for homeostasis in their original paper, Eldredge and Gould relied on arguments of the geneticist I. Michael Lerner, who in turn relied on ideas of W. B. Cannon, one of Henderson's Spencerian buddies at Harvard. In short, punctuated equilibria is as American as apple pie and (Gould will appreciate this) baseball.[11]

APPENDIX OF EMPIRICAL DATA

I present in this appendix my raw data from the *Citation Index* together with other pieces of information used in my essay. I should say that, having come to the end of this, my most empirical paper, I have considerably more respect for scientists, including social scientists, than when I went in. The number of citations is given in parentheses after references.

Citations for the period 1965–9

Dobzhansky (1951) (111)
Eldredge (1968) (2)
Gould (1966) (14)
Hamilton (1964a) (19)
Hamilton (1964b) (12)
Hubby and Lewontin (1966) (53)
Jacob and Monod (1961a) (955)
Jacob and Monod (1961b) (263)
Lewontin and Hubby (1966) (87)
MacArthur and Wilson (1967) (29)
Vine (1966) (151)
Vine and Matthews (1963) (139)
White and Gould (1965) (8)
Williams (1966) (23)

Citations for the period 1970–4

Dobzhansky (1951) (79)
Dobzhansky (1970) (127)
Eldredge (1971) (9)
Eldredge and Gould (1972) (14)
Gould (1966) (51)
Hamilton (1964a) (42)
Hamilton (1964b) (22)
Hubby and Lewontin (1966) (107)
Jacob and Monod (1961a) (543)
Jacob and Monod (1961b) (95)
Lewontin and Hubby (1966) (185)
MacArthur and Wilson (1967) (177)
Vine (1966) (205)
Vine and Matthews (1963) (147)
White and Gould (1965) (8)
Williams (1966) (54)
Wilson (1971) (74)

Citations for the period 1975–9

Dawkins (1976) (100)
Dobzhansky (1951) (88)
Dobzhansky (1970) (205)
Eldredge (1971) (24)
Eldredge and Gould (1972) (110)
Gingerich (1976) (16)
Gould (1966) (80)
Gould (1977a) (3)
Gould (1977b) (40)
Gould and Eldredge (1977) (27)
Hamilton (1964a) (245)
Hamilton (1964b) (85)
Hubby and Lewontin (1966) (89)
Jacob and Monod (1961a) (381)
Jacob and Monod (1961b) (264)
Lewontin (1974) (401)
Lewontin and Hubby (1966) (142)
MacArthur and Wilson (1967) (519)
Oster and Wilson (1978) (5)
Stanley (1975) (53)
Vine (1966) (50)
Vine and Matthews (1963) (84)
White and Gould (1965) (11)
Williams (1966) (262)
Williams (1975) (147)
Wilson (1971) (331)
Wilson (1975) (481)
Wilson (1978) (6)

Citations for the period 1980–4

Dawkins (1976) (261)
Dobzhansky (1951) (89)
Dobzhansky (1970) (230)
Eldredge (1971) (20)
Eldredge (1980) (96)
Eldredge and Gould (1972) (181)
Gingerich (1976) (38)
Gould (1966) (125)

Gould (1977a) (10)
Gould (1977b) (253)
Gould (1980b) (24)
Gould (1980c) (81)
Gould (1982) (47)
Gould and Eldredge (1977) (183)
Gould and Lewontin (1979) (173)
Gould and Vrba (1982) (31)
Hamilton (1964a) (376)
Hamilton (1964b) (105)
Hubby and Lewontin (1966) (60)
Jacob and Monod (1961a) (197)
Jacob and Monod (1961b) (32)
Lewontin (1974) (491)
Lewontin and Hubby (1966) (106)
Lumsden and Wilson (1981) (49)
Lumsden and Wilson (1983) (4)
MacArthur and Wilson (1967) (738)
Oster and Wilson (1978) (130)
Stanley (1975) (62)
Stanley (1979) (169)
Vine (1966) (50)
Vine and Matthews (1963) (51)
White and Gould (1965) (24)
Williams (1966) (351)
Williams (1975) (291)
Williamson (1981) (70)
Wilson (1971) (389)
Wilson (1975) (682)
Wilson (1978) (44)

Citations for the period 1985–90

Dawkins (1976) (210)
Dawkins (1982) (110)
Dawkins (1986) (47)
Eldredge (1971) (10)
Eldredge (1980) (161)
Eldredge (1985a) (50)
Eldredge and Gould (1972) (161)
Gingerich (1976) (25)

Gould (1966) (215)
Gould (1977a) (20)
Gould (1977b) (377)
Gould (1980b) (24)
Gould (1980c) (69)
Gould (1982) (53)
Gould (1985) (29)
Gould (1989) (5)
Gould and Eldredge (1977) (169)
Gould and Lewontin (1979) (350)
Gould and Vrba (1982) (32)
Hamilton (1964a) (470)
Hamilton (1964b) (119)
Hölldobler and Wilson (1990) (10)
Hubby and Lewontin (1966) (41)
Lewontin (1974) (380)
Lewontin and Hubby (1966) (67)
Lumsden and Wilson (1981) (44)*
Lumsden and Wilson (1983) (18)
MacArthur and Wilson (1967) (695)
Oster and Wilson (1978) (197)
Stanley (1975) (43)
Stanley (1979) (151)
Vrba and Gould (1986) (19)
White and Gould (1965) (21)
Williams (1966) (371)
Williams (1975) (295)
Williamson (1981) (55)
Wilson (1971) (500)
Wilson (1975) (443)
Wilson (1978) (35)

* There were many more references to this book in the *Social Sciences Citation Index*. (A similar pattern was found for Gould's *Mismeasure of Man*, which between 1981 (the year of its appearance) and 1990, got 74 references in the *Science Index* and 196 references in the *Social Sciences Index*.)

Total references made to particular articles and books

Dawkins (1976) (1976–90)	571
Dawkins (1982) (1982–90)	110
Dawkins (1986) (1986–90)	47
Dobzhansky (1951) (1965–84)	367
Dobzhansky (1970) (1970–84)	562
Eldredge (1971) (1971–90)	63
Eldredge (1980) (1980–90)	257
Eldredge and Gould (1972) (1972–90)	466
Gingerich (1976) (1976–90)	79
Gould (1966) (1966–90)	485
Gould (1977a) (1977–90)	33
Gould (1977b) (1977–90)	670
Gould (1980b) (1980–90)	48
Gould (1980c) (1980–90)	150
Gould (1982) (1982–90)	100
Gould (1985) (1985–90)	29
Gould and Eldredge (1977) (1977–90)	379
Gould and Lewontin (1979) (1979–90)	523
Gould and Vrba (1982) (1982–90)	63
Hamilton (1964a) (1965–90)	1152
Hamilton (1964b) (1965–90)	343
Hubby and Lewontin (1966)	350
Hölldobler and Wilson (1990) (1990)	10
Jacob and Monod (1961a) (1965–84)	2076
Jacob and Monod (1961b) (1965–84)	454
Lewontin (1974) (1975–90)	1272
Lewontin and Hubby (1966) (1966–90)	587
Lumsden and Wilson (1981) (1981–90)	93
Lumsden and Wilson (1983) (1983–90)	22
MacArthur and Wilson (1967) (1967–90)	2158
Oster and Wilson (1978) (1978–90)	332
Stanley (1975) (1975–90)	158
Stanley (1979) (1980–90)	320
Vine (1966) (1966–84)	456
Vine and Matthews (1963) (1965–84)	421
Vrba and Gould (1986) (1986–90)	19
White and Gould (1965) (1965–90)	72
Williams (1966) (1966–90)	1061
Williams (1975) (1975–90)	733

Williamson (1981) (1981–90)   125
Wilson (1971) (1971–90)   1294
Wilson (1975) (1975–90)   1606
Wilson (1978) (1978–90)   85

Table 3.1 Total overall citations

	1965–9	1970–4	1975–9	1980–4	1985–90
Dawkins			254	734	874
Dobzhansky	1219	1027	1448	1560	
Eldredge	2	44	231	500	616
Gingerich		26	260	501	688
Gould	33	145	610	1876	3330
	(41)	(167)	(731)	(2081)	(3531)
Hamilton	90	250	870	1560	1839
	(78)	(228)	(795)	(1455)	(1720)
Jacob	3060	2040	1472	1088	
Lewontin	470	830	1350	1820	1593
	(523)	(937)	(1439)	(2053)	(1984)
Stanley		93	410	728	836
Vine	420	605	278	155	
Vrba				136	354
Williams	85	384	750	1260	1284
Williamson				105	104
Wilson	390	650	1550	1880	3102
	(419)	(827)	(2074)	(2801)	(4056)

The figures given in brackets on the rows below those of Gould, Lewontin, and Wilson represent the cumulative totals if one includes all of the mentioned publications on which they appeared as second authors. I appreciate that there are other such publications which are going unrecorded, but I doubt that their omission makes too much difference at the level of accuracy that I require. I suspect that Stanley's figures would have been much inflated if I had included the textbook that he co-authored with Raup; but given that others had also published textbooks, I decided not to include any such figures. The bracketed figures below those of Hamilton represent the totals if one regards (as I am inclined to think one should) Hamilton's seminal kin selection papers as but one continuous argument.

Table 3.2   Citation patterns for Hubby and Lewontin (1966) and
Lewontin and Hubby (1966)

	Hubby and Lewontin (1966)		Lewontin and Hubby (1966)	
	Genetic	Evolutionary	Genetic	Evolutionary
1965–9	27	0	39	3
1970–4	34	7	70	12
1975–9	30	12	48	12
1980–4	18	4	39	8
1985–90	9	2	24	5

'Genetic' includes *Genetics, Canadian Journal of Genetics, Biochemical Genetics, Genetika, Heredity, Journal of Heredity, Genetical Research, Annual Review of Genetics, Japanese Journal of Genetics, Journal of Medical Genetics.* 'Evolutionary' includes *Evolution, Journal of Molecular Evolution, Evolutionary Biology, Journal of Human Evolution* and *Genetics, Selection, and Evolution.*

Table 3.3   Total citations made to Gould in *Paleobiology*

	A	B	C
1975	6	3	–
1976	6	3	–
1977	6	6	11
1978	37	9	–
1979	27	5	–
1980	24	8	–
1981	49	14	13
1982	41	8	–
1983	12	7	2
1984	25	4	–
1985	33	4	11
1986	32	7	10
1987	13	3	5
1988	20	2	–
1989	18	–	–
1990	12	2	–
Totals	361	85	52

A   Total citations to Gould, excluding self-citations; *B*   Total number of articles (by all authors) citing at least one punctuated equilibria article (defined as Eldredge and Gould 1972; Gould and Eldredge 1977; Gould 1980b – Eldredge 1971 was never cited alone, without one of these three articles); *C*   Total self-citations.

Total number of articles in *Paleobiology* in the years 1975–90: 723

Total number of articles making reference to punctuated equilibrium: 85
Articles referring favourably to punctuated equilibrium: 31

Articles referring unfavourably to punctuated equilibrium: 20
Articles having a neutral stance: 34
(These figures were determined by a content analysis.)

Hence, about 12 per cent of articles refer to punctuated equilibria; about 4 per cent favour it.

Circulation of *Paleobiology* as of 1993: 2200

Table 3.4 Total citations made to Gould in *Evolution*

	A	B	C	D
1970	–	–	–	
1971	3	–	3	–
1972	2	–	2	–
1973	8	–	4	1
1974	7	–	6	4
1975	2	7	2	1
1976	3	–	3	1
1977	3	–	3	–
1978	4	–	3	3
1979	11	3	6	2
1980	8	1	5	1
1981	13	–	11	1
1982	37	–	20	14
1983	15	–	13	3
1984	28	–	15	3
1985	27	9	15	1
1986	34	–	14	2
1987	32	6	19	1
1988	23	–	14	1
1989	24	12	11	2
1990	28	–	16	1
Totals	312	38	185	41

A Total citations to Gould; *B* Self citations; *C* Articles referring to Gould; *D* Articles (by all authors) referring to punctuated equilibria articles (defined as Eldredge and Gould 1972; Gould and Eldredge 1977; Gould 1980b).

Articles referring to punctuated equilibria: (1970–90) 41
                                          (1975–90) 36

Articles favourable to punctuated equilibria: 3 (including one by Stanley)
Articles unfavourable to punctuated equilibria: 7
Articles neutral to punctuated equilibria: 31
(These figures were determined by a content analysis.)

Number of articles in *Evolution* (1975–90): 2016

Hence, comparatively, roughly 22 per cent of articles referring to Gould refer to his punctuated equilibria papers.

Absolutely, roughly 9 per cent of articles refer to Gould, 2 per cent of articles refer to his punctuated equilibria papers, and the number explicitly favourable to the theory is insignificant.

Circulation of *Evolution* 1992/3: 4500

Addendum on non-punctuated equilibrium citations to Gould in *Evolution*

Most common citations: Gould (1977b) 47; Gould (1966) 35; Gould and Lewontin (1979) 28; P. Albrech, S. J. Gould, and D. Wake (1979) 'Size and shape in ontogeny and phylogeny' 19; Gould (1980b) 13; S. J. Gould (1971) 'Geometric similarity in allometric growth: A contribution to the problem of scaling in the evolution of size' 10; S. J. Gould (1975) 'Allometry in primates, with emphasis on scaling and the evolution of the brain' 10; Gould (1982) 7; S. J. Gould and R. F. Johnson (1972) 'Geographic variation' 7.

All other citations appear less often (usually much less often). *Ever Since Darwin* and *The Mismeasure of Man* have but one citation each.

Table 3.5   Citations made to Eldredge in *Paleobiology*

	Citations (excluding Eldredge and Gould 1972 and S C)	Eldredge and Gould 1972	S C
1975–9	27	19	3
1980–4	30	33	0
1985–90	17	15	0

These figures are for Eldredge as first author.

Table 3.6 Citations made to Eldredge in *Evolution*

	Citations (excluding Eldredge and Gould 1972 and S C)	Eldredge and Gould 1972	S C
1970–4	3	1	5
1975–9	2	6	0
1980–4	6	15	0
1985–90	10	8	0

These figures are for Eldredge as first author.

Table 3.7 Citations made to Stanley in *Paleobiology*

	Citations (excluding S C)	S C
1975–9	59	7
1980–4	93	23
1985–90	134	27

These figures are for Stanley as first author.

Table 3.8 Citations made to Stanley in *Evolution*

	Citations (excluding S C)	S C
1970–4	1	3
1975–9	3	0
1980–4	27	5
1985–90	31	0

These figures are for Stanley as first author.

NOTES

1 The allopatric model is due primarily to Ernst Mayr, who argued that isolation of a small 'founder population' would lead to a rapid genetic revolution within the group, as an atypical selection of organisms drawn from a larger (parent) group shook down to enforced co-existence. Although Mayr was approaching this idea over a number of years, notably in his classic *Systematics and the Origin of Species*, the key paper is Mayr (1954). In that paper, he actually draws precisely the implication for the fossil record that Eldredge is promoting, almost twenty years later.

2 Trying to tease apart the reasons for the better success of the Lewontin-Hubby work than the Eldredge-Gould work, two not necessarily separate hypotheses come to mind. First, that anything to do with genetics has a bigger potential for impact than anything to do with straight evolution in itself, and that anything to do with straight evolution has more potential than anything to do with palaeontology. Second, that Lewontin-Hubby were giving people a tool to work with,

in a sense that the more 'philosophical' Eldredge-Gould theorizing was not. The empirical information that I offer, both on the Lewontin-Hubby work and the Eldredge-Gould work suggest that the first hypothesis has much merit, but I would not discount the claim that this feeds straight into the second hypothesis, given the logic of the case where evolution depends so crucially on genetics, whereas palaeontology is more a derived science – even though I shall suggest that this was precisely what Gould was hoping to change. (For more on the logic of the case, see Ruse 1973b and 1982.)

3 I cannot overemphasize how significant is gradualism for the Darwinian. Selection can only work if variation is slight, otherwise one gets out of adaptive focus. Darwin, who at one early point contemplated 'hopeful monsters', quickly stepped back in line (Ruse 1979a). Fisher's *The Genetical Theory of Natural Selection* (1930) makes the definitive Darwinian case for gradualism.

4 Checking every tenth reference to *Sociobiology* in the *Index* between 1975 and 1980, some forty plus in all, the absolutely uniform impression is that people did *not* cite Wilson for or against sociobiology, but as a background source. This suggests that in this case – what I think we might also find for punctuated equilibria – most of the controversy was about science rather than within it. It is true that if one were to go to the *Social Science Citation Index* one might find more controversy.

5 Although the review in *Science* (Woodruff 1980) was reasonably positive, the review in *Paleobiology* (Lande 1980) was critical, and the review in *Evolution* (Templeton 1980) was not one to which an author draws attention. It is noteworthy that the criticisms were coming from population geneticists who thought simply that the claims of Stanley, based as they were on palaeontology, were irrelevant or mistaken in the light of modern population genetics.

6 I exclude the hypothesis that this was simply an artifact of the increased scope of the *Index*. It is true that the total source items were rising through the period discussed, from 273,870 in 1966 to 590,841 in 1990, but so also were the numbers of authors, from 473,658 in 1966 to 1,300,086 in 1990. The main point is that the number of citations per author rose moderately (6.36 to 8.91), suggesting that those who were getting increased attention were doing so for substantive reasons.

7 In fairness, I must add that the work of Wilson that was generally judged extreme tended not to get major attention. This is true particularly of the two books he co-authored with Lumsden. Note that the first of these books, directed more at the professional audience, did, nevertheless, get some attention in the social science community.

8 I must note that there are one or two references to punctuated equilibria in *Ontogeny and Phylogeny*. But the references are fleeting and certainly do not constitute a full discussion.

9 Jean Gayon (1990) makes the strong claim that thinking or not thinking in terms of hierarchies actually makes no difference whatsoever to one's scientific theorizing. 'I strongly recommend that any naturalist

who would believe that being "for" or "against" hierarchy is of primordial importance read Kant's "Second Antimony of Pure Reason" and its "solution" as given in *The Critique of Pure Reason* (Kant, 1781)' (35).

10 As noted in the last essay, I have been able to trace this link through a series of letters written, while he was a young man, from Sewall Wright to his brother Quincy.

11 I am not going to extend this essay by opening up a whole new realm of philosophical discussion, but I am sure you can see how, if I were to do so, I would follow the path of the immediately previous essay of this collection and set my discussion within Putnam's (1981) philosophy of internal realism. This is not to disavow the insights I think I achieved in my previous discussion of punctuated equilibria (Ruse 1989), when I set my discussion in the context of a modified Kuhnianism. I am, incidentally, aware that if what I claim about the ancestry of punctuated equilibria theory is well taken, then there is something a little odd about Gould's present violent anti-progressionism. One could of course simply say (what I am sure is true) that he now repudiates one part of his heritage. It is worth noting that until the late 1970s, including (especially including) the writing of *Ontogeny and Phylogeny*, he was sympathetic to progressionism, changing not because of the fossil record but because he was persuaded that biological progressionism supports the very racism he saw epitomized by human sociobiology. However, as you will learn from other essays in this collection, I am not sure that (for all his vehemence) Gould is today entirely consistent in his anti-progressionism.

Part II

EVOLUTIONARY EPISTEMOLOGY

INTRODUCTION

As I explain in the essays which follow, there are two main approaches that people have taken in trying to bring evolutionary thinking to bear on philosophical problems of knowledge and epistemology. The first is to argue by analogy from the main evolutionary mechanism of natural selection to the supposed way in which knowledge, particularly scientific knowledge, arises and develops. The second is to argue literally, from the way in which natural selection has shaped us humans as thinking beings to the kind of knowledge claims that we would make.

Here, as elsewhere, I express a pretty strong preference for the second kind of approach, feeling that there are some major points of disanalogy between the growth of organisms and the growth of science. However, for two reasons my hitherto firm opposition to the first kind of evolutionary epistemology has weakened. First, as one who takes so seriously the significance of metaphor, I now think that I ought to take more seriously a philosophy which begins, continues and ends on an analogy. It is true that there are points of disanalogy, but this is true for any metaphor or analogy. At least, I ought to be more charitable. Second, some really first-class analyses of science have been produced in the past decade by people working under and from the analogy. I refer here particularly to the writings of David Hull and Robert Richards. As a naturalist, I am always open to the pragmatic argument that the proof of the pudding is in the eating.

It is in this spirit that I offer the first two essays of this section – not convinced but more open. The first essay, in fact, explores in some detail the whole attempt to draw analogies between different fields, so you will see in detail my feelings – positive and negative – about the idea of knowledge itself as evolutionary. The second essay, which I stress now as I do within its pages, is offered as no more than as (what I think is) a bright suggestion, is an attempt to take the fight to the opposition. If we are to work by analogy, then (in the words of Popper) let us have a lot of 'bold conjectures' – being aware that 'rigorous refutation' is the fate of most. In fact, if any of my readers are inspired to refutation, I shall think my time well spent. Only if the essay is met with silence shall I realize that it is a failure.

The third essay lays out my own position on evolution and epistemology, arguing for the second approach, namely that it is by taking seriously our evolved nature that we can start to get a true perspective on the nature of (scientific) knowledge. You will see that, as in the essays in Part I, I find myself pointed towards the kind of position endorsed by Hilary Putnam (although you will find a more detailed discussion of Putnam's philosophy in the earlier essays). The fact that Putnam himself has been a severe critic of naturalistic approaches to knowledge I take to be at least one good reason why it is worth offering my discussion. I do not think that you advance philosophical discussion by dismissing everything held by those on the other side. Rather, true progress comes, as with a consilience in natural science, by bringing together the strengths of all sides. (This is one reason why I am not desperately keen on the analogical approach to evolution and epistemology, for I am not sure that hybridization is the key to real change in the world of organisms.)

In a way, 'The view from somewhere: a critical defence of evolutionary epistemology' is the lynchpin of this whole collection – not necessarily the best or the most important for me, but the essay which provides the clearest statement of my background position. Let me therefore admit that this is the essay which I suspect will have the shortest shelf-life in the sense that it will most quickly need revision. I think the general philosophy is right and will endure, but it is crucially dependent on very contingent claims about the nature of physical reality (including here claims about the nature of our own cognitive abilities). I think we stand on the edge of a revolution about our understanding of the way in which the brain works and the ways in which humans, as evolved primates, absorb, process, and use information – perhaps indeed we are already into that revolution. Hence if there are those readers who want to take me to task on empirical grounds, I shall be their strongest supporter, asking only that they revise what I have done for the benefit of all.[1]

NOTE

1 If asked for specific references for the would-be student of evolutionary epistemology, I would commend the magnificent overview of philosophical naturalism by Philip Kitcher (1992). This will give you both background and a stimulus, for although Kitcher has himself written brilliantly in defence of evolutionary biology, as a philosopher he feels so little enthusiasm for evolutionary epistemology he dismisses it in less than a page of an over fifty-page survey. At the more empirical level, no would-be evolutionary epistemologist should now ignore the seminal work by Leda Cosmides and John Tooby, linking our reasoning abilities with our adaptive heritage (see, for instance, Cosmides 1989). And I simply must recommend Plantinga (1991), written by a man who is so far from naturalism that he is a Creationist, but which centres in on the circularity problems of the evolutionary naturalist with a force that I have seen expressed nowhere else.

4

A THREEFOLD PARALLELISM FOR OUR TIME?

Progressive development in society, science and the organic world

In the middle of the nineteenth century, the Swiss-American palaeoichthyologist, Louis Agassiz (1842, 1859), proposed and argued for a threefold parallelism: the order of living beings, the ontogenetic development of individual organisms, and the history of life as seen in the fossil record. Moreover, claimed Agassiz, the unifying thread is that of *progress* – from simple to complex, from the uniform to the highly differentiated, from monad to man. Thus in the living world – especially the living world of animals – it is possible to order beings along some kind of *scala naturae*, from the invertebrates up through the primates, and eventually to humankind. This mirrors the embryological sequences of a simple organism, which also starts with the primitive and (in one species, at least) culminates in full intelligence. And, although Agassiz was never an evolutionist, he thought that God's creative power unfurls down through time until we reach those organisms made in his image.

I shall not stop here to discuss the intrinsic merits of Agassiz's parallelism or its subsequent fate. Suffice it to say here that, for all its problems – particularly with the thorny question of branching – it had an influence beyond that which Agassiz envisioned, or altogether desired (Bowler 1976, 1984; Ruse 1979c). It was to prove a tool without compare in the hands of those whom Agassiz anathematized, the transmutationists! My aim here, rather, it to look at a modern-day possible threefold parallelism, different in many respects but similar in making central the notion of progress. This is a parallelism between the development of society, the development of science, and the development – the evolutionary development – of organisms. I am not sure that there is one prominent enthusiast for this parallelism, mirroring Agassiz as it were, but I do detect varying degrees of advocacy and acceptance. My primary purpose is sympathetic understanding, so I shall stress the disinterested explication of plausible positions. But, as it seems appropriate, particularly towards the end, I shall move into critical comment.

Because the notion of 'progress' is so crucial to the discussion, it will be useful to have some idea about this before we start, although part of the need for such an exercise as mine is precisely the fact that most discussions calmly presuppose some sort of pre-analytic notion and let matters get worse from there. Following the biologist Francisco J. Ayala (1974, 1982, 1988), one person who has made some effort with the notion, I take it that progress requires change, and that this in some sense involves change in a linear direction. Mere cyclical change could not qualify as progress, even though there is perhaps some flexibility about how directional one must be. One might insist that the change could never falter or double back, particularly at the end. Or one might allow a little backsliding: 'There is progress, but we're in a bit of a lull or dip right now.'

What is important, whether one be strict or not about reversals, is the recognition that directionality alone is not enough. Progress is a *value* notion (Ayala 1988: 76–9). Progress implies that things are in some sense getting better or more desirable – at least, progress in any absolute sense has this implication. 'There has been a terrific amount of progress but we're all far worse off' is a contradiction in terms. But, going beyond Ayala, it is useful to distinguish between evaluation and valuing (Nagel 1961). Only the latter is absolute. The former occurs against any arbitrarily specified standard. 'To the detriment of us all, humankind has made much progress in its capability for nuclear warfare' is not contradictory – although it may or may not be false.

Talk of the fact of progress (meaning, when used without qualification, the absolute sense) raises questions about causes. These and other matters will have to be kept in mind. For now, however, we can turn to the task in hand and start unpacking the threefold parallelism.

THE DEVELOPMENT OF SOCIETY

Suggestions that there might be general laws governing the development of society, 'historicism', tend to be treated with (at best) amused contempt (Popper 1974). To quash such thoughts, it is generally thought enough merely to mention the name of Arnold Toynbee, the last great practitioner of this *genre* of historical philosophizing. Yet the fact remains true that there is a tradition in the West, at least since the early part of the eighteenth century, of thinking that the course of society is not entirely random. For all the admitted backslidings, and few would want to say that there have been none at all, things – generally meaning, things for a goodly proportion of the members of Western society – have got better. Material benefits, education, freedom (more or less) have improved. Hence, it is generally thought that there is reasonable expectation of continued progress. We might hope for further improvements. There will be more material benefits, more education for those who want it, and more freedom (more or less).

> As Phlogiston is displaced by Oxygen, and the Epicycles of Ptolemy by the Ellipses of Kepler; so does Paganism give place to Catholicism, Tyranny to Monarchy, and Feudalism to Representative Government, – where also the process does not stop. Perfection of Practice, like completeness of Opinion, is always approaching, never arrived; Truth, in the words of Schiller, *immer wird, nie ist*; never *is*, always is *a-being*.
>
> (Carlyle 1896: 38)

The idea of (societal) progress was not espoused by the Ancients, nor indeed was it one which could flourish while Christianity had a dominant hold on the human psyche. There is that in the biblical story of the Fall and of subsequent possibility of salvation through the sacrifice of Jesus which cuts strongly against the notion that there could be any genuine secular improvement of life here on earth (Bury 1920). But, with the coming of the Scientific Revolution, belief in our own abilities to better our lot started to grow, most particularly in the country which spearheaded the Enlightenment and whose intellectuals had the strongest interest in seeing the present order of things overthrown – France. Moreover, as the writings of Condorcet, one of the noblest of all such thinkers, show well, it was these very advances in science and technology which supposedly supply the causal fuel for societal progress.

> As preventative medicine improves, and food and housing becomes healthier, as a way of life is established that develops our physical powers by exercise without ruining them by excess, as the two most virulent causes of deterioration, misery and excessive wealth, are eliminated, the average length of human life will be increased and a better health and stronger physical constitution will be ensured.
>
> (Condorcet [1795] 1956: 199)

There were national differences in thinking about progress. In Britain, secure in its establishment and plunging headlong into an industrial revolution, progress tended primarily to be thought of in economic terms – forces and benefits. Adam Smith ([1759] 1976, [1776] 1937) and like thinkers argued that progress occurs when the state avoids interference, allowing market forces free play, thus letting the 'Invisible Hand' maximize benefits for us all. A major part of this thinking is that there will occur a natural 'division of labour' with society growing more complex as tasks are assigned to experts. (Note how complexity might be a mark of progress, even though one may not value complexity in its own right.)

Germany, to the contrary, was the land of idealists – at least in thought. Lacking a unified state and many of the material and political desiderata that the British took for granted, it emphasized a world spirit working its way inevitably up the path of progressive advance. Thus, according to Kant:

> The History of the Human Species as a whole may be regarded as the unravelling of a hidden Plan of Nature for accomplishing a perfect state of Civil Constitution for Society . . . as the sole State of Society in which the tendency of human nature can be all and fully developed.
>
> (quoted by Pollard 1968: 86)

Hegel, as is well known, made a full political philosophy out of the upwardly rising world spirit. Thesis leads to antithesis and thus to synthesis. Marx, in turn, although a materialist, never stepped off the transcendentalist escalator of German Idealism. Progressionism was, therefore, built right into his system.

By the middle of the nineteenth century, national ideas of societal progress began to twist and entwine together. This was particularly so, as they were transplanted to North America (Wagar 1972). One often finds a belief in the socio-economic theories of the British (courtesy particularly of Herbert Spencer) combined with a German-like faith in the upward, God-intended, destiny of the nation. However, it is important to note that progress always had its critics. In Britain, for instance, the idea took a long time to recover its popularity after the horrors of the French Revolution. And, as the nineteenth century drew to a close, the darker side of industrialism, the hollowness of colonialism, and the fear of militarism began to make their marks. People did not necessarily give up on progress, but increasingly they looked for ways to put it back on track. Henry George's ([1879] 1926) immensely popular proposals for communal land ownership were typical of Utopian remedial schemes.

In this century, it seems fair to say that beliefs in progress have never engendered the enthusiasms that they did in previous times (Almond *et al.* 1982). Two world wars, the rise of Nazism, and the failure of the glorious promise of the Soviet Revolution have seen to that. Moreover, today, given the threats of nuclear and other kinds of warfare, global pollution, an apparently uncontrollable population explosion – not to mention such themes as international terrorism, continued religious strife (Northern Ireland, Israel, the Punjab), and AIDS – in the view of many it seems almost immoral to talk of progress, let alone to hope for it. The words of Reinhold Niebuhr, written in the dark times of 1940, still seem appropriate.

> History does not move forward without catastrophe, happiness is not guaranteed by the multiplication of physical comforts, social harmony is not easily created by more intelligence, and human nature is not as good or as harmless as had been supposed.
>
> (quoted in Chambers 1958: 211)

Yet humans are optimists, and it would be a bad mistake to end this section by suggesting that the idea of social progress is a spent force, with as little appeal as other obsessions of yesteryear. Whatever may be the gloomy fears of intellectuals and fellow travellers, survey after survey suggests that if recent American presidential elections prove anything, US citizens at least refuse to elect anyone who does not think in a like manner.

Elsewhere in the world also, hopes of progress ride high. After all, what else can leaders offer but such hopes? In these rapidly changing times, one hesitates to make any pronouncements on the official (or unofficial) thoughts on progress in Eastern European countries. What one can say is that, in Russia until very recently, it was still very much part of the state philosophy. Quoting from a recent textbook:

> Marxists are convinced that if the development of morality is approached dialectically, the very dynamics of its contradictions reveal steady progress. Marx noted, with full justice, that the concept of progress is not to be taken in the usual abstract form typical of a metaphysically clumsy mentality. Progress inevitably faces contradictions and the struggle of opposites (in morality, the most common pair of opposites are good and evil), but it does not cease to move towards higher and better ideals.
>
> (Bakshtanovsky *et al.* 1989: 89. Note the name of the publisher!)

Whatever else the present upheavals may spell, it does not seem likely that they will be read as a retreat from progress. If anything, the faith that a better time can come, must come, and will come, seems set fair to flourish.

THE DEVELOPMENT OF SCIENCE

Science is Heraclitean, always moving. No one would deny that, although, conversely, no one would deny that science moves irregularly – now leaping forward, now sluggish. Where one branch may be teeming with excitement – major discoveries, eager students, a proliferation of publications – another may be dull and humdrum, polishing up old discoveries and hoping listlessly for major innovations.

But is there any meaning to the movement? Does the flux of science make sense? Is there any pattern? Is science, not to mince words, progressive, and if it is, what is the nature of this progress and what is the cause? Let me start at the beginning and state about as categorically as one can that speaking of scientists *qua* scientists – that is, excluding the things, often very silly, that scientists say when being self-reflective – they are strongly committed to the belief that their subject-matter does have a pattern and that it does make sense. In particular, scientists believe in progress (of

117

science), and by progress they mean getting closer to the truth (Davies 1986).

Moreover, scientists *qua* scientists are philosophical realists, and by getting closer to the truth they mean getting their theories in better correspondence with the facts of the case. Molecular genetics is better than Mendelian genetics because the unit of inheritance really is the DNA molecule, which in turn really is a double helix. Scientists show their realism-based progressionism by their supreme indifference to history, except as a guide for the very young or a hobby for the very old. And even then they usually care only for history to some Whiggish end. After all, why should one care about the past, if it is not as good as the present?

How far are these views about science well-taken? One might want to look at them with a sceptical eye, if only because the ideology of the progressive nature of science seems so important an element in the successful prosecution of science – externally against rivals for human allegiance, such as religion, and internally to keep people going against all of the daunting obstacles that ignorance and nature seem to throw up. Although it is true that the dispute about whether, independently of our observation, a real world truly exists 'out there' is as old as philosophical debate, and although it is true also that this dispute has (and does) reflect itself into thinking about science, it seems true also that the general progressivist view of science is one which has been widely accepted by commentators on science (Losee 1972). At least, this was and is true of those closest to the philosophical end of the spectrum, although recently belief in scientific progress has come under attack from radical thinkers from history, sociology, literary theory, and the like.

Consider, to take an articulate position from the past, the view of William Whewell (1837, 1840), one of the towering figures in the history of the philosophy of science, also one of the great historians of science, and indeed an active scientist in his own right (Butts 1965; Ruse 1976). Whewell was no naive realist, thinking that what you see is what there is. Rather, he was a sophisticated Kantian (later veering towards Platonism), who saw science as a complex fusion of raw experience and mind-giving organizing principles – 'Fundamental Ideas'. But, within this context he saw science as unambiguously, albeit not always smoothly, progressive, as through a series of 'inductive epochs' scientists strive to achieve complete understanding. On the one hand, the theoretical must be articulated ('explication of conceptions'); on the other hand, the empirical must be collected ('colligation of facts'); then the two are brought together in an 'inductive' leap.

Important for Whewell is the belief that the products of induction can then themselves serve as facts, for a new round of inductive leaping. This goes on until finally one reaches the limit of a Fundamental Idea, at which stage apparently one has established necessary truth. (Although he does not use this language, this is at least the necessity of the Kantian synthetic *a priori* – something which Whewell, an ardent Anglican, would have thought backed by God.) For Whewell, a major mark that one's science is progressing properly, guided by the right Ideas, is when different branches of scientific activity are brought together beneath one hypothesis.

> Accordingly the cases in which inductions from classes of facts altogether have thus *jumped together*, belong only to the best established theories which the history of science contains. And as I shall have occasion to refer to this peculiar feature in their evidence, I will take the liberty of describing it by a particular phrase; and will term it the *Consilience of Inductions*.
>
> (Whewell 1840: 2, 230)

Whewell remarked that a consilience is *simplicity* by another name, since one is reducing the required number of explanatory factors.

Let us jump now to the present. The two most influential living commentators on the nature of science are, undoubtedly, Karl Popper (1959, 1963) and Thomas Kuhn (1962). The former's analysis differs in significant respects from Whewell's, but is no less committed to progressionism. As is well known, Popper believes that the mark of science – the 'criterion of demarcation' – is falsifiability, and he believes that science moves forward as scientists face problems, propose tentative solutions ('bold conjectures') and then have others attempt to knock them down. Even in the process of destruction ('refutation'), progress is made, and a body of as-yet-undefeated knowledge grows (Popper 1972). Unlike Whewell, Popper denies that you can ever get to the truth (or, if you do, that you can ever know that you have done so), but there does seem to be an asymptotic approach to some sort of absolute (or 'objective') knowledge. Popper denies also that one can ever know there is a reality, but he is prepared to assume that there is one. In this sense, he is a 'hypothetical realist'.

Prima facie, Kuhn's philosophy seems very different, although his constant complaints about misinterpretation should warn one against slick readings. As well known as Popperian falsifiability is the Kuhnian 'paradigm', a kind of world picture in which the scientist functions and is generally trapped. (As it happens, later elaboration has shown that the kind of world a paradigm is picturing might be pretty small.) Every now and then, a paradigm seems to come apart, 'normal science' is no longer possible and, if you are lucky, a new paradigm is produced and there is a 'revolutionary' switch. Since paradigms set their own rules, scientific revolutions in some sense stand outside logic – they require rhetoric and emotive persuasion, like political revolutions.

Kuhn is sometimes read as a non-realist, but it is fairer perhaps to read him in a kind of Kantian way, as seeing reality in an important sense defined and created by the inquiring mind. He is certainly not a Whewellian in seeing the aim and end of science as some kind of finished absolute knowledge. There is always room for another paradigm switch. Yet, in a passage which is often ignored or down-played (or misunderstood), Kuhn, no less than Popper, stakes out a commitment to progress.

> The analogy that relates the evolution of organisms to the evolution of scientific ideas can easily be pushed too far. But with respect to the issues of [this book] it is very nearly perfect. The process described [by me] as the resolution of revolutions is the selection by conflict within the scientific community of the fittest way to practise future science. The net result of a sequence of such revolutionary selections, separated by periods of normal research, is the wonderfully adapted set of instruments we call modern scientific knowledge. Successive stages in that developmental process are marked by an increase in articulation and specialization. And the entire process may have occurred, as we now suppose biological evolution did, without benefit of a set goal, a permanent fixed scientific truth, of which each stage in the development of scientific knowledge is a better exemplar.
>
> (Kuhn 1962: 172–3)

Admittedly, this is not a comfortable absolute progress, in the sense of travel towards firm knowledge of objective reality, but it is progress of a kind. Perhaps at the least Kuhn intends a sort of relativistic progress, where the standards by which paradigms are judged involve such virtues as predictive fertility, coherence, consilience, simplicity and more. These virtues are often called 'epistemic values' (McMullin 1983); invoking them as standards may perhaps put Kuhn more in the line of one who is evaluating against chosen criteria than valuing against anything absolute.

I confess that I am not absolutely sure about this last point. How arbitrary is the choice of something like predictive fertility? What I am sure of is the relativism of recent commentators who try to 'deconstruct' science, using the tools of sociology, literary theory and the like. These people argue that just about any scientific theory is compatible with the facts, whatever these latter may be (Collins 1985). The driving force of scientific change is, therefore, not the real world, but a host of cultural factors – epistemic values, certainly, but also non-epistemic values like politics, sex and gender, religion, status, race, and more.

In the eyes of these critics – Marxists, feminists, gay and civil rights activists, and others – talk of progress towards knowledge of reality is not simply ridiculous, but itself part of the ideology to be ripped away from modern science (Haraway 1989). It is often not easy to decide if there is indeed a reality in the eyes of such critics – at an important level, they do not care. It is equally difficult to decide if there is belief in any kind of progress. Some, at least, seem to think so; but, their kind of progress is to be measured strictly in terms of advance towards greater manifestation of appropriately sought and held standards – more sensitivity to legitimately desired demands of feminism, for instance, or to gay rights. I take it that such progress as this is unambiguously relativistic. Although activists hold their values dear, others – not all of whom are obviously ignorant or incorrigibly corrupt – do not.

This must suffice for a survey of the situation in science. Overall, despite critics and detractors just mentioned, it does seem true to say that beliefs in progress are a lot stronger and more generally held than such beliefs are held about society. I shall return later to more discussion about the question of causes.

THE ORGANIC EVOLUTIONARY PROCESS

Organic evolution means change. That is a tautology. And almost as close to the tautological is the fact that, with very minor exceptions, such change does not double back on itself. It is true also that adaptation is a significant mark of the organic – some would say it is *the* significant mark – and that although there may well be other causal factors, natural selection brought on by a struggle for existence is the reason for such adaptation and hence for organic evolution generally.

What of the overall pattern? Almost by definition, in the more than three-and-a-half billion years since life first appeared on this planet, there has been a rise from the simple to the complex, a process that really caught fire about 600 million years ago at the beginning of the Cambrian. But does all of this add up to progress of any kind? This is the key question.

It cannot be denied that people have thought that there has been progress. Early evolutionists were progressionist to a person. The French evolutionist Jean Baptiste de Lamarck ([1809] 1963), for instance, was so keen on progress that he proposed two upward ladders, one for plants and one for animals. Needless to say, we humans come at the peak of the animal ladder, remarkable for a complexity which puts us ahead even of the orangutan.

Other evolutionists of the time were no less progressionist. Listen, for instance, to Dr Erasmus Darwin:

> Organic Life beneath the shoreless waves
> Was born and nurs'd in Ocean's pearly caves;
> First forms minute, unseen by spheric glass,
> Move on the mud, or pierce the watery mass;
> These, as successive generations bloom,
> New powers acquire, and larger limbs assume;
> Whence countless groups of vegetation spring,
> And breathing realms of fin, and feet, and wing.
>
> Thus the tall Oak, the giant of the wood,
> Which bears Britannia's thunders on the flood;
> The Whale, unmeasured monster of the main,
> The lordly Lion, monarch of the plain,
> The Eagle soaring in the realms of air,
> Whose eye undazzled drinks the solar glare,
> Imperious man, who rules the bestial crowd,
> Of language, reason, and reflection proud,
> With brow erect who scorns this earthy sod,
> And styles himself the image of his God;

Arose from rudiments of form and sense,
An embryon point, or microscopic ens!
(Darwin 1803: 1, 295–314)

Until the day of Dr Darwin's grandson, half-a-century later, the theme was the same. Then, however, many think that the tune changed dramatically. Supposedly, Charles Darwin had no time for biological progress and excluded it rigorously from his published writings. After all, what else could he do, given the mechanism of selection? What wins is what wins, and given the right combination of circumstances it could just as easily be the weedy little runt as the magnificent, prancing, prize specimen which has all of the offspring. It could just as easily be the simple as the complex.

As one who used to interpret Darwin this way, let me now rush to say that I think this is all quite wrong (Ospovat 1981). It is true that Darwin recognized that branching is a crucial part of the evolutionary process. It is true also that Darwin denied any simple upwardly progressive force in evolution. It is true, thirdly, that Darwin saw that selection would lead most naturally to a kind of relativistic progress, where one improves particular adaptations, like muscles for speed or teeth for attack ('comparative highness'). But, when this is all said, it remains true that Darwin thought relativistic progress would slide over into absolute progress, where the mark is complexity (Darwin 1859). Unambiguously, Darwin saw humans – primarily white, Anglo-Saxon, male humans – at the top of the list (Darwin 1871; Greene 1977).

With some doubts (to be mentioned later) belief in evolutionary progress has continued down to the present. Only now have formidable critics arisen. Most forceful among these has been George C. Williams, especially in his 1966 classic, *Adaptation and Natural Selection*. He points out that all proposed measures of progress fail, and that they even yield counter-intuitive results. If one judges complexity over the whole of ontogeny – and why should one do otherwise? – a good case can be made for saying that the liver fluke is a higher life form than humans!

You may think (I used to think) that this is the end of matters. Biological progress has gone the way of Lamarckism. Certainly, there is no shortage of voices prepared to give this impression. Stephen Jay Gould (1989) is simply the loudest and most persistent. However, matters are not this straightforward. Biological progressionism is a hardy plant (or weed, if you prefer). Relativistic progress of an explicitly Darwinian kind, presupposing evaluation against a standard, rides high. I will return to this point later. For now, I want to remark how endorsement of a fairly absolute kind of progress – monad to man – can be found readily in the biological literature. Listen, for instance, to E. O. Wilson:

> We should first note that social systems have originated repeatedly in one major group of organisms after another, achieving widely different degrees of specialization and complexity. Four groups occupy pinnacles high above the others: the colonial invertebrates, the social insects, the nonhuman mammals, and man.

> (Wilson 1975: 379)

And then:

> The typical vertebrate society ... favors individual and in-group survival at the expense of societal integrity.
> Man has intensified these vertebrate traits while adding unique qualities of his own. In so doing he has achieved an extraordinary degree of cooperation with little or no sacrifice of personal survival and reproduction. Exactly how he alone has been able to cross to this fourth pinnacle, reversing the downward trend of social evolution in general, is the culminating mystery of all biology.

> (Wilson 1975: 382)

Why should there be this kind of progress? How does one move, especially if one is a Darwinian, from pattern to process? The most articulate explanation has come recently from the pen of John T. Bonner (1987), who argues that there has been and always will be a kind of biological pressure towards increase in bodily size. Bigness has its virtues. So also does smallness, true. But the scale at the top is open-ended in a way that the scale at the bottom is not. For instance, when the mammals went back to the sea, the ecological niches for small animals were crowded. But there was masses of room for really big animals. Hence we got the whales.

Continuing this theme, Bonner points out that size requires internal support systems – the greater the size, the greater the needed support. This led to increased complexity, where this can be defined simply in terms of the different number of types of component part – such different parts splitting up the tasks at hand and thus leading to a classic division of labour. Complexity in turn leads to improved adaptations, most importantly sophisticated social skills. Hence, as in traditional accounts, one sees primates – humans in particular – coming out at the top. The things we value most, by just about any standard, are the winners in life's struggles. Progress reigns!

COMPARISONS: SOCIETY/SCIENCE

Let me turn now to similarities and differences between the three developmental processes just discussed: society, science and biology. There are three interfaces, so let us start with that between society and science.

The question is whether there is any similarity of pattern and, if there is, whether this points to any similarity of process, referring now to the causal level. Fairly obviously, many people will answer the first part of the question in the negative, and that will be an end to it. Society is not progressive. Science is. The two processes are clearly different. But what if one sees some pattern parallelism? This could be because one sees society as progressive, at least in some respects, or because one sees science as less than progressive, at least in some respects.

The strongest way to promote parallelism, perhaps, is to make both of these moves. One might argue that (relatively) society certainly advances in certain respects, especially with respect to some values one holds dear. Conversely, one might argue that thoughts of an absolute scientific progress to disinterested knowledge of reality are chimerical, but there is still hope of a (relativistic) progress as one incorporates ideologically acceptable values in a better fashion. Society might become more sexually sensitive. Hence, science might become more sexually sensitive. (I am not saying that either does or will.)

What then of causes? There are those, drawn, I suspect, mainly from the scientific community, who see a direct causal connection. Improved science leads to improved technology to improved society. Note, however, that this sequence does not presuppose any parallelism in the processes. One might well (if one takes this sequence seriously, one probably will) think that science is a value-free endeavour, progressing towards knowledge of reality. Society, on the other hand, improves and advances inasmuch as desired values are achieved.

Even the fundamental mechanisms need not be the same. One could think that science requires unreflective creative genius, whereas societal improvement demands uninspired hard grind. (One probably will think this if one holds to the usual parodies of eccentric creative scientists and boring civil servants.) But suppose one does want to go on to parallelism of causes: on what grounds might one base a case? I think, in the literature, there are hints of at least three.

First, one might highlight some sort of *laissez-faire* causal process, leading to an unrestrained struggle for existence, from which the best will emerge. As we have seen, this was the view accepted by the British political economists of the eighteenth century as that best suited to promote societal progress. It was also a highly popular view in the nineteenth century and, as is only too well known, has enjoyed a considerable resurgence recently. It is also a view which has had considerable support in the past century as the way that science works, or at least as the way that science works best if it is to advance. Thus Darwin's great supporter Thomas Henry Huxley wrote:

> Now the essence of the scientific spirit is criticism. It tells us that whenever a doctrine claims our assent we should reply, Take it if you can compel it. The struggle for existence holds as much in the intellectual as in the physical world. A theory is a species of thinking, and its right to exist is coextensive with its power of resisting extinction by its rivals
>
> (Huxley 1893: 229)

Recently, Popper (1974) has been interpreting (or reinterpreting) his position in this light. He argues that the method of bold conjecture and rigorous refutation is *laissez-faire* by another name. It is at least a struggle for existence, with the best rising to the top. And, more generally, there is a whole school of 'evolutionary epistemology' which believes that science advances by throwing up variants, new ideas, and then letting them fight for survival in the public arena – this latter being the laboratory, the conference, the journal (Ruse 1986).

Central to this vision of progress is the need for struggle, for competition. Pointing to a second way of getting a society/science causal parallel, we find that not all feel that society (at least) advances best through naked aggression. Such people look for different, perhaps softer, methods of change; methods which, they

126

argue, lead to truer and more lasting advances. Co-operation of one sort or another is usually involved here and various motives for such co-operation are suggested. A recent case of this kind has been proposed by the sociobiologists, who argue that although life may be a struggle, you can often get more out of it if you are prepared to work with your fellows (Ruse 1985).

The same is true in science, argues at least one theorist, David Hull (1988a, b). He sees perpetuation of one's ideas as the driving force behind scientific effort. There is, therefore, the consequent need to co-operate – especially to cite the ideas of others – if one wants to be taken seriously oneself. This perhaps sounds somewhat cynical (this is perhaps somewhat cynical!) but Hull argues that it is not only the way science functions, but also the reason why science functions so very well. There is, for instance, a high premium on honesty, not because scientists are particularly nice people but because fraud spoils the game for everyone and hence is very heavily penalized. One might forgive but one can never forget.

Sociobiological ideas are highly controversial. Many deny them absolutely for society, and Hull's proposals for science also have their critics. This swings me, therefore, to the opposite end of the spectrum, towards the third proposal for promoting the parallelism. What if Marxism is right? Would one not have a similarity of pattern and process in that case? At the societal level this involves the well-known Hegelian dialectic, with thesis going to antithesis, and then the contradiction dissolving into synthesis – advance, and a new, higher point from which to start again.

Recognizing that a Marxian 'contradiction' is essentially one of opposition (master and slave are hardly logical contradictories), do we get something similar in the progress of science? Suffice it to say that some have certainly thought so. Richard Lewontin (1974), for instance, sees the development of population genetics as one of position, counter-position, and then resolution – with advance, but with the creation of a whole set of new problems which, in turn, call for renewed application of the dialectic. The classical position in population genetics of Hermann Muller was opposed by the balance position of Theodosius Dobzhansky. The dispute was dissolved by the coming of gel electrophoretic techniques; but, as the controversy over Japanese thoughts on drift shows only too well, the issues have not gone. They have simply been moved

127

to a higher plane. We know more than we did, but there is always more to know.

Here, then, we have three ways of promoting the parallelism, at the levels of pattern and process. What can be said by way of critical comment? My own oft-expressed feeling is that analogies are a bit like spinach – either you like them, or you don't. One can point out all kinds of health-giving, or life-threatening, properties, but, ultimately, it all comes down to a matter of taste. However, even within these bounds some critical comments can be made. After all, a preference for French cooking over English cooking is a matter of taste, but it is not entirely without some objective foundation.

For myself, the big problem with all purported parallelisms between societal and scientific change is the very much stronger sense of progress one has (I have!) in the case of science over society. I appreciate that there may have been times and places when (absolute) societal progress seemed obvious. But, even if it is true that society progresses, it is not obvious today. Science does, however, seem to progress. Darwinism over Creationism is an advance. Against those who doubt what I am saying, let me make three points. First, like G. E. Moore's proof of external reality, the conviction of scientific progress is so strong that I prefer to think arguments to the contrary must be flawed (Stroud 1984). Which do you relinquish first? The belief that your hand in front of you really exists or the sceptic's argument? The belief that science really progresses or the sceptic's argument? Second, doubters raise questions about the infiltration of values into science, but this (which I fully accept) is far from saying that science does not advance. Perhaps science advances despite, or because of, the values. Third, even if one concludes that science does *not* advance, one is still left with the fact that it *seems* to. (None of these points implies that one must endorse an extreme philosophical realism. Indeed, elsewhere I have agreed that such a realism is meaningless (Ruse 1986).)

But assume for a moment that the pattern parallelism is sufficiently strong to go on to ask about process. What then? The first suggested analogy, centring on *laissez-faire* market forces, has all the problems that lie behind every reference to such forces. At least, it is far from obvious that at the societal level, such forces lead to positive advance. One can say that even the most ardent proponents of *laissez-faire*, then and now, usually find reason for all sorts of exceptions. And in any case, the most successful societies around today are precisely those which properly balance individual freedom with government planning – this holds whether one's criterion of 'success' is based on social welfare (as in Scandinavia) or on material gain (as in Germany or Japan).

There are difficulties also with the *laissez-faire* idea applied to science. Apart from the problems of working out what, in science, represents a new innovation exactly comparable to a successful innovation in society – is one small successful experiment the equivalent of a new brand of detergent? – it is no more obvious here that unrestrained competition is or would be a good thing. Epistemologically, one might want to shelter an idea for a while (by suspending criticism), if it promises to bear great fruit. Sociologically, it is well known that the 'Matthew effect' operates strongly – new ideas from successful scientists get more attention and respect than new ideas from unknown workers (Cole and Cole 1973). Moreover, it is not obvious that this is such a very bad thing: most scientists would defend it strongly.

Let us move on to the sociobiological analogy. There are so many questions here, especially about the application of sociobiology to society, that I need hardly stop to detail them – although for the record I should say that I am probably more sympathetic to human sociobiology than most. What I do want to state is that Hull's (1989) application of sociobiology to the workings of science probably leads to real insight – he himself is his own best advocate in his analysis of the recent history of systematics. Nevertheless, it must be agreed that, inasmuch as Hull's model works, it does raise questions about the sort of success that the progress of science achieves. If what counts is the getting of others to take your ideas seriously, then at least in theory it is possible that a false idea (judged against the best evidence) gets accepted and a true idea rejected, simply because the false idea is promoted by the scientist with the superior political skills (Ruse 1995).

To the radical sociologist of science this is probably an acceptable conclusion – although, applying a reflexive argument, why then should we rush to agree with them? Here I will merely note it as a challenge. One can certainly agree that there is a kind of relativism to the progress of science; but, unless one wants to go all the way over to total relativism, it is necessary to show that the kinds of political factors Hull highlights can be reconciled with rationality and an approach to knowledge of reality.

129

Finally, there is Marxism. Let me say simply that I for one am not convinced that recent events in Eastern Europe show the total collapse of Marxism as a viable epistemology, and that in the case of both society and science it still offers a powerful tool for penetrating insight. Lewontin's analysis alone shows this. But, speaking now of the latter, to quote Aristotle, one swallow does not a summer make. It is far from obvious that all scientific advance requires 'contradiction' – or if it does, 'contradiction' is probably being used in such an elastic sense as to be virtually meaningless. At the very least, we need a more extended discussion with more examples.

There are other questions also. A Marxist approach to science is often thought to endorse a holistic philosophy, as opposed to 'reductionism', whatever that might mean (Ruse 1982). At a minimum, particularly given the successes of such sciences as quantum mechanics and molecular biology, this is a position which needs argument before acceptance. Lewontin the scientist raises serious questions for Lewontin the philosopher. However, I stress that I raise questions such as these as questions and not as definitive refutations. No one can (no one should) deny that Marxist analyses of science and its history have been some of the most fruitful of our generation. One does not have to accept the philosophy to appreciate the results – especially those underlining the extent to which social factors do get into science.

These then are some critical reflections on the society/science purported parallelisms. Overall, I am not a great enthusiast, but in detail there are some stimulating signposts.

COMPARISONS: SOCIETY/BIOLOGY

I turn next to compare the development of society with the development – the evolution – of organisms. What one can say is that, at the level of pattern, there is a long history of seeing close analogies between the development of society and the development of organic life, and often this has been taken over to discussions about process.

It is indeed not too much of an exaggeration to say that organic evolutionary theorizing was conceived in the eighteenth century out of beliefs in societal progress. What was seen (or hoped for) in society, was seen (or hoped for) in organisms. Then the latter was taken as support for the former! Moreover, the distinctive national patterns (and processes) of societal progress were read into and out of the organic world. In France, societal progress was something fuelled by the intellect, as ideas were developed and then (if useful) passed from one to another (Pollard 1968). In crucial respects, this was precisely the biological theory of Lamarck, who was incidentally an enthusiast for views about societal progress. He thought organisms develop new features in response to needs, and these are then transmitted as part of heredity. The end result is organic progress.

Erasmus Darwin also blurred together his support for the economic factors of societal progress with the changes he believed to occur in the world of organisms (McNeill 1987). Crucial for him were ideas about complexity and the division of labour, and just as supportive of the case was the example of Germany. Here the metaphysics was idealism, and societal progress was seen as the working of the spirit through time. Likewise, in biology we see German thinkers among those most inclined to developmentalism and change, as the spirit works its powers. Although, somewhat paradoxically, because for an idealist it is the *idea* which matters, we find that German thinkers rarely felt the need to endorse full-blown actual material organic evolutionism. Thus Hegel:

> Nature is to be regarded as a *system of stages*, one arising necessarily from the other and being the proximate truth of the stage from which it results: but it is not generated *naturally* out of the other but only in the inner Idea which constitutes the ground of Nature. *Metamorphosis* pertains only to the Notion as such, since only *its* alteration is development. But in Nature, the Notion is partly only something inward, partly existent only as a living individual: *existent* metamorphosis, therefore, is limited to this individual alone.
>
> (Hegel 1970: 20)

The point could not be clearer, and it is made again in his students' lecture notes:

> It is the necessity of the Idea which causes each sphere to complete itself by passing into another higher one, and the variety of forms must be considered as necessary and determinate. The land animal did not develop *naturally* out of the aquatic animal, nor did it fly into the air on leaving the water,

131

nor did perhaps the bird again fall back to earth. If we want to compare the different stages of Nature, it is quite proper to note that, for example, a certain animal has one ventricle and another has two; but we must not then talk of the fact as if we were dealing with parts which had been put together.

(Hegel 1970: 21)

Charles Darwin also was a progressionist about society – how could he fail to be, coming from a rich, liberal family, with roots deep in the nonconformist, industrial British Midlands? – and this progressionism was taken explicitly into his biology.

What is interesting is the story of evolutionism after the *Origin*, when, although beliefs in societal progress ran high, doubts were starting to emerge – the already mentioned costs of industrialism, sterility of colonialism, and rise of militarism were making manifest their effects. The worries of intellectuals about these sorts of phenomena found their way right into the theorizing of biologists. Typical in this respect was the work of E. Ray Lankester, follower of Huxley, and professor, first in London and then at Oxford. He saw society, British society in particular, in grave danger of decline, primarily because of its lack of attention to science and engineering. Almost immediately, then, we find Lankester stressing that decline – 'degeneration' – is a widespread phenomenon in the organic world also, the implication being that we humans should not sit back complacently. Across the Atlantic, meanwhile, the Cambridge (MA) biologist, Alpheus Hyatt (1893), was making a similar case for much the same reasons.

Let us turn the clock now rapidly forward to today. I think one can find the same connections drawn between the development of society and that of organisms. George Williams is an interesting counter-example who proves the case, for he complements his organic non-progressionism with a somewhat gloomy view of society (Williams 1988). E. O. Wilson (1978, 1984), to the contrary, is optimistic both about society and about organisms. ('Optimistic' is not quite the right word, for Wilson is desperately concerned about ecological issues. 'Hopefully confident that society can stay on course, given good will and effort' would be a better characterization.) Gould, however, runs an interesting twist on this scenario. He believes in societal progress but thinks that one of its greatest obstacles is racist thinking about the superiority of some peoples over others (Gould 1981). Since he takes

132

evolutionary views on progress to be some of the greatest supports of racism, he opposes organic progressionism – precisely to make way for societal progressionism (Gould 1989).

Grant now that at the level of pattern, people see parallelisms. Today, as in the past, there is often a straight transfer across when it comes to process. Again, Wilson's name springs immediately to mind, for he thinks the same sociobiological forces govern the forward movement of society as have governed the upward rise of organisms. Interestingly, although he denies that evolution is progressive, Gould (1979) sees the same dialectical forces driving forward society and lying behind his biological theory of punctuated equilibria – at least, he did. (Which point leads me to wonder just how truly non-progressionist in biology Gould truly is.)

Asking now the critical questions, let me invoke our original distinction between absolute progress and some kind of relativistic progress. With respect to the former, I have expressed little confidence in its existence in society and I confess now to feeling little more in its existence in evolution. Let me put things this way: I do not see that the enthusiasts for progress (thinking now biologically) adequately answer critics like Williams. Perhaps some functional measure of complexity can be formulated – a measure which confirms our preanalytic intuitions – but none seems yet to have been produced. DNA content of individual cells or in total bodily content looked promising, but failed the test.

Bonner's (1987) attempt is the most recent and one of the most honest to argue for organic progress and to offer a causal explanation. But there are some worrisome gaps in his argument. In the first place, the assumption that there will always be an ecological niche for the larger organism seems questionable. Apart from anything else, one might argue that niches do not exist passively, waiting to be occupied. In dynamic fashion, they are created by their occupiers. (Did the Innuit discover a niche in the Arctic or create one?) In the second place, the link between complexity (as Bonner defines it) and size seems loose. Is the giant whale so much more complex than the tiny mouse? In the third place, there is a big move from structural complexity to developmental and (important to us) social complexity. All of these reasons, at the least, make Bonner's case 'not proven'.

I see little pattern and less process. The interesting question is why evolutionists (including the very best) do. I believe there are at least two reasons. One is a version of what is now called the 'anthropic principle'. We humans are part of the evolutionary process, and – inasmuch as we ask 'Is there progress in evolution?' – we are necessarily at the end of the process (to date) and are able to ask 'Is there progress in evolution?' This distorts our answers, making us think we *must* have emerged progressively from the process. The second reason is that evolutionists are scientists. They see progress in their science. They read this into society, and then read it into their biology. There is a crucial case of biased sampling affecting the very set of people who think most about evolution.

Turn now to the question of relativistic progress. I have been happy to grant that this occurs in society. Of course it does, sometimes for good and sometimes for bad. (Whether once relativistic progress has started it keeps going indefinitely is another question.) It clearly occurs also in biology. This is Darwin's comparative highness, and today is the basis of the trendy notion of a biological arms race. Without inquiring too deeply into process (the developments in society raise question of intention, akin to those which will come up in the next section), there may well be a really useful analogy here. Consider, indeed, how someone like Richard Dawkins – discussing the ends of arms races – mixes together the social and the biological.

> How do arms races end? Sometimes they may end with one side going extinct, in which case the other side presumably stops evolving in that particular progressive direction, and indeed it will probably even 'regress' for economic reasons soon to be discussed. In other cases, economic pressures may impose a stable halt to an arms race, stable even though one side in the race is, in a sense, permanently ahead. Take running speed, for instance. There must be an ultimate limit to the speed at which a cheetah or a gazelle can run, a limit imposed by the laws of physics. But neither cheetahs nor gazelles have reached that limit. Both have pushed up against a lower limit which is, I believe, economic in character. High-speed technology is not cheap. It demands long leg bones, powerful muscles, capacious lungs. These things can be had by any animal that really needs to run fast, but they must be *bought*. They are bought at a steeply increasing price. The price is measured as what economists call 'opportunity cost'. The opportunity cost of something is measured as the sum

of all the other things that you have to forego in order to have that something. The cost of sending a child to a private, fee-paying school is all the things that you can't afford to buy as a result: the new car that you can't afford, the holidays in the sun that you can't afford (if you're so rich that you can afford all these things easily, the opportunity cost, to you, of sending your child to a private school may be next to nothing). The price, to a cheetah, of growing larger leg muscles is all the other things that the cheetah *could have done* with the materials and energy used to make the leg muscles, for instance make more milk for cubs.

(Dawkins 1986)

I think there are many more questions to be asked at this point. I am certainly not pleading for uncritical acceptance of the analogy. But, in concluding this part of the discussion, I do suggest that here our parallelism might yield interesting insights, of both pattern and process.

COMPARISONS: SCIENCE/BIOLOGY

The final putative parallelism is between the development of science and the development or evolution of biology. It is a very popular analogy today, with respect both to pattern and cause, with (as we have seen) both Popper and Kuhn trying to locate themselves beneath it. (I confess to some shock at Kuhn's gall here, given that his notion of paradigm switches is about as anti-evolutionary as it is possible to be – although perhaps he could draw on the Eldredge–Gould theory of punctuated equilibria, since it too makes abrupt change central.)

Since this kind of 'evolutionary epistemology' has been written about extensively, including by myself, I shall be brief. The claim is that the pattern of change in science and life is evolutionary and usually also that the process is a shared one of Darwinian struggle and selection. Stephen Toulmin's account is one of the best.

Science develops ... as the outcome of a double process: at each stage, a pool of competing intellectual variants is in circulation, and in each generation a selection process is going on, by which certain of these variants are accepted and incorporated into the science concerned, to be passed on to the

135

next generation of workers as integral elements of the tradition.

Looked at in these terms, a particular scientific discipline – say, atomic physics – needs to be thought of, not as the contents of a textbook bearing any specific date, but rather as a developing subject having a continuing identity through time, and characterized as much by its process of growth as by the content of any one historical cross-section. . . . Moving from one historical cross-section to the next, the actual ideas transmitted display neither a complete breach at any point – the idea of absolute 'scientific revolutions' involves an over-simplification – nor perfect replication, either. The change from one cross-section to the next is an *evolutionary* one in this sense too: that later intellectual cross-sections of a tradition reproduce the content of their immediate predecessors, as modified by those particular intellectual novelties which were selected out in the meanwhile – in the light of the professional standards of the science of the time.

(Toulmin 1967: 465–6)

He emphasizes:

In talking about the development of natural science as 'evolutionary', I [am not] employing a mere *façon de parler*, or analogy, or metaphor. The idea that the historical changes by which scientific thought develops frequently follow an 'evolutionary' pattern needs to be taken quite seriously; and the implications of such a pattern of change can be, not merely suggestive, but explanatory.

(Toulmin 1967: 470)

I have two things to say about this analogy. The first is philosophical. At the level of pattern, I consider the analogy to be weak. Science is progressive in a way that organisms are not. At least, science appears progressive in a way not apparently so (to me) in the organic world. This takes us straight to process, where the reason for the disanalogy is obvious. The variants of science are intensional, and the selection of science is teleological, in ways that the variants and selection of biology are not. Darwin's coming up with his views on evolution was part of a purposeful mental process, and the acceptance of his views by biologists was equally reflective. Conversely, however, there is nothing directed about the arrival of a new biological variant, whatever its success. Moreover, success itself is a function of the needs of the moment, without thought to the long-term future.

This all accounts for the direction of science (whatever Kuhn and the sociologists might say to the contrary) and for the non-direction of biology (whatever Wilson and Bonner might say to the contrary). Moreover, the end points of the two processes show how different they are. Agree that biology promotes complexity. However this might be defined, there seems consensus that this involves a division of labour. Yet as Whewell (1840) shows, brilliantly, scientific advances centre on a flight from complexity. The great scientific theory is the truly simple theory. It is the theory where there is no division of labour, because all the work is done by one hypothesis.

Philosophically, therefore, the parallelism is weak, which brings me to my second point. Notwithstanding the philosophical arguments, some of the best recent history of science uses the parallelism as its historiographic model! I refer, in particular, to the work of David Hull (1989) and even more to that of Robert Richards (1987). The latter in particular has used the model skilfully to tell the tale of the development of evolutionary theories of mind and behaviour for the past two hundred years. I could now say that an even better job might have been done without the model. I could now point out that some great works have been written despite, or because of, their author's pretty funny philosophical ideas (Tolstoy and Dostoevsky spring to mind). But that all sounds like sour grapes. So let me conclude simply by reiterating that I do not like the analogy, but that ultimately it is all a matter of taste. One person's philosophical poison is clearly another person's historical food.

CONCLUSION

What, if anything, remains to be said? Just this. Agassiz's threefold law had its critics and ultimately was not destined to survive, at least in the form proposed. But it was a powerful factor in the forward movement of the science of his day, and moreover remnants survive in the thinking of our day. Perhaps the same will hold of the threefold law I have been discussing. If so, that is not such a bad fate.

5

SCIENTIFIC CHANGE IS A FAMILY AFFAIR!

For well over a hundred years, and perhaps longer, people have been using biological models to illustrate and explain scientific change. The most obvious, and probably the most common, is one which sees change in science as being akin to change through time in organic life – that is to say, as being 'evolutionary' (Campbell 1972). The best-known, indeed notorious, exponent of this theme was the nineteenth-century English writer, Herbert Spencer. So enthused was he with this idea, he even saw the connection between scientific change and organic evolution as no mere analogy but a manifestation of one greater all-encompassing general law of the universe. (For Spencer's own views, see especially his famous essay 'Progress: Its law and cause', first published in 1857; also Spencer 1904. Comments on Spencer include Ruse (1986) and Richards (1987).)

But Spencer was not alone, then or today. For instance, we find Darwin's 'bulldog' – Thomas Henry Huxley – endorsing similar themes. He argued that just as change in the world of ideas is driven by a struggle for existence, so also is change in the world of animals and plants (Huxley 1888). Likewise in our own time, we find biologists and philosophers – a spectrum encompassing people with views as widely divergent as Karl Popper (1972) and Thomas Kuhn (1962) – suggesting that all development follows roughly similar patterns, for roughly similar reasons. Perhaps the most ardent and stimulating of thinkers in this vein in recent years have been the well-known philosophers/historians of biology David Hull (1988a, b) and Robert Richards (1987). (One might almost refer to them as belonging to the 'Chicago School', for others connected with the Windy City and with an enthusiasm for this kind of thought have included Campbell (1972), Toulmin (1972), and Wimsatt (1986, 1987).)

Of course, even if one is an 'evolutionary epistemologist' of this kind, one does not necessarily have to see things in Darwinian terms, as analogous to processes driven and shaped by natural selection; that is as analogous to processes driven and shaped by the differential reproduction of organisms through time. Spencer, for instance, had always a somewhat uneasy relationship with this particular mechanism, for all that he himself hinted at the very idea before Darwin (and Wallace) went public on the subject (Spencer 1904). However, today, Darwinism has won, and one now generally (perhaps always) finds people trying to interpret scientific change in a Darwinian fashion. Nor is there much surprise in this, for science lends itself readily to such an interpretation – so long as one begins in a Huxley-like fashion with a battle between concepts, and then goes to the survival of the fittest manifesting itself in terms of one theory being adopted and another rejected. (See especially Toulmin 1972 for detailed discussion of such a Darwinian approach.)

Even critics of this position – and I am one – have to agree that it yields penetrating insights. Philosophically, it highlights the way in which science is a fluid, ongoing process. It is the very epitome of Heracleitian change. You cannot step into the same river twice, nor apparently can scientists of different generations hold to the same theories. As historian after historian implies, there is far more difference between (say) the Darwinian theory of the *Origin* and the Darwinian theory of today, than would be experienced by the mid-nineteenth-century bather in the Seine and that bather's great-grandchild today.

Historically, the position has led to some of the most stimulating work in recent years by those analysing the history of evolutionism itself. To refer simply to those mentioned above, Hull has analysed in great detail the story of the taxonomic wars of the past two decades, showing how Darwinian principles of social evolution (so-called 'sociobiology') throw much light on the ways in which scientists network, forming alliances and combating perceived foes. Richards in his turn has opened up a hitherto virtually unknown vein of German influence on the ideas of evolution, showing how transcendentalist ideas (so-called '*Naturphilosophie*') worked their ways into the most orthodox of theorizing, perhaps lasting down even unto this day.

But there are problems with the approach, most obviously that biological change is non-directed, in the sense that the raw building-blocks of evolution ('mutations') are random. They occur in directions quite unrelated to the needs of their possessors. In the world of science, to the contrary, although there is certainly some randomness and chance, most of the raw building-blocks ('discoveries') have been anything but random. One has only to look at the laborious story told by the private notebooks of Charles Darwin himself to see this. Through eighteen intensive months (early 1837 to late 1838) he worked through an absolutely massive amount of material drawn from sources as disparate as animal breeding and political economy, before finally he came to his major mechanism of natural selection. His discovery was the apotheosis of direction or teleology. (There are many – too many – discussions of this route to discovery: my own contribution can be found in my *The Darwinian Revolution*; rival accounts, with references to even more, can be found in Kohn 1985.)

It must be emphasized that this difference between the randomness of biological variation and the non-randomness of scientific variation is no trivial difference. Most significantly, it lies at the heart of the major dissimilarity between the course of science and that of the world of organisms, namely that whereas organic evolution is essentially without end or goal, science has just such a unique end, namely the disinterested truth about objective reality. (This is so, even if one believes like Popper (1959, 1972) that such truth can never be achieved or at least can never be known to be achieved; or if one believes, as do I (Ruse 1986), that truth ultimately is coherence rather than correspondence.)

For myself, this is an end to matters. I want no part of this philosophy (Ruse 1986). For people like Hull and Richards, this is the place to start. They argue that you always have disanalogies when you first compare two different things, whether they be countries or processes of change. The point is to recognize such disanalogies, keeping them in their proper perspective. Indeed, one should let the creative tension caused by such disanalogies work for you, in pointing to hitherto-unappreciated connections and points of similarity.

But although I set up people like Hull and Richards as foils against my own beliefs, I am not now in the business of criticizing others. My aim rather is to present an alternative model of scientific change. Having been dismissive of other people's model of change, let me rush at once to cover myself and to assure you that however successful I may be in my presentation, my goals now are very modest. I am going to base my discussion on but one case study, which may or may not be applicable elsewhere. And whether applicable or not, I do not pretend to be digging down into some profound level of reality and understanding. But I do think that my model highlights some important aspects of one major episode in science – in an important branch of science – and if this be true, our time is anything but wasted.

My case study is (like Hull and Richards) the history of evolutionary theory itself, from its origins in the middle of the eighteenth century right down to the present day. I am going to make a number of stark historical claims; but as far as this paper is concerned I shall not really attempt to defend them. This is not because I have any doubt as to their truth – the opposite in fact. But I (and others) have looked at and argued for the claims elsewhere, at great length. So, because my interests in this paper are essentially philosophical, as I go along I shall simply state the history and then take it for granted.

And, because this is not a detective story where it is dramatically important to keep you from knowing my conclusion, let me tell you now that my key historical claim is that the history of the concept of evolution has been entwined with the history of the concept of progress – the belief that things (societies, moral codes, knowledge) in this world do and can get better and better, through human effort. My key philosophical claim will be that this relationship between evolution and progress is illuminatingly illustrated by the model of the typical development of a human family. In other words, whereas the Chicago school uses a phylogenetic model of scientific change, I am going to propose an ontogenetic model of scientific change. (The main source for the historical material is Ruse (1995). Other essays by me, speaking to the issue, include Ruse (1988b, 1993). Look also at Bowler (1983) and Richards (1992).)

EVOLUTION IS THE CHILD OF PROGRESS

Breaking things down, my first historical (sub-)claim is that evolution – the belief that all organic beings, quick and dead, have natural origins and are produced by the normal laws of nature – was an idea which first appeared and started to be accepted from the middle to the end of the eighteenth century. And my second historical (sub-)claim is that it was not chance that evolution appeared at this time, nor was it chance that the same idea (in somewhat different versions) appeared in France, England and Germany. This was a century which invented, developed and promoted the idea of progress – the belief that it is possible to improve aspects of human existence, and that this improvement can come about through human effort and ability – and the birth of the one idea (progress) brought about the birth of the other (evolution).

For the traditional Christian, the metaphysic of history was providentialism – the belief that God controls the destiny of the world, and judges the fate of the denizens thereof. The eighteenth century exploited the secular opportunities made possible by the Scientific Revolution, and (as we now realize, working as much from as against a notion of Providence) argued that change can and will come about by human efforts and abilities. Moreover, this is change for the better. But just as people were developing such progressivist sentiments, they were realizing that the world of organisms is far richer and more mysterious than previously recognized. Through exploration, through agriculture, through mining, and through diverse other activities, directly scientific and indirectly technological, the full cornucopia of life was being uncovered. And this demanded explanation which progress seemed ready to provide (Bury 1920; Moore 1979; Almond *et al.* 1982; Spadefora 1990; McNeill 1987).

Why progress? In major part because the more that was learnt of the world of organisms the more it was realized that it is a world of change. Apart from increasingly successful human attempts at change in the worlds of animal and plant breeding, there was an ever-growing list of biological phenomena which seemed to point to perpetual becoming rather than stable being. Most obviously, there is the fossil record with its revelation of fabulous beasts of yesterday which seem not to have any living counterparts (Greene 1959; Bowler 1984; Rudwick 1972). Combined with all this, there was the long-standing tradition of viewing the organic world as one ordered by a chain of being, going from the most simple to the most complex. This was a belief which goes back at least to Aristotle's *De Anima*, and it was one which was reinforced by theological and philosophical arguments through to and including the century of the Enlightenment (Lovejoy 1936).

As a consequence, there was therefore an easy swing from belief in change in the world of culture and society and science to a belief in change in the world of organisms – 'monad to man'. And, especially given that the progressionists were no less keen than the providentialists to judge our own species as the epitome and crowning triumph of creation, it was felt natural to read the improvement of culture right into the processes and products of organic change. Evolution (I use this term somewhat anachronistically) was therefore seen as progressive, with *Homo sapiens* as the end point. At which stage, equally naturally, people turned right round and read the progressiveness of the biological record back into society. Thus they felt able to use evolution as support for their beliefs and aspirations about the course of history! (See Bowler 1975 and Richards 1992 for discussions of the history of the word 'evolution'.)

Evolution was the child of progress – and like human children, it showed its parentage proudly and without embarrassment. One can demonstrate this fact through countless individual cases – Jean Baptiste de Lamarck in France, Erasmus Darwin in England and Lorenz Oken (inasmuch as he or any of his countrymen were genuine evolutionists) in Germany. Moreover, just as people are inclined to attack the children through their parents (and conversely), so we find that people attacked evolution through progress (and conversely). Georges Cuvier despised both evolution and progress. As also did the English geologist and cleric Adam Sedgwick, who made no bones about the links he drew between the two vile doctrines. And a similar stance was taken by the Swiss-American ichthyologist Louis Agassiz. (For Lamarck, see Burkhardt 1977 and Corsi 1988; for Darwin, see McNeill 1987; for the German thinkers, see Richards 1987; for Cuvier, see Coleman 1984, Outram 1984, and Appel 1987; for Sedgwick, see Clark and Hughes 1890; for Agassiz, see Agassiz 1859.)

Evolution existed because of and as an extension of progress. Indeed, like a human child, it could not exist without its parent. The solid evidence for the truth of evolution was thin, especially in the early years. Its main appeal was as a corollary of progress. In fact, even as the nineteenth century pulled to its mid-point, we find the Scottish evolutionist, the anonymous author of *The Vestiges of the Natural History of Creation*, Robert Chambers, ultimately defending his evolutionary beliefs by appeal to progress. Faced by withering criticism, he pleaded that if you believe in progress – as did most of his readers – then it is only reasonable to believe in evolution. They are a package deal (Secord 1989):

> The question whether the human race will ever advance far beyond its present position in intellect and morals, is one which has engaged much attention. Judging from the past, we cannot reasonably doubt that great advances are yet to be made; but if the principle of development be admitted, these are certain, whatever may be the space of time required for their realization. A progression resembling development may be traced in human nature, both in the individual and in large groups of men.... Now all of this is in conformity with what we have seen of the progress of organic creation. It seems but the minute hand of a watch, of which the hour hand is the transition from species to species. Knowing what we do of that latter transition, the possibility of a decided and general retrogression of the highest species towards a meaner type is scarce admissible, but a forward movement seems anything but unlikely.
>
> (Chambers 1846: 400–2)

In the terms of this essay, I read Chambers as I read the others before and of his generation. He regarded progress and evolution as part of the same family, the former the parent of the latter.

EVOLUTION GROWS UP

I do not want to claim that the change of status of evolution from that of mere epiphenomenon of belief in progress to that of established scientific fact was solely the work of one man. Even I, as an Englishman, feel somewhat uncomfortable with the boast that Charles Darwin, unaided, in his *Origin of Species*, proved evolution as something beyond reasonable doubt. Yet there is no doubt that Darwin, with varying degrees of help (intentional and unintentional) did move evolution over from the speculative and quasi to the reasonable and respectable.

Thanks to the *Origin*, the onus was now on the critic to show why evolution should not be taken as true – a challenge which diminishingly few wanted to accept. Nor was this changed status of evolution any more a matter of chance than the original appearance of the idea. Skilfully, Darwin bound together many different strands of biology – palaeontology, biogeography, embryology, systematics, anatomy, and more – into one unified theory, with evolution as its 'true cause' (its *vera causa*). Moreover, although many had doubts about its full application, Darwin made evolution even more reasonable by providing a causal mechanism: natural selection. He was thereby able to explain one of the most puzzling aspects of the organic world, that which had hitherto convinced many that any naturalistic explanation of origins is forever barred. Selection speaks to the design-like nature of organisms – their 'adaptedness' (Ruse 1979c, 1982).

The implication that I want to stress here is that, after the *Origin*, it was no longer necessary to appeal to progress to support one's belief in evolution. It was enough to appeal to the wide range of evidence in the world of biology. Darwin had provided what the philosopher of science William Whewell (1840) called a 'consilience of inductions', thus making the support of progress unnecessary (Ruse 1975c). It is in this sense that I want to argue that evolution had grown up. Like a human adult, it no longer needed its parent to exist, to live and to make its own way in the world. It was quite possible for someone to accept evolution even if they had never heard of progress – even if they rejected it. Just as I am independent of my parents, so evolution was independent of its parent.

EVOLUTION STAYS IN THE FAMILY

And yet, like a great many human families, evolution did not pick up its belongings and leave home. Less metaphorically, it did not break away from progress, even though it no longer needed progress for its very existence and support. Evolutionists continued to be progressionists just as ardently after the *Origin* as they had before. More so in fact. Indeed, even in the first edition of the *Origin* there were strong intimations of Darwin's own progressionism. This came through most clearly in the book's final flowery paragraph.

> Thus, from the war of nature, from famine and death, the most exalted object which we are capable of conceiving, namely, the production of the higher animals, directly follows. There is grandeur in this view of life, with its several powers, having been originally breathed into a few forms or into one; and that, whilst this planet has gone cycling on

according to the fixed law of gravity, from so simple a beginning endless forms most beautiful and most wonderful have
been, and are being, evolved.

(Darwin 1859: 490)

This passage, incidentally, is a fascinating example of Darwin using
non-evolutionist material for his own ends, showing just the historical connections I have been postulating. Consider the following
– highly providentialist – passage from an article by the Scottish
man of science, David Brewster.

> In considering our own globe as having its origin in a gaseous
> zone, thrown off by the rapidity of the solar rotation, and
> as consolidated by cooling from the chaos of its elements, we
> confirm rather than oppose the Mosaic cosmogony, whether
> allegorically or literally interpreted . . .
> In the grandeur and universality of these views, we forget
> the insignificant beings which occupy and disturb the planet-
> ary domains. Life in all its forms, in all its restlessness, and
> in all its pageantry, disappears in the magnitude and remote-
> ness of the perspective. The excited mind sees only the
> gorgeous fabric of the universe, recognises only its Divine
> architect, and ponders but on its cycles of glory and deso-
> lation.

(Brewster 1838: 301)

We know that Darwin read this just before he discovered natural
selection and that he was much moved by it. (The resemblance is
even stronger in the 'sketch' of his theory, which Darwin penned
in 1842.

By the time of the third edition of the *Origin* (1861), Darwin
knew that his evolutionary ideas were a basic success, and thus he
relaxed and wrote much more explicitly about his belief that evolution is essentially an upward drive towards that organism that we
all love and cherish.

> If we look at the differentiation and specialisation of the
> several organs of each being when adult (and this will include
> the brain for intellectual purposes) as the best standard of
> highness of organisation, natural selection clearly leads
> towards highness; for all physiologists admit that the special-
> isation of organs, inasmuch as they perform in this state their
> functions better, is an advantage to each being; and hence the

accumulation of variations tending towards specialisation is within the scope of natural selection.

(Peckham 1959: 222)

This explicit Darwinian commitment to progress comes as a surprise to many who believe that natural selection, being opportunistic, can never result in directed change. However, although this is a view to which I personally subscribe (a view backed by the already-mentioned non-directed nature of mutation), such was not Darwin's belief. He thought that selection results in what today we call 'arms races', with competition between lines, resulting eventually in the production of beings with brains and other attributes distinctive of us humans. There may not have been the necessity to progress that we associate with the full-blown teleology that we find in the writings of someone like Teilhard de Chardin (1955) – although he himself had no adequate theory of heredity, Darwin took a hard line on the non-directedness of new variation – but progress was there nevertheless. And by the time that Darwin had finished with it, it was of the pretty old-fashioned variety which leads up to our own species. (It is to the late Dov Ospovat (1981) that we owe the definitive proof of Darwin's progressivism. 'Arms races' are discussed in Dawkins and Krebs (1979); Dawkins (1986); and Vermeij (1987). I give a brief overview of Darwin's position, relating it to modern thought, in Ruse (1993).)

It is true that not many followed Darwin along the precise path that he took, at least until this century when the arms race idea came into its own (Huxley 1912; Huxley and Haldane 1927; Cott 1940). But, Darwin was far from alone in his progressionism. Although one must allow that some (like E. Ray Lankester 1880) imposed a degenerationist theme on top of the main melody, until the turn of the century I have found (almost) no evolutionist who was not at heart a progressionist. People like Herbert Spencer (1857) in England and Ernst Haeckel (1866, 1868) in Germany, not to mention all the evolutionists in other parts of the world from Russia to America, were as fanatical in their progressionism as any eighteenth-century French secular philosopher. As intimated in the last section, with rare exceptions, natural selection lay slightly on the average evolutionist; but let there be no mistake as to the genuine depth to the commitment to some form of evolution. That such forms tend not to be highly regarded today is irrelevant to our story. (See Bowler (1983) for the general picture; Richards (1987) for Germany; Vucinich (1988) for Russia; Pusey (1983) for China; and Russett (1976) and Rainger (1991) for America. Wagar (1972) is excellent on progressionism after Darwin.)

What many do not realize is that this state of affairs – evolution *and* progress – continued well into this century. The second myth about their relationship, after the first tale that they were torn asunder by natural selection, is that the divorce was made final by the coming of Mendelian genetics, with its non-directed units of change ('mutations'). Conceptually this should have occurred: it is the basis of my critique of traditional evolutionary epistemology. But, historically, it no more happened for the post-Mendelians than it did for Darwin. The great mathematicians who synthesized Darwinian selection with Mendelian genetics – R. A. Fisher (1930), J. B. S. Haldane (1932), and Sewall Wright (1931) – were all ardent progressionists. They saw no incompatibility between their evolutionism and progressionism, even though they did work hard to show how the two could be made mathematically harmonious. Fisher was the most blatant and remarkable. At the heart of his classic *The Genetical Theory of Evolution* lay his self-styled 'fundamental theorem of evolution', which was intended explicitly to counter progressively in the organic world the degenerationist tendencies of the second law of thermodynamics in the inorganic world (Turner 1985; Kruger 1987).

In the light of these undoubted historical facts, I argue that although – thanks to Darwin and the *Origin* – evolution reached adulthood in the mid-nineteenth century, it never left the family home. Evolution was the child of progress and, notwithstanding the lack of necessity, for nearly a hundred years it was happy to acknowledge the relationship – proudly to flaunt it, in fact. The generations lived together (Ruse 1988b).

EVOLUTION BECOMES INDEPENDENT

Nevertheless, as happens in human families, the time did come when evolution – that is, evolutionists – wanted to sever the family ties. At last, people in increasing numbers wanted to work with an evolutionism shorn of progressionist sentiments. It was not that they gave up being progressionists – far from it – but that they realized that so inherently a value-laden concept as progress was incompatible with their aspirations, as scientists, to be taken seriously as *professionals*. If evolutionists were to get the respect that they craved, not to mention the grants and departments and the students and the status of subjects like genetics and embryology, they just had to drop all the talk about 'higher' and 'lower', and 'upward rise', and 'humans at the pinnacle' and so forth. This was mere pop science, fit for the museums at best. To be real scientists, evolutionists had to become *prima facie* value-free researchers just like everybody else.

And so they did. Men like Theodosius Dobzhansky and George Gaylord Simpson and Ernst Mayr and G. Ledyard Stebbins – those who wanted desperately to raise the status of evolutionary studies to the status of professional science – set out deliberately to cleanse their work of progressionist language and descriptions and mechanisms and conclusions. At least, they set out to cleanse their professional work of such sentiments. As a matter of fact, they all remained progressionists; but they kept this kind of reading of evolution to their leisure hours and their private correspondence or to books and articles clearly labelled 'popular' or 'public'. (We are only just starting to open up the history of this period. Apart from the seminal Mayr and Provine (1980), a very impressive study is Cain (1993). For the professional popular divide compare Dobzhansky (1937) and (1967); Simpson (1944) and (1950); Mayr (1942) and (1988); and Stebbins (1950) and (1969).)

In the terms of my model, therefore, I argue that between the years of (approximately) 1930 and 1960, evolution broke away from its parent, progress. The professionalizers of evolution (often known as the 'synthetic theorists', because they formulated the 'synthetic theory of evolution') severed the bonds. Evolution had been capable of standing on its own two feet for nearly a hundred years; but until there was reason for it to do so, it failed to make the break. Or, perhaps, the language of failure is inappropriate. Many people, parents and children, see no reason why there should be a break until there is a need. Evolutionists felt much the same way.

(The exception is the case that proves the rule. In England, Julian Huxley tried to be both a progressionist and an accepted professional evolutionist. This was clearly the intent of his *Evolution: The Modern Synthesis* (1942). The simple fact is that people did not respect him as a professional scientist, and he was very much marginalized into the role of a popularizer: good for a television programme, but not as a serious researcher.)

FAMILY TIES RUN DEEP

Evolutionists achieved their ends. They did set up their own professional discipline of evolution. Progress was thrown out, or driven underground. Moreover, as in human families, once the break had been made, and the reasons for the break fully internalized, increasingly the tendency grew to claim that no one had ever wanted anything very much to do with the old parent anyway. I am afraid that we all know of people who are deeply ashamed of their family origins. The fact that these people are usually thoroughly insecure themselves is often the reason, even if it is but little excuse. The same is much the case for evolution.

To be honest, I suspect that many of today's evolutionists have little interest in progress. They look upon it as some funny old relic of the past, forever being resurrected by historians. It is quite irrelevant to modern professional evolutionary studies. Although, in this context – apart from the fact that old values have a way of being replaced by new values (equilibrium is the trendy value of many of today's evolutionists, who find in it just the kind of sentiment one needs for the ecologically conscious) – one should not forget that, for all that evolution may be a professional discipline, no one can pretend that it is a particularly secure or dominant one. Evolutionists have to fight for their professional place in the sun, along with molecular biologists and physiologists and the like. And often they get but the crumbs.

Nor does one have to be unduly cynical to recognize that things are going to remain this way, at least until evolutionists can claim that they too hold the key to the cures of cancer or some such thing. This being so, even those with progressionist tendencies – probably especially those with progressionist tendencies – are wont to deny any enthusiasm for the old ways. They argue that such geriatric notions of the past should remain confined to the nursing home of history, which (before they are carried off to the graveyard of philosophy) is their only proper resting place. (Look at the rude comments made by working evolutionists at a recent Field Museum symposium on progress: Nitecki 1988.)

And yet, as we all know, in the human world it is so often those very folk who talk and behave in this way who are most prone to reveal precisely that which they are denying – often as they are right in the middle of the very act of denial. In the half-light a familiar profile from the past is sensed. A long-forgotten tone is heard. A distinctive mannerism is glimpsed. Whether it be biology or culture or both, family roots do run deeply.

The same is true of evolution and progress. As one trolls through the work of today's evolutionists, one is often reminded of the discipline's past. Sometimes, indeed, the reminder is very obvious and explicit. For example, Edward O. Wilson, the Harvard ento-mologist and sociobiologist, wears his progressionism very close to the surface. He talks happily of 'peaks' of evolution, and no prizes are offered for guessing which species of organism sits atop the highest peak. For him, evolution and progress will never be far apart.

> Four groups occupy pinnacles high above the others: the colonial invertebrates, the social insects, the nonhuman mam-mals, and man. Each has basic qualities of social life unique to itself. . . . Man has intensified [the] vertebrate traits while adding unique qualities of his own. In so doing he has achieved an extraordinary degree of cooperation with little or no sacrifice of personal survival and reproduction. Exactly how he alone has been able to cross to this fourth pinnacle . . . is the culminating mystery of all biology.
>
> (Wilson 1975, 379–82)

What is fascinating, however, is how such reminders of the past echo down in the work of others, including in the work of those most eager to deny progress. Stephen Jay Gould (1989), for instance, has been vehement in his attack on progress, thinking it a pernicious shadow of nineteenth-century racism. Yet his own pet theory of 'punctuated equilibrium', seeing organisms held homeostatically in balance until such time as they break and jump to other patterns, has a direct line to precisely that which he denies. Even the name of his theory sounds like that of the arch progressionist Herbert Spencer, who argued that organisms are held in balance until such time as they move to another plateau – a state which he referred to as 'dynamic equilibrium'. (For more on these and related points, see Ruse 1988b, 1989, 1995, and of course Chapter 3 in this collection.)

(Something which I think needs closer examination is Gould's attitude to the status of our own species. On the one hand, as in

Wonderful Life, he denies vehemently that we do have special status. On the other hand, there are comments elsewhere suggesting that our culture makes us very special organisms indeed, and surely Gould's ardent critiques of all and every attempt to read humankind from a biological perspective – especially as personified by the human sociobiologists – suggest that, paradoxically, he thinks us just as distinctive as do those that he criticizes. (For his arguments against our special status, see especially Gould 1981 and 1989.) But compare also Gould 1980 and 1982. And, most particularly, see the recent book on life's history, edited by Gould (1993). We go all the way from primitive organisms in the first chapter to a bare-breasted Cro-Magnon beauty at the end of the final chapter – 'blobs to boobs', to rework a phrase.)

I do not want to strain my point beyond credulity. I am not saying that every evolutionist is a progressionist. But I do deny that it is as absent as some would claim. Like humans, the sensitive observer recognizes ancestry.

CONCLUSION

My story is finished. I shall not argue for my model of change. Either you think it is appropriate and illuminating, or you do not. If I have not convinced you now, I never shall, for I have given you all the evidence that I have. All that I can say is that – almost despite myself, for I have a distrust of these sort of models – I do find that it helps me to understand what went on in the history of evolutionary biology. For me, the picture has become clearer.

And with this said, I shall conclude. I simply do not know if this model applies elsewhere. Moreover, I do not know if the disanalogies are crippling. Humans are bisexual. They have two parents, and if they are to perpetuate themselves they must find a mate. I have made no attempt to identify any parent for evolution other than progress. It was not virgin born, for as I have mentioned there were other factors like the development of the biology of the eighteenth century. But how far this constitutes an equivalent parent escapes me. As also does the answer to the question at the other end, about the status and love-life of evolutionism now and in the future. Evolution did not break from progress to blend with another science – nor does it seem ready to do so today.

Points like these may matter; they may not. I shall be interested in the reactions of my readers. I would only say that even limited models have their uses. For this reason, I commend my family history model to you!

6

THE VIEW FROM SOMEWHERE
A critical defence of evolutionary epistemology

Charles Robert Darwin, the father of modern evolutionary theory, hit upon his mechanism of evolution through natural selection somewhere towards the end of September 1838 (Ruse 1979c; Ospovat 1981). At once, he started to think of its possible applications to our own species. Indeed, the very first explicit writings on selection that we have in Darwin's private notebooks, occurring around the end of October 1838, consider possible implications of the mechanism for human thought processes. However, when Darwin finally published his evolutionary speculations in *On the Origin of Species* in 1859, he said little about our own species, simply noting that his general views would have specific applications for *Homo sapiens*.

This silence was not cowardice. Darwin never wanted to conceal the implications of his ideas, but he was concerned first to make as full a case as he could for the general theory. Finally, in 1871, Darwin turned to human beings in their own right and accorded them detailed treatment in his *The Descent of Man*. By this time, of course, many other evolutionists had taken up the subject, most notably Darwin's great supporter Thomas Henry Huxley, who, in his *Evidence as to Man's Place in Nature* (1863), solidly established human evolutionary origins with detailed comparisons between ourselves and the so-called higher apes. Darwin, therefore, was free to devote his efforts to discussion of mechanisms, especially (what he took to be the crucial notion of) sexual selection.

Despite this fairly fast start, the study of human nature from an evolutionary perspective, specifically from a Darwinian perspective, making full use of the explanatory power of selection has always lagged somewhat behind other areas of evolutionary inquiry (Bowler 1984, 1986). There are reasons for this. Internal to biology, there is the fact that much spade work had to be done on developing the general theory of evolution and particularly on the implications of evolution for behaviour of various kinds. Without such development, there was little hope of throwing much explanatory light on such a species as our own (Mayr and Provine 1980). External to biology, there was the fact that with the general decline of the importance of Christianity in the nineteenth century, there grew up a number of substitute ideologies that had little or no place within them for an evolutionary perspective on humankind. I think here, particularly, of various movements in and around the social sciences, most notably Marxism and then, at the beginning of this century, Freudianism. As it happens, both Marx and Freud themselves were sympathetic to evolutionary ideas – even to Darwinian ideas – but their followers tended to take them as exclusive alternatives to evolutionism. Thus, for many years in influential circles there was no real place for a biological perspective on humankind (Caplan and Jennings 1984).

In the past twenty or thirty years, things have started to change. In part this has been because the rival views have generally failed to deliver on much that they promised. But, also, there has been a newfound vigour within evolutionary studies and this is a vigour which has extended over into the biological study of humankind. Palaeoanthropologists have made many exciting studies about human origins, underlining in particular our close affinity with the apes. We now know, for instance, that we have been separated from the chimpanzee a mere six million years (Pilbeam 1984). Indeed, were we taxonomists from an alien planet, all evidence would impel us to classify humans and chimpanzees in the same genus. At the same time as some evolutionists have been working on the paths leading to our present state, so others have been working on mechanisms. In particular, the students of the evolution of social behaviour, so-called 'sociobiologists', have not only been developing their theory at the general level, but also applying it to humankind. This has not been without controversy. Nevertheless, already some solid results are coming in (Ruse 1979b; Betzig *et al.* 1987).

As a philosopher one cannot be (at least one should not be) indifferent to these various happenings. Philosophy draws always on advances in other subjects, particularly on advances in the sciences. This is not a sign of weakness, but a mark of the symbiotic relationship that the philosophical enterprise has with other areas of human inquiry. I believe that, in fact, this new understanding about the biology of human nature has profound implications for the philosophical enterprise. This is not a new thought. Indeed, Darwin himself was always groping to connect his biology, particularly his evolutionary biology, with the major problems in the theory of knowledge and in the theory of moral behaviour. For instance, in a private notebook in 1837 (that is, at least a year before he hit on the notion of natural selection) Darwin was wrestling with epistemology when he wrote 'Plato . . . says in Phaedo that our *imaginary ideas* arise from the pre-existence of the soul, are not derivable from experience – read monkeys for pre-existence'. Later when he turned in detail to human nature in *The Descent of Man* and in other works, Darwin continued to explore the implications of his science for the problems of philosophy. Nor was Darwin alone in this. Huxley was always working and writing on the questions of philosophy. And even more was Herbert Spencer, who is well known for having devised a whole evolutionary perspective on life (Ruse 1986).

However, although the evolutionary approach to philosophy is of fairly long standing, it is also of fairly disreputable standing, at least in the eyes of most professional philosophers. There are reasons for this, not the least being the fact that, thanks to the fragmenting nature of our education, most philosophers today, certainly in the Anglo-Saxon world, grow up in ignorance of (if not outright hostility to) science. I want to counter this ignorance and hostility. I cannot hope to convert everybody at once, but in this paper I shall try to make a start by arguing that modern evolutionary biology, specifically modern neo-Darwinian evolutionary biology, throws significant light on questions that have to do with the theory of knowledge.

Although in a minority, I am not alone in my enthusiasm for what Donald Campbell (1974, 1977) has labelled 'evolutionary epistemology'. Already there is a small but growing body of literature devoted to the subject (Campbell *et al.* 1986). It is true that much of the reaction to this literature has been fairly critical. Yet, perhaps, the very fact that people think it worth criticizing shows that the evolutionary approach is commanding respect or attention of a kind. I believe, however, although I am an enthusiast for the evolutionary approach as such, that the movement stands in some danger of collapsing in on itself from a sterile refusal to ask or answer difficult questions. Therefore, in this essay, although what I intend to do is offer a defence of evolutionary epistemology, it will be a *critical* defence. I shall take issue with supporters of the idea, as much as with opponents.

To accomplish my ends, I shall begin with a short sketch of what I take to be the correct evolutionary approach to the theory of knowledge. Here I shall be covering more quickly some of the ideas that I explore in my recent book, *Taking Darwin Seriously: A Naturalistic Approach to Philosophy* (1986). Then I shall comment critically on a number of recent discussions on and around evolutionary epistemology. My aim, as always, will be positive. I am not particularly interested in besting opponents. I want rather to use both support and disagreement to tease out further some of the implications of the evolutionary approach. In conclusion, I shall pose a number of questions arising from the discussion which I think must be faced by evolutionary epistemologists if we are to have an ongoing vibrant study. An idea that leads to no new developments is as barren as an organism without offspring.

INNATE CAPACITIES

I begin with the fact that organisms are the end products of evolution and that the major mechanism of evolution is Darwinian natural selection (Ruse 1986; Dobzhansky *et al.* 1977). By this, I mean that because more organisms are born than can possibly survive and reproduce, there will be a differential reproduction and a constant winnowing or selecting of those with characteristics particularly advantageous in life's struggles. The overall effect is change, but change of a particular kind, namely, in the direction of adaptive efficiency. Organisms do not just exist; they have features – 'adaptations' – which enable them to perform well, or at least better than the unsuccessful.

I take it also that this view of life applies to human beings. At the physical level, such a claim is (I presume) fairly uncontentious. No one who knows anything of modern science would deny that we are the product of evolution or that our features have been forged with a view to adaptive efficiency: eyes, teeth, ears, penises, vaginas, all of these things aid in the battle for reproduction. I believe also that natural selection reaches into our brains and minds (whatever the connection between these two) and that thus the ways in which we think and act are themselves reflective of

157

the ever-present pressure towards reproductive efficiency (Isaac 1983). In non-biological circles, this claim is of course a great deal more contentious than those made previously, so let me unpack in a little detail precisely the nature and extent of what I would argue. (I speak for myself here, but in biological circles – certainly in Darwinian circles – I do not think I am being particularly forward or controversial in what I claim.)

It is clear that humans have, in some sense, if not escaped their biology then at least turned it into altogether new channels. Obviously we humans have a cultural dimension, which if not unique, is very much more developed than anywhere else in the organic world (Boyd and Richerson 1985). This means that we have the power to transmit information more rapidly and with less regard to immediate ends than would be possible were everything to be passed on in conventional biological ways. What this all adds up to is that we get cultural changes and variations that are far too fast-moving and too drastic to be directly and completely controlled by the biological forces of selection. However, this in no way implies that biology is irrelevant. Rather, culture in a sense sits on top of a bed of biological constraints and dispositions. If you like, culture is the flesh which adheres to the skeleton of biology. Less metaphorically, what I would argue is that the human mind is not a *tabula rasa* but is informed by various capacities, constraints, and dispositions, which come to us innately. We have these capacities or dispositions because it has proven biologically advantageous for our ancestors to have them. Culture, then, works within the constraints put on us by these dispositions. In the mature being, culture expands out to the forms of thought and behaviour that we have (Wilson 1978).

In speaking of 'innate' capacities, let me emphasize that neither I nor any other Darwinian evolutionist would argue for innate ideas of the kind rejected by the philosopher John Locke (1975) in his classic critique. No one believes that a human grows to maturity, knowing innately that God exists, or that $2 + 2 = 4$. Rather, the claim is that there are underlying channels, as it were, into which culture must flow. (Locke himself seems to have acknowledged the existence of these.) These dispositions have been known by various names. Recently the sociobiologists Edward O. Wilson and Charles Lumsden have labelled them 'epigenetic rules', which is perhaps as good a name as any (Lumsden and Wilson 1981, 1983). However, I would emphasize that in thus arguing for innate dispositions I do not thereby want to commit myself to all that has been said on their behalf, on every occasion by every biologist. In particular, I see no reason to tie oneself to the fairly deterministic view of human nature favoured by Wilson and Lumsden. They argue that the epigenetic rules can change in but a few generations, with profound implications for culture. This, it seems to me, is an empirical matter and certainly not yet decided. It is not one on which a true Darwinian need take a stand.

Thus far, I want to emphasize that I do intend my claims to be taken as genuinely empirical and part of natural science. These are not supposed to be mere philosophical musings; although I will admit that, being towards the forefront of science, our knowledge about these matters is not always definitive. Nevertheless, there is a growing body of evidence explicating the nature and substantiating the existence of the innate dispositions. Wilson himself notes the backing behind a number of such dispositions, or rules. One that he details at some length concerns the way in which humans perceive colours (Lumsden and Wilson 1981). It now appears that, far from seeing a gradual spectrum or from categorizing according to specific cultural variation, all humans break up colours in certain universal patterns (Berlin and Kay 1969). This partitioning is apparently a direct function of the most basic aspects of the physiology of vision, although the precise adaptive virtues of such partitioning are still somewhat murky – they may perhaps be connected with the general abilities of higher primates to perceive in colour. These abilities, in turn, have something to do with our origins as arborial creatures. (Note that here, as often, the Darwinian is not necessarily claiming immediate adaptive virtues for some particular function. What is important to the Darwinian is that, at the time of origin and development, features had virtues which proved themselves in the ongoing struggles for life (Maynard Smith 1981).)

Another disposition that Wilson discusses is one that has been treated at length by many authors recently. I refer to the incest barriers that seem to exist between close relatives. These occur in virtually all societies without exception (notwithstanding certain special cases, like the Egyptian pharaohs). The adaptive advantages to incest barriers are obvious and strongly confirmed. Close inbreeding leads to horrendously deleterious biological effects. There must surely have been very strong selective pressures against intra-family mating in our evolutionary past (Alexander 1979; van den Berghe 1979, 1983).

Completing my examples, yet more dispositions of the kind being supposed here surely lie in the area of linguistics. Although the work of Noam Chomsky (1957, 1966) and his associates is controversial, there is growing acceptance of his central thesis that languages are not purely culturally developed, but instead reflect a 'deep structure', which is shared between the peoples of the most diverse backgrounds. It is true that Chomsky himself does not give a fully Darwinian explanation of these underlying structures, but the general thesis fits well with the kind of position that I am advocating and endorsing. Although the variation of language is given by culture and can change rapidly, as we know indeed it does, and can vary from society to society, as again we know it does, there is an underlying biological foundation on which the spoken word rests. This foundation is one of innate capacities put in place because of their adaptive virtues. (Pertinent in this context is the way in which people like Philip Lieberman (1984) have taken up Chomsky's thesis and related it to modern biological thought.)

THE MAKING OF SCIENCE

Now the question before us here is how we are to connect all this up to epistemology, the foundations of knowledge. I believe that Darwin, in the already-quoted notebook passage, again leads the way. Knowledge as such is part of culture, and changes rapidly without being tied tightly to adaptive advantage. But knowledge is structured and informed by underlying principles or norms – Plato's 'imaginary ideas' – and, as Darwin said, these are part of our evolutionary heritage. The norms of knowledge relate to selective advantage.

To make my case, I shall seize on what is today often taken as the epitome of knowledge, namely science – although I believe that the Darwinian position is applicable generally. As a start I shall pick up on a fact about which, among philosophers and others who have examined and discussed the nature of science, there is almost unanimous agreement: there are certain principles or rules which govern the production of science. There is, in other words, a generally shared *scientific methodology* (Nagel 1961; Hempel 1966).

Of course there are disagreements about the exact nature of this methodology, but in outline it is fairly universally recognized. The scientist does not try simply to produce ideas of any kind. He or she takes seriously the notion that the world works in a fairly regular sort of way and that it is the aim of the scientist to try to capture this regularity within scientific theories or hypotheses. In particular, science attempts to achieve understanding by reference to laws, that is to say, by reference to regularities that govern the happenings of events. Such laws are believed not to hold merely occasionally or spasmodically, but to be entirely regular. In other words, they have some sort of necessity. Generally this necessity is taken to reflect a system of powers or forces, known as causes. (Whether there are genuine powers or forces behind causes is another question. The point is that science thinks of phenomena happening because of certain effecting powers, which they call 'causes'.)

How, then, does the scientist try to tie together his or her discoveries about the causal regularities of the world? Here, crucially important, are the various principles of formal reasoning. I refer, of course, to logic and to mathematics. The scientist (just like anybody else) believes that there are certain rules of inference which confer validity on arguments that one might want to make, binding together hitherto disjoint pieces of knowledge (Salmon 1973). Thus, for instance, in logic one has the basic laws of necessity like the law of identity and the law of excluded middle. Together with these, one has certain inferences which one is allowed to make, like *modus ponens* (if p, then q, p, therefore q) and disjunctive syllogism (p or q, not p, therefore q), to be distinguished from invalid inferences like the so-called 'fallacy of affirming the consequent' (if p, then q, q, therefore p). Together with logic one has, particularly in modern science, the whole apparatus of the mathematician. The scientist relies on the laws of mathematics. For instance, the basic laws of arithmetic ($2 + 2 = 4$, $7 - 5 = 2$) together with principles of algebra and geometry ($x + y = y + x$, the square on the hypotenuse in a right-angled triangle is equal to the sums of the squares on the other two sides), and again various rules of inference (if $x = y$ and $y = z$, then $x = z$).

Given the basic principles and inferences of logic and mathematics, a scientist can work with his or her discoveries about causal regularities and thus try to put together developed theories. It is often thought that these are axiom systems, at least in principle, although (as is well known) in recent years many philosophers of science have argued that matters are perhaps a little more complex than this (Suppe 1974). But, whatever the resolution of this particular philosophical squabble, all agree that, once completed, a scientist can turn to the task of checking and verification and extension and rejection of a theory. (I speak now at the conceptual level, recognizing fully that as practised the various tasks of discovery and verification are mixed up and what is conceptually prior might not necessarily be temporarily prior.) The precise form of such check and extension has been much discussed. If one takes seriously the Popperian vision of science, one of the most important things for the scientist to do is to check his or her theories against the real world, being prepared to reject the theories if they do not correspond to reality (Popper 1959, 1963). This, as is well known, is called the principle of falsifiability, although not all today would give it quite the high status of the Popperian (Kitcher 1982).

Other principles are also important, perhaps even more important. Without taking a strong stand myself, I will simply note that a crucial cannon in the scientist's arsenal seems to be what the nineteenth-century British philosopher William Whewell (1840) referred to as the 'consilience of inductions'. What scientists try to do is bind together separate areas of their knowledge into one overall thesis, connected by one or a few high-powered hypotheses. This is, for instance, what Isaac Newton did in his mechanics, and it was also done extremely successfully by Charles Darwin in *On the Origin of Species*, as he argued for his evolutionary perspective. Scientists feel that a successful consilience shows that the truth of what one has achieved is something independent of one's own subjective wishes or dispositions. They sense that a consilience could not have occurred unless it 'truly is telling you about reality'.

I will not go into further details about scientific methodology. These can be gleaned from virtually any elementary textbook in the philosophy of science. The point I want to make is clear. Science is not a random subjective phenomenon or activity, but is rather governed and evaluated by certain commonly accepted rules and criteria. And I am sure that you can guess now what move I am about to make. I argue that these rules and criteria used by the scientist are not subjectively decided on by the individual scientist, nor even by a group of scientists. Neither are they reflections of absolute reality or some such thing. They are rather the principles of reasoning and understanding that we humans use because they proved of value to our ancestors in the struggle for existence.

In other words, what I argue is that the principles of science (and I include here mathematics and logic) are reflections of the innate dispositions, or epigenetic rules, which are burned into the thinking processes of every mature normal human being. We believe that $2 + 2 = 4$, not because it is a reflection of absolute reality, or because some of our ancestors made a pact to believe in it, but because those proto-humans who believed in $2 + 2 = 4$, rather than $2 + 2 = 5$, survived and reproduced, and those who did not, did not. Today, it is these same selectively produced techniques and rules which govern the production of science.

Note that I am not saying anything so crude as simply that science is adaptive and that which we consider better science is more adaptive than worse science. This is obviously false. Mendel, to the best of one's knowledge, died childless and yet in respects he had a better grasp of the nature of heredity than any of his fellows. Darwin, to the contrary, had many children but this had nothing whatsoever to do with his brilliance as a scientist. Darwin's reproductive success was a function of his comfortable and privileged position in Victorian society, not to mention his fortune in finding a fertile and supportive wife. However, science – and, I would argue, the rest of human knowledge – is connected in a very vital way to our biology. The connection comes through the criteria and methods which we use in producing and evaluating science. Although science reaches up into the highest dimensions of culture, its feet remain firmly rooted in evolutionary biology.

One could say more in support of the case that I am making; in particular, one could (and one should) say more about the empirical evidence for the case that I am making. Is there reason to think, for instance, that logic and mathematics, not to mention the rules of scientific methodology, are in some sense innate, rather than purely learned? (I feel a little uncomfortable about thus opposing innate to learned. In fact, as you must by now realize, I do not see this as an exclusive alternation. Although the epigenetic rules may be innate, in order to become aware of scientific methodology, learning and culture are crucially important (Bateson 1986).) As it happens, I believe that there is empirical evidence supporting the sort of case that I am endorsing. Most suggestive in this context are recent studies by primatologists, showing that our closest living relatives, the chimpanzees, have unambiguous powers of reasoning (De Waal 1982; Gillan 1981; Gillan *et al.* 1981). Moreover, these powers seem as much a function of biology as of learning, either from fellow chimpanzees or from humans. No one pretends the chimpanzees can reason in anything like as sophisticated a fashion as humans, but they certainly seem to have rudimentary awarenesses of logic and mathematics, as well as of principles of reasoning like transitivity and symmetry.

I believe that some of this empirical work is taking us well beyond heuristic and into the realm of solid justification. However, having (I trust) whetted your appetite, I shall say no more here about evidence. I have gone into these matters elsewhere recently in some detail (Ruse 1986). In any case, my primary concern at this point is with the arguments of others. What I will say, however, is that in addition to any present-day empirical evidence, the kind of thesis that I am proposing meshes nicely with our general understanding of the evolutionary process. It is not at all implausible to suppose that a proto-human who had a ready grasp of elementary mathematics would be better suited for life's struggles than one who did not; and the same goes for the basic principles of scientific method. Consider, for instance, two proto-humans, one of whom takes seriously consiliences and the other who does not. They both go down to the river to drink. They notice about them signs of a struggle – feathers, blood, paw marks in the mud, and growls in the nearby undergrowth. The one proto-human exclaims, 'Ah, it looks as though tigers were here and are still here, but obviously this is just a theory, not a fact'. The other says nothing, but disappears rapidly from view. Which one of these was more likely to be your ancestor?

Evidence apart, you have now in essence the evolutionary epistemology that I endorse. It is simple and straightforward, but I look upon this as a virtue, not a fault. I do not pretend that it is particularly original with me; certainly there are others who have written very much in the same vein – beginning with Darwin himself. If what I have to say has any special merit, it lies only in my realization of the very close connections between recent claims of the human sociobiologists and the needs of the epistemologists. I shall not pause here to congratulate myself, or to apologize for failings. Rather, as promised, I shall now turn at once to the writings of others, comparing and contrasting them against what

I have endorsed. (In the course of this discussion I shall be making reference to several whose ideas are – more or less – close to mine.)

THE PROBLEM OF SCIENTISM

I want to begin with some claims by the well-known philosopher, Thomas Nagel, given in his recent and much-acclaimed book *The View from Nowhere* (1986), the title of which obviously provided the inspiration for the title I have used for this discussion. Although Nagel does not provide a full and searching critique of evolutionary epistemology, he does have things to say briefly that are certainly pertinent to the enterprise and which I strongly believe must be considered by the supporter of the approach. I pick out two arguments for particular consideration.

First, Nagel accuses the evolutionary epistemologist of what he calls 'scientism':

> Philosophy is also infested by a broader tendency of contemporary intellectual life: scientism. Scientism is actually a special form of idealism, for it puts one type of human understanding in charge of the universe and what can be said about it. At its most myopic it assumes that everything there is must be understandable by the employment of scientific theories like those we have developed to date – physics and evolutionary biology are the current paradigms – as if the present age were not just another in the series.
>
> Precisely because of their dominance, these attitudes are ripe for attack. Of course, some of the opposition is foolish: antiscientism can degenerate into a rejection of science – whereas in reality it is essential to the defense of science against misappropriation. But these excesses shouldn't deter us from an overdue downward revision of the prevailing intellectual self-esteem. Too much time is wasted because of the assumption that methods already in existence will solve problems for which they were not designed; too many hypotheses and systems of thought in philosophy and elsewhere are based on the bizarre view that we, at this point in history, are in possession of the basic forms of understanding needed to comprehend absolutely anything.
>
> (Nagel 1986: 9–10)

In response to this criticism, all I can say is that as it is framed I agree with it entirely! Nagel is quite right to be appalled at the ever-present willingness of human beings to think that they uniquely, at this point in space and time, have grasped absolute truth, whereas none of the silly deluded human beings previously or elsewhere have ever done so. Anyone with the slightest sensitivity towards the historical process – and who is to be sensitive about the historical process, if not an evolutionist? – will realize that claims of omniscience and infallibility rarely have a half-life long enough to hold true even until they get into print. Therefore let me say absolutely and unambiguously that if any word of what I have said in the last sections holds true when considered in the light of knowledge a hundred years hence, I for one will be extremely surprised. I fully expect just about everything which I have had to say will be at best revised, and at worst rejected.

However, having now been so modest, let me next start to take it all back! It is indeed true that knowledge, including scientific knowledge, is tentative and ever liable to revision if not outright rejection. Indeed, I would go so far as to say that this is virtually a mark of the scientific. Nevertheless, it is quite wrong to conclude that this is all that there is to be said on the matter. Science does, in a very real sense, progress: we build on what has gone before, incorporating, adjusting, revising, rejecting, but in some sense retaining a spark of what led our predecessors to claim as they do.

Take, for example, the Copernican Revolution. Copernicus and his fellow heliocentric theorists threw out much that had been held since the days of Aristotle and (somewhat later) Ptolemy. Yet Copernicus did not start absolutely again. He took many of the results and methods of the ancient astronomers and incorporated them within his system. He took seriously, for instance, the notions that there are heavenly bodies going around in circles, that some of these heavenly bodies are significantly different from others (I refer to the distinction between the planets and stars), and that certain principles of motion and causality and so on apply to the workings of the universe. Then, having accepted these notions from the old system, Copernicus built his own (Kuhn 1957).

In turn, Copernicus' ideas proved faulty in many respects. His empirical data were badly in need of revision. He saddled himself unduly with beliefs about circularity of motion. He thought that the universe is finite in size; and so on. All of these ideas and more were in turn chipped away at and revised by those who came after. But surely no one would want to say simply that Copernicus was false? No one would want to put Copernicus' work on a par with someone who, for instance, said that the planets go in squares, or that the moon is a cube. Rather, what we have is a progressive improving of the data, and this reflects itself into our knowledge getting stronger and more secure.

Similar things can be said about every other branch of science. Does anyone, for instance, genuinely believe that the discovery by James Watson and Francis Crick that the DNA molecule occurs in a double helix and that it is made up of just a few repeatable basic building-blocks, was not a significant improvement on our previous knowledge of heredity? Or does anyone believe that the work that has been done in molecular genetics since the Watson–Crick discoveries of 1953 has not produced significant advances? I am not now claiming that we have the complete truth about heredity, any more than we have complete truth about astronomy, but we have made advances.

Whether these are advances that will ever come to an end, whether we can ever claim to know with reasonable confidence all that there is to be known, is, of course, another matter. I myself rather doubt it. But the point is that it would be foolish to pretend that the scientific method is totally on a par with any other method, or that the products of science are of no greater or lesser worth than other human products, be these religion, superstition, folk technology, or whatever. It is ludicrous to be seduced by some misguided yearnings for equality into suggesting that the primitive magic and technology of preliterate people is necessarily of equal worth to that of the knowledge of Western civilized human beings. This is not to say that preliterate people might not know things that we do not know. The point is that being under-impressed by the achievements of science is no less a distortion or sin than being over-impressed by such achievements. (A fact that Nagel himself seems to acknowledge, but then promptly ignores.)

The conclusion to be drawn, therefore, is not that the evolutionary epistemology that we have today – the evolutionary epistemology that I have just endorsed – is absolutely perfect. It is obviously very incomplete and much work must be done, even before it will be a fully functioning paradigm, or whatever it is that you aspire to. I very much expect, for example, that as our knowledge of the brain improves, and our awareness of how the brain effects our thinking likewise advances, we shall learn much that is presently unknown about the nature of the innate dispositions that guide our thinking generally and our science in particular (Churchland 1984).

At the moment, the most I can suggest in an area like mathematics is that maybe the innate dispositions encode for something like Peano's axioms. Once we have these, then we know at least we can get elementary arithmetic. But I should not be at all perturbed if it were to transpire that the way we really think is not in terms of these axioms *per se*, but perhaps in terms of some other constraints that in some convoluted way give rise to the axioms themselves. A suggestion like this seems to me much more in tune with what we know of the evolutionary process. Natural selection never produces the perfect, obvious answer. Rather, unlike a good designing God of natural theology, natural selection works in a gerry-building fashion, making do with what it has at hand. It would not at all surprise me to learn that the way the human brain functions is through all sorts of compromises brought about by the contingencies of past evolutionary events, and that the roots behind our most logical thinking start with very unlikely foundations.

Incomplete though all of our present knowledge may be, this is a far cry from saying that it is totally worthless. The knowledge we have at the moment is incomplete. Yet, as best we know, it is on the right track. This is not everything, but it is a lot more than nothing. And taking this sort of attitude is the complete answer to Nagel's criticism. We do not have absolute knowledge today; yet there is no reason to give way in a welter of self-denial and abrogation. We have made progress in science and, as a philosopher, one is entitled to ride the crest of that particular wave. Not to do so is not a mark of philosophical humility, but of scientific stupidity.

THE PROBLEM OF RATIONALITY

Of course, what I have said in response to Nagel does rather presuppose that I have got today's science right. I have said already that I doubt my position is particularly controversial among orthodox biologists, especially Darwinians. But can one (should one) dismiss the critics so readily? I will not here get into a general discussion of the virtues of the sociobiological approach in itself. I have defended them at length before (Ruse 1979c). However, it does seem to me that there is one aspect of the critique which should be raised and mentioned. This is the suggestion that there must be something insecure about the kind of position I am advocating, because we now know, thanks in particular to the work of psychologists, that the way in which humans reason and think in fact has little to do with the ideal structures and inferences explicated in the textbook of philosophers of science (Stich 1985).

It is argued that rarely, if ever, do normal human beings rely on such methods of inference as *modus ponens* and that indeed even scientists (some would say especially scientists) are in real life a lot less prone to using logical inferences than they and others pretend they are. It is true perhaps that when it comes to writing up a scientific paper, logic and methodology figure largely and carefully, but the real work, as everyone knows (or if not everyone, as the sociologists and psychologists of science know), is done by people thinking in altogether different ways. For this reason, therefore, it is naive in the extreme to think that the methodology of the philosophers could ever truly be embedded in the epigenetic rules of the evolutionary biologist. Far better to suggest that we have innate dispositions to affirm the consequent, for this is what we seem to do most of the time (Wason and Johnson-Laird 1972).

I suspect that, heavy handed though this criticism usually is, there is much truth in it. I, for one, would certainly not pretend that humans generally and scientists in particular think always in the idealized way that we philosophers suppose they do. Indeed if they did, then as a philosopher-teacher I would be out of a job because much of my time is spent teaching people about inferences that they seem not to have grasped innately! If nothing else, therefore, an empirical study of the epigenetic rules in everyday (or scientific) reasoning is required. And a position like mine has to take this kind of point into account. However, having said this much, surely it is far too extreme to suggest that logic, methodology, mathematics and all the rest of the prescriptions of the philosopher's textbook are totally irrelevant either to everyday life or to the way of the scientist? Better surely to suppose that much of the time we do not think particularly carefully or logically, simply because it is not really necessary to do so, but when pressed we can do so and for very good reasons, namely, that those who could not tended not to survive and reproduce?

At least, let me put matters this way without going into any great argument. If it is indeed the case that by and large humans do not think in the way that the methodologists of science suggest they do, on what authority can the psychologists and sociologists presume to tell us how people really do think? If we think fallaciously, then is not the very claim of these critics (or cynics) themselves likewise infected by fallacy? One suspects that such critics would argue that it is possible to pull back in some way and employ a proper methodology. But if in fact one allows this much, then it seems to me that it is possible for the evolutionary epistemologist to make his or her case. To argue that the way that we really think is a lot more rough and ready than the way that the philosophers suppose seems to me to be evidence for the evolutionists rather than an argument against the impossibility of ever giving our reasoning an empirical base. (In this context, I note with some interest how psychologists can often get us to commit fallacies when we are presented with problems in unfamiliar artificial situations, whereas we have no difficulty with problems of the same formal structure when they occur in everyday situations. Somehow, I feel that this is evidence for the evolutionist rather than against him or her.)

CAN BIOLOGY EXPLAIN PHYSICS?

Nagel's second argument against evolutionary epistemology makes reference to the highly sophisticated nature of modern science. Essentially, he wonders how anything that was forged in the jungle (or more precisely in the descent from the jungle) could be sufficiently sensitive to produce such magnificent edifices as quantum mechanics.

> The question is whether not only the physical but the mental capacity needed to make a stone axe automatically brings with it the capacity to take each of the steps that have led from there to the construction of the hydrogen bomb, or whether an enormous excess mental capacity, not explainable by natural selection, was responsible for the generation and spread of the sequence of intellectual instruments that has emerged over the last thirty thousand years. This question is unforgettably posed by the stunning transformation of bone into spaceship in Stanley Kubrick's *2001*.

I see absolutely no reason to believe that the truth lies with the first alternative. The only reason so many people do believe it is that advanced intellectual capacities clearly exist, and this is the only available candidate for a Darwinian explanation of their existence. So it all rests on the assumption that every noteworthy characteristic of human beings, or of any other organism, must have a Darwinian explanation. But what is the reason to believe that? Even if natural selection explains all adaptive evolution, there may be developments in the history of species that are not specifically adaptive and can't be explained in terms of natural selection. Why not take the development of the human intellect as a probable counterexample to the law that natural selection explains everything, instead of forcing it under the law with improbable speculations unsupported by evidence? We have here one of those powerful reductionist dogmas which seem to be part of the intellectual atmosphere we breathe.

(Nagel 1986: 80–1)

This argument is not quite as original as Nagel seems to think that it is. To the best of my knowledge it was first made in the 1860s by natural selection's co-discoverer Alfred Russel Wallace (1870), who thought that it showed the impossibility of natural selection ever accounting adequately for the evolution of the human mind. Obviously that it is an ancient objection does not mean that it should not be answered, and in fact I think that it does indeed pose a serious challenge to the evolutionary epistemologist. However, having said this, I would argue that it is a challenge and not a refutation. No one argues – certainly not I – that human beings evolved special techniques for doing quantum mechanics, or other esoteric aspects of modern science. But it is not necessary for the evolutionist to mount such an argument. If you look at the way in which a non-evolutionary philosopher would tackle the production of modern science, what he or she would attempt to do is to break down the work into simpler steps and inferences, and ultimately what one would argue is that sophisticated science, no less than simple science, relies ultimately on the same processes of inference. The same reductive moves are open to the evolutionist.

The theorist in quantum mechanics does not cease to use mathematics, or logic, or falsifiability, or consiliences. Anything but. It is just that he or she has taken the process that much further (Nagel 1961). And if one argues this, then why can one not continue to argue that the ultimate rules of methodology were themselves given by the evolutionary process? The claim is not being made that a knowledge of quantum mechanics in some sense gives an advantage in life's struggles. The claim being is that the elementary principles and methods of inference gave such advantage. If one allows that these principles, even for the sophisticated scientist, ultimately reduce to the simple ones of everyone else, then the evolutionary epistemological case is secure.

I would add two points to this. On the one hand, I would note with some interest that modern science, for instance quantum mechanics and relativity theory, leads one right beyond the realm of the imaginable. Moreover, when one turns to mathematics, one gets into areas and results that to the nineteenth-century thinker would be totally paradoxical. I think here particularly of Gödel's incompleteness theorem. But surely mind-stretching areas of modern science and unimaginable theses are precisely what the evolutionary epistemologist expects. Only the person who is still stuck with the good God of Archdeacon Paley expects the world to work perfectly and comprehensively to the ordinary human mind. The evolutionary epistemologist rather believes that our way of thinking was that which suited us as we evolved from lower organisms. The fact that now, when we peer into the unknown, we find it inconceivable and paradoxical is what you would expect. Why should there be any guarantees that arithmetic is complete? The surprise, if anything, is that arithmetic takes you as far as it does.

On the other hand, however, having said this much, I do not think that the evolutionary epistemologist can just leave matters at this point. I think it is incumbent upon such an epistemologist to put in time and effort showing exactly how it is that the methodology of science can lead to modern physics and the sorts of challenges that it poses. I think, for instance, that it is necessary to look at the reasons why something like Heisenberg's uncertainty principle is invoked – where, apparently, what one is doing is rejecting the law of excluded middle, in some sense. Does this point to the fact that the law of excluded middle is not really rooted in our biological dispositions? Or is there some other less drastic alternative?

Parenthetically, I am inclined to think that something like the law of excluded middle is indeed rooted in our biological propensities, but that we recognize some sort of ordering of these propensities with perhaps the law of non-contradiction as more fundamental (Ruse 1986). When (as when dealing with something like electrons) we seem to be in danger of violating the law of non-contradiction by supposing electrons to have contradictory properties, simultaneously, in order to avoid such tensions, we pull back. We invoke something like Heisenberg's uncertainty principle, which bars the asking of awkward questions (Hanson 1958). I should say, in this respect, my thinking is very much in line with the mathematical intuitionist (Körner 1960). (A point I note, to be remembered later, is that mathematical intuitionism is a direct outgrowth of Immanuel Kant's thinking about mathematics.)

As you will see from the last passage I quoted, Nagel also supposes that perhaps our reasoning abilities are in some sense epiphenomena upon our other adaptive abilities. This of course may be so. The Darwinian evolutionist accepts that there are certainly non-adaptive features and that these have a variety of causes (Simpson 1953; Ruse 1973a). For instance, they may be mere vestiges of past adaptive features, or they may be byproducts of the physical production of other features that are indeed adaptive, and so forth. However, having already countered Nagel's argument that our biologically evolved abilities simply could not lead to modern science, the need for his epiphenomenal supposition becomes much less pressing. I should say, nevertheless, that even if it were not at all obvious how our innate dispositions might lead to modern science, I would still be uncomfortable about supposing that so fundamental an aspect of human nature as our reasoning abilities was entirely a non-adaptive byproduct of the evolutionary process. This is simply not the way that evolution works. When you have major features which seem to have adaptive virtues – and if reasoning does not have such virtues, I do not know what would – then you expect to find natural selection has been at work (Dawkins 1986).

Furthermore, contrary to Nagel's supposition, commitment to adaptation at this point is not mere 'reductionist dogma'. Rather, it is a proper inference from one of the most powerful of scientific theories (Ayala 1985). We know that humans were part of the evolutionary process. We know also that, thanks to natural selection, evolution does not work by dropping things and starting anew. Rather, it works with what you have – and what you have is usually something that began life for adaptive reasons. On *a priori* grounds, therefore, it is simply sensible science to suppose that our reasoning abilities are, in some very real sense, rooted in our biology. (But as you have seen, I do not rest my case for evolutionary epistemology simply on general Darwinian principles. Even in this brief discussion, I have made reference to some pertinent empirical evidence. My point here is merely to counter the sneer of 'reductionism'.)

In leaving Nagel, I might note that Wallace countered Darwin's selectionism with hypothesis of his own, one based on his spiritualist beliefs that the Great Mind in the sky was positively interfering in the evolutionary process and bringing about the production of humans. If you reject evolutionary epistemology, it is surely incumbent upon you to suppose some alternative of your own. Would Nagel have us adopt the position of Wallace? Strange as it might seem, he almost hints that this could be so. 'What, I will be asked, is my alternative? Creationism? The answer is that I don't have one and I don't need one in order to reject all existing proposals as improbable'(81). I confess that I find this response disingenuous. If Nagel had an empirical argument against the evolutionist's case, then perhaps he could conclude that the position is 'improbable'; but at best all he does is to point out that Darwinism does not logically imply that all characteristics, including human reasoning abilities, are adaptive. But we knew this fact already.

SCIENCE AS NETWORKING

I turn now to a philosopher with a very different intent. David Hull, today's leading philosopher of biology, has in recent years been strongly championing an evolutionary approach to our understanding of scientific knowledge. Nevertheless, I suspect that he will find my account of evolutionary epistemology thoroughly unsatisfying. He may or may not disagree outright with what I have to say. What he will claim is that I have altogether missed the main thrust of the proper evolutionary understanding of human knowledge (Hull 1988).

As several commentators have noted, most recently and in most detail Michael Bradie (1986), there are two ways in which you can attempt to bring our knowledge of evolution to bear on our understanding of knowledge. The first way, the way that I have endorsed, starts with the human mind as a product of evolution through natural selection, and then works from there to try to understand the nature and development of science. The second way, which incidentally has roots at least as far back as the first way, sees the whole of existence as in some sense a developing phenomenon, with organic evolution as but one manifestation. There are many other dimensions to existence than the organic, and in these other dimensions, inorganic and cultural to name but two, one likewise sees an ongoing process of development. Moreover, argue supporters of the second approach, there is every reason to think that the causal forces lying behind the evolutionary movements in all dimensions share significant similarities, if indeed they are not part and parcel of the same world force.

There seems to be a range of attitudes people take to the two epistemologies. Some, like myself, endorse one but not the other. I accept the evolutionary epistemology which starts with the naturally selected brain and reject the conceptual approach to evolutionary epistemology. Stephen Toulmin (1967, 1972), on the other hand, seems to take the diametrically opposed approach. Others seem happy to accept both kinds. One would include here Karl Popper (1972) and Donald Campbell (1977). Hull is inclined to take a middle position, but not one which is particularly ecumenical. He is not very sympathetic to the biologically based approach, which I embrace. However, he does want to go beyond pure concepts, bringing in real people, specifically scientists. He writes that the task of evolutionary epistemology is 'to present a general analysis of evolution through selection processes which applies equally to biological, social and conceptual evolution' (Hull 1982: 304).

How is this to be done? Adopting Richard Dawkins' (1976) view of cultural elements – what Dawkins calls 'memes' – as things akin to the biological units of heredity, the genes, Hull argues that these are held by, and passed around between, scientists. Moreover, like biological elements the memes are subject to selective forces and are therefore part of an overall evolutionary picture. Hull supposes no particular biological input by the scientists: for instance, there are no claims that scientists are innately disposed to accept certain ideas rather than others, or constrained in similar fashions as one might expect were the epigenetic rules at work. Hence, although scientists play a crucial role in Hull's picture, inasmuch as they are the carriers of memes, his picture is essentially one of cultural evolution. There is no special supposition that biological evolution is evolved.

Let me say at once that Hull develops his ideas with great subtlety. I find particularly stimulating the way in which he explicates the functioning of a scientific community. He argues, and I am sure he is right in this, that one should not think of a particular community or movement like, say, Darwinism in the 1860s, as being composed of a set of men and women with identical or near-identical ideas. In fact, this was simply not true in the case of Darwinism. Nor, for that matter, is it true of other movements, including those around us today (Ruse 1979a).

Hull shows that we do much better to think of scientific movements as networks of people bound together by shared goals, working with each other because there are scientific and cultural advantages to so doing. Unless one aligns oneself with a particular movement, one will be an isolated freak that no one will take any notice of. What one must do is work with other scientists, send them preprints and offprints, refer to their work, quote them, help their students, and in return one can expect reciprocation. If one does not get it, very quickly one ceases to help and the offender becomes an outcast. Hull argues with some vigour that what really counts in science is not so much the disinterested truth, but the success of your ideas, and he notes that if a scientist fails entirely to convince anyone of his or her theories, then he or she is simply judged a failure, by scientific terms.

What then leads to change and to success? Simply passing on one's ideas and having them picked up and adopted by others. The process is exactly analogous to the organic world. What succeeds in that realm? Once again, it is simply a question of having one's information – in this case one's genes – picked up, that is to say, inherited by other organisms, and passed on. But how is this to be done? What succeeds in the organic world is having some feature which is better than one's competitors. Does this mean it is better to be white, rather than black? No, not necessarily. In certain circumstances being white rather than black is clearly of adaptive advantage: if one is in the Arctic and the predators can pick out black objects, one will be better adapted if one is white. On the other hand, if one is living in an area of rather dark sand, then one will presumably be better off if one is dark brown or black, rather than white. Success depends on the particular contingencies of the case. Likewise, argues Hull, success in science is and is no more than the particular contingencies of the case. The scientist who is successful in pushing his or her ideas wins. The scientist who is unsuccessful fails. This is not so much cynical as realistic.

There is much that one could say in response to this view of the development of scientific knowledge, so let me begin by praising it. In many respects, I find the general approach that Hull takes to be insightful and the specific approach that Hull himself takes to be particularly insightful. As I have noted elsewhere, taking such an evolutionary approach to the development of science certainly draws attention to much that conventional philosophies miss or purposefully avoid. Anyone who has spent any time working on the history of science soon learns that science is a much more fluid or dynamic phenomenon than elementary textbooks lead one to suppose. There really is no such thing as 'Darwinism', or 'Punctuated Equilibria Theory'. Rather, there are groups of people who hold some of the ideas some of the time in some form. These ideas are held in different ways by different people in different forms, by the same person at different times, and so on. Freezing the picture to get a snapshot effect may be necessary at times, but it is important always that this is a distortion and sometimes a serious distortion. An evolutionist like Hull reminds us of this. (I am keenly aware of this fact myself from having written a paper on the new palaeontological theory of punctuated equilibria, and having found extreme difficulty in pinning down the exact official line and who, if anyone, would believe in it: Ruse 1989.)

Particularly insightful in this context is Hull's own treatment of the scientific community. He does well to drive home how important is the development of interpersonal relationships within the community, and how much even the greatest – especially the greatest – scientist depends on networking in various ways. Charles Darwin himself was a paradigmatic example of this. People often compare Darwin with Wallace and complain that Wallace has been unfairly treated by history in being regarded as a junior partner. However, although it is indeed true that Wallace did hit upon the same ideas as Darwin, I have always felt that it is Darwin who rightfully receives the greater treatment. Not only was he earlier than Wallace in discovering the theory and not only did he develop it at much greater length than Wallace did, at least by 1859, but also Darwin went out of his way deliberately to cultivate a group of supporters – including such influential thinkers as the botanist

Joseph Hooker and the already-mentioned zoologist Thomas Henry Huxley (not to mention people who, although not entirely committed, were favourably disposed, like the geologist Charles Lyell). Anyone who thinks that this is a mere ripple on the surface of science simply has not studied the subject properly. They do not understand the success of Darwinism. It is as important to take into account Darwin's friendship with Huxley as to acknowledge his treatment of the evidence of biogeography (Ruse 1979a). The way Hull's philosophy draws our attention to this and like facts is altogether admirable.

THE PROGRESS OF SCIENCE AND THE NON-PROGRESS OF EVOLUTION

Nevertheless, as many have noted before, such an approach as Hull's does face serious difficulties, and to be candid I see nothing in Hull's work which gets around them. Most crucially, in my opinion, Hull's treatment of science fails to account for the already-noted sense of progress that we have – that I certainly have – about science. Science is not only not a static phenomenon but seems to be a teleological phenomenon in the sense that it is going somewhere, whether the somewhere be the truth or not, and whether or not its goal will ever be achieved. It makes good sense to say that Mendel was ahead of his predecessors, just as Watson and Crick were ahead of their predecessors. Yet, as Darwinian evolutionists are perpetually telling us, our biological evolution is not progressive (Williams 1966). Appearances to the contrary, it is a rather slow process, going nowhere. Any notions of progress are illicit imports from pre-Darwinian Christian Providentialism. Progress is impossible in the world of Darwinism, simply because everything is relativized in the sense that success is the only thing that counts.

At this point, there are a couple of counters. On the one hand, one might argue that although there is no inevitable progress in biology, there is surely some kind of progress. It is just plain wrong to deny that humans are in some sense more advanced than microbes (Wilson 1975). On the other hand, one might argue that, appearances to the contrary, science is not really progressive (Kuhn 1962). Although it seems to be, if we look at it in some detail, we see that it is really as relativized as the organic evolutionary process. People have taken both of these approaches. Some, like Julian

Huxley (1942) and C. H. Waddington (1960), have argued for progress in biology. Following on them, we find that some evolutionary epistemologists argue that one gets a like sense of progress in science – perhaps not a unidirectional monad-to-man type progress of the old kind, but progress nevertheless. Others, like Thomas Kuhn, have argued that appearances to the contrary there is a Darwin-type progress in science, and in fact Kuhn (1962) himself has drawn the analogy in this respect with the biological world. All I can say (and I realize that I am stating rather than arguing) is that I find neither response particularly convincing. More importantly, I find no effective response to the work of Hull himself.

Certainly we can say this much: those biologists who have argued for progress in biology have generally failed to put up convincing arguments. This applies particularly to the work of someone like Julian Huxley, whose definition of progress is so blatantly self-serving as to be almost laughable. Likewise, although certainly not laughable, the philosophy of those who deny that there is progress in science has proven to be less than convincing. I hardly need detail here all the difficulties that have been revealed about Kuhn's epistemology (Lakatos and Musgrave 1970). Apart from anything else, in the present context given that Kuhn argues that there are such sharp breaks between the theories or paradigms of science, it would be ironic to the point of hypocrisy were an evolutionary epistemologist to appeal to Kuhn for support. (I rush to add that this is not something Hull does.)

In any case, these general considerations apart, there is a clear and crucial point of disanalogy between the Hull-type approach to the conceptual change of science, and the evolution of organisms in the biological world. This is that the new elements of science seem in some sense to be directed or teleological, whereas the whole point about the new elements of the organic world is that they are not so directed or teleological (Cohen 1973; Thagard 1980). New variations in the biological world appear without rhyme or reason (not that they are uncaused), and certainly without any connection to their possible utility. The whole point about science is that this is not so, notwithstanding the supposed lucky guesses of people like Alexander Fleming when he hit upon penicillin.

When, for instance, Niles Eldredge and Stephen Jay Gould (1972) produced their theory of punctuated equilibria, they were not stabbing blindly in the dark but trying to answer a specific problem as they saw it, namely, the fact that the fossil record does not exhibit gradualism but periods of non-change ('stasis') broken by points of rapid change. Punctuated equilibria theory may be many things, and I suspect that some of these are not as complimentary as its proposers would wish, but it was certainly not a random variant. There was therefore not quite the same need for natural selection to work upon it – though I would not deny that some process akin to selection might take place once it appears (Ruse 1989).

However, when a new variant appears in the organic world, since it appears without respect to the needs of its possessors, natural selection must do all the designing (Ruse 1982). It is, of course, for this reason that organic evolution is not teleological, or progressive, or goal directed in the way that one thinks that science is. When a scientist produces a new variant, it is not merely that he or she is trying to produce something which is adequate to the problem, but rather that the aim is in some sense towards the 'truth' (whatever that word might mean ultimately). Because scientific variants are directed phenomena, science is more than just a relativistic pragmatic phenomenon, in a way that the products of organic evolution have to be. For this reason, there is no compulsion to adopt what strikes me as clearly overstated to the point of falsity, namely, the extreme sociological relativism of Hull's position. A scientist who does not attract the attention of his or her fellows will certainly not win the Nobel Prize. He or she might well be right, nevertheless.

Hull is obviously not unaware of the sort of points that I have just been making. Recently he has written as follows.

> Another apparent difference between biological evolution and conceptual change is that biological evolution is not clearly progressive while, in certain areas, conceptual change gives every appearance of being progressive. At a glance, biological evolution appears to be as clearly progressive as conceptual evolution in the most advanced areas of science, but appearances are deceptive. Thus far biologists have found it surprisingly difficult both to document any sort of biological progress in the fossil record and to explain what it is about the evolutionary process that might lead phylogenetic change to be progressive . . .

180

Conceptual development in certain areas of human endeavor, especially in certain areas of science, gives even a stronger appearance of being progressive. Although science is not progressive in the straightforward way that earlier enthusiasts have claimed, sometimes later theories are better than earlier theories even on the criteria used by advocates of the earlier theories. Science at least appears to be more clearly progressive than biological evolution. Of greater importance, we have good reason to expect certain sorts of conceptual change to be progressive.

Intentionality is close to necessary but far from sufficient in making conceptual change in science progressive. It is not absolutely necessary because sometimes scientists have made what turn out to be great advances quite accidentally. Chance certainly favors a prepared mind, but a scientific advance is no less of an advance because the problem which a scientist happens to solve was not the one he or she had intended to solve. . . . Conceptual evolution, especially in science, is both locally and globally progressive, not simply because scientists are conscious agents, not simply because they are striving to reach both local and global goals, but because these goals exist. If scientists did not strive to formulate laws of nature, they would discover them only by happy accident, but if these external, immutable regularities did not exist, any belief a scientist might have that he or she had discovered one would be illusory.

(Hull 1988: 40–2)

I have trouble with this passage, not because I cannot understand it, but because I think I do understand it and it seems to say exactly what I myself have just been saying! As I read Hull, he is admitting explicitly what I have been arguing, namely, that science does seem to be progressive in a way that the organic world is not progressive. Moreover, this progression is, in part at least, due to the intentions of scientists; such intentions are bound up with the fact that, in some sense, science has a goal of finding out the truth, whether or not this can ever be truly achieved or whether the truth is ever quite what we think it is. Allowing all of this is simply to admit and drive home the very disanalogy I have just been proposing.

Of course, you can admit the disanalogy and just go on as

though nothing has happened, and this I think is what Hull does, not to mention other evolutionary epistemologists of his ilk. His attitude seems to be that although biological evolution ɪⁿ ⁱ conceptual evolution are very similar, one certainly expects some differences. (After all, you have to admit that there are some, if only the speed at which conceptual evolution occurs.) One is still left with many points of great similarity and many insightful relationships. All I can say is that, although I recognize the virtues of the analogy, the dissimilarities are so great as to be make me very unwilling to embrace this form of evolutionary epistemology as a viable research programme.

I appreciate that analogies are a little bit like vegetables – some people like spinach where others cannot stand it, and who is to say one is right and the other wrong? Likewise, some people like the Hull-type approach to evolutionary epistemology. Others, like myself, do not like it. Neither preference is *a priori* right, or *a priori* wrong. Nevertheless, one can try to move discussion beyond blind preference. In particular, as someone like myself can be challenged to find evidence of the epigenetic rules, so I in turn can challenge the enthusiast for Hull's approach to go ahead with his or her work and to produce insightful conclusions. By this I mean to offer analyses of actual episodes in the history of science that are made more meaningful by an evolutionary analysis. Let me hold on this point for the moment. I will return again briefly to it in my conclusion.

THE THREAT OF CONVENTIONALISM

I turn back now to a critic – a gentle critic, but perhaps all the more formidable for that. Barry Stroud (1981) worries about the status of the claims that someone like myself finds embedded in the evolutionary process, as mediated through the epigenetic rules. How would an evolutionary epistemologist like myself regard the claims that these rules yield? What is the truth-status of beliefs about logic and mathematics and scientific methodology?

Fairly obviously, the answer is that the evolutionary epistemologist (from now on, since there will be no ambiguity posed by 'evolutionary epistemologist', I mean the kind that I am rather than the kind that Hull is) wants to think that such principles or rules are in some sense *necessary*. We may not draw the analytic/synthetic distinction in the conventional way – in fact, I am not sure that we could draw the analytic/synthetic distinction in the conventional way – but we do want to think in terms of some beliefs as 'having to be' or binding in some way. This is obviously a notion of necessity of some kind or another. The evolutionary epistemologist believes that the scientist obeys the law of non-contradiction and Peano's axioms and the urge to consilience, not out of some whim or arbitrary choice, but because this is the way that one *must* think and behave if one is to do good science.

What the evolutionary epistemologist argues is that this sense of mustness, or necessity, lies not in some disinterested objective set of values but rather in our evolutionary past. Those of us who did not think in this way simply did not survive and reproduce. I think, incidentally, that this points to the fact that the evolutionary epistemologist must believe in some form of projection going on here. Although there may not be an objective necessity in the world in quite the sense that the Leibnizian thinks, it is part of our evolved nature that we are inclined to think that there is such a necessity in the world. Because we are thus deluded by our biology, we act in ways that are advantageous to us. If we did not project in this fashion, then we would be inclined often to ignore the dictates of reason – to our own misfortune. (See Mackie 1979 for an analogous point about ethics.)

Lumping evolutionary epistemology with conventionalism (which is not entirely unfair, since although the evolutionary epistemologist does not think that necessities were made by human decision, he or she does believe that necessities lie in human nature rather than 'outside' somewhere), Stroud makes the following objection:

> Consider something that we believe to be necessarily true, for example 'If all men are mortal and Socrates is a man then Socrates is mortal.' Does conventionalism, or indeed any view according to which necessary truth is in some sense our own 'creation,' imply that the truth of that statement is due solely to our present ways of thinking or speaking in the sense that if we had thought or spoken in certain other ways, or had adopted relevantly different 'conventions,' then it would not have been true that if all men are mortal and Socrates is a man then Socrates is mortal? If that is an implication of conventionalism, then to accept conventionalism would be to concede that under certain (vaguely specified

but nevertheless possible) circumstances it would not have been true that if all men are mortal and Socrates is a man then Socrates is mortal. But we take that familiar conditional to be necessarily true, and so we cannot allow that there are such circumstances – that there are in that sense alternatives to its truth. Acknowledging possible alternatives to the truth of p is incompatible with regarding it as necessarily true that p. Therefore we cannot accept what appears to be an implication of conventionalism while continuing to believe that it is necessarily true that if all men are mortal and Socrates is a man then Socrates is mortal.

(Stroud 1981, 242–3)

There are two responses that one can make at this point, and both of them have been adopted by evolutionary epistemologists. However, as will become apparent, I think only one is truly adequate. One response, perhaps the most obvious response, is that of the Kantian. Here one argues that although it can be necessary, truth never lies in objective reality. Nevertheless, necessary truth is more than mere convention. The Kantian argues that necessity, as in the famous $5 + 7 = 12$, lies in the conditions for thinking rationally at all. For this reason, the Kantian denies that there are alternatives to the truth of necessary statements. It simply does not make sense to say that $5 + 7$ does not equal 12. Hence the kind of objection that Stroud brings is simply not relevant to the evolutionary epistemological programme. (The Kantian, of course, would distinguish between the truths of logic and the truths of mathematics and of scientific methodology, but for the purposes of this discussion I shall ignore this distinction.)

Now I am not sure that Stroud would be particularly worried at this point because, with some justification, he could point out that Kantianism is really not conventionalism, and thus was not the target of his attack. This then raises the question of whether or not the evolutionary epistemologist can thus dissociate himself or herself from conventionalism. Can the evolutionary epistemologist rightfully put himself or herself in the Kantian camp and thus be immune to such criticisms? It has to be admitted that many evolutionary epistemologists think that they can. Most notable among them is the famous Austrian ethologist, Konrad Lorenz (1941) and his many followers, including Rupert Reidl (1984). They argue (with me) that thinking is constrained in various

184

innately preprogrammed ways – the sort of picture that I have sketched using the epigenetic rules. They argue that these ways are in fact to be identified with Kantian type categories, where (like Kant) they think that the categories are in some sense *a priori* given. However, like me but unlike Kant, Lorenz, Reidl and others locate the origin of the categories in our evolutionary past. But having done this, they still feel that then they can argue that such necessities as are yielded by evolution have the strength of Kantian necessities, inasmuch as their denial is simply not conceivable.

I bow to no one in my respect for Lorenz. He was thinking in evolutionary terms and applying them to epistemology long before we philosophers had grasped how fruitful an approach this is. Nevertheless, in thinking of himself as a neo-Kantian, I believe Lorenz is just plain wrong. I do not, of course, deny that there are significant similarities between the philosophy of Kant and the philosophy of the evolutionary epistemologist. They do both share the conviction that our thinking is in some sense constrained by our minds, rather than simply and directly given in experience. For this reason, I was happy to note the way in which my position meshes with the thinking of mathematical intuitionists. But Kant himself wants to do far more than the evolutionary epistemologist can possibly allow. And one place where the two philosophies come apart is over this very question of necessity.

Think back for a moment about what we have already learned of the evolutionary process. One thing is absolutely fundamental: there is no progress. It is simply not the case that evolution led unidirectionally – or indirectly with any inevitability – towards the human species. We are what we are because of the contingencies of the process and we might not have evolved at all, or we might have evolved in a very different way. As a Darwinian, it is altogether too much to claim that the only rational animals which could possibly have evolved are those that think and behave like us humans. Given our position on this earth, it may well be the case that rationality on this same earth is constrained by our existence and thus would have to simulate our rationality; but, were evolution to occur somewhere else in the universe, I see no reason for rationality of the human kind (Ruse 1994).

EXTRATERRESTRIAL THOUGHT PATTERNS

Now, as Stroud points out, quoting C. I. Lewis with some approval, if one is to make the kind of case that I am making it is incumbent upon me to suggest precisely how some other rational but non-humanlike thinking being might come into existence. Of course this is virtually impossible, given that I am a human-type being, thinking in a human-type way, but let me make at least one suggestion. We think that fire burns because of the causal connection between the hot flame and the sensitive human skin and various nerve ends, and so on. There is a connection here between, I suppose ultimately, the energy of the molecules within the flame and the physical constitution of human flesh. The burning and the consequent pain happen because of the excited molecules. Thus we learn that there are very good reasons not to put one's hand into a hot fire.

Suppose somewhere else in the universe there were other beings and that these beings had physiologies somewhat comparable to ours. I take it that there would be strong selective pressure against their putting their hands in the flame. (It is no circularity in my supposing this. I am talking about how *I* perceive the situation. I do not in any sense imply that *they* would be aware that there is strong selective pressure against putting one's hand in the flame.) Of course, we ourselves recognize that sometimes you can put your hand in the flame without getting burned. In such cases, we do not deny the causal connection, but invoke other deflecting circumstances. However, rather than associating fire with burning, in a human causal way, such extraterrestrials might make the exceptions the norm. They think that there is no such necessary connection, but that when one does put one's hand near flame, the gods get angry and punish us. In their minds, there is no binding connection between fire, pain and burning. Nevertheless, these beings from outer space go through the same sorts of motions as we. In such a case as this, it seems to me that such beings think in an entirely non-human sort of way. Certainly, it is not in any sense apparent that a necessary condition of their thinking is that they think in a causal fashion. I suppose at this point one could deny that such beings are rational, and thus save the Kantian case. But, this is surely an illicit *ad hoc* move. If such beings can conduct their lives in much the way that we do, there is no reason whatsoever to deny them the attribute of rationality.

186

I argue therefore that the Kantian option is not open to the evolutionary epistemologist. Does this mean, then, that we are thrown back into conventionalism and impaled on Stroud's critique? I think not. I would argue that the evolutionary epistemologist does indeed stand in the tradition of one of the major philosophers of the eighteenth century, but rather than Kant this father figure is the great Scottish philosopher, David Hume (1978). Without wanting to draw unwarranted connections, it seems to me that Hume's 'dispositions', which he supposed to govern our thinking, are very much in line with the rules of thinking that the evolutionary epistemologist believes were yielded by the epigenetic rules (Wolff 1960). And, incidentally, I find confirmation of my supposition about the connections between evolutionary epistemology and the philosophy of Hume in the thought of Stroud himself. As Stroud notes, contrary to the claims of many commentators, Hume certainly did not intend to deny the notion of necessity:

> The genetic explanation is thought to expose the idea of necessity as superfluous, or as a confusion to be jettisoned in the name of clarity. But that was not Hume's own reaction, and to suppose that it was is to misconstrue the relation between his philosophical theory of causality and the behaviour of human beings in their ordinary and scientific pursuits. Despite his philosophical 'discoveries' Hume did not abandon the idea of causality or necessary connection when he thought about the world as a plain man, or indeed as a general theorist of human nature. He sought causal explanations of why human beings think, feel, and act in the ways they do, and in particular he thought he had found a causal explanation of our thought about causality. According to that explanation, it is inevitable that human beings with certain kinds of experience will come to think in causal terms, and Hume himself was no exception to the 'principles of human nature' he discovered. It was inevitable, then, that he too would continue to think in causal terms despite his philosophical 'discoveries.'
>
> (Stroud 1981: 246)

Without accepting the details of Hume's psychology – although there are many places in his writing where Hume gets close to an evolutionary understanding, I would certainly not claim that he was a full-blown evolutionist – I argue that the evolutionary episte-mologist's understanding of necessity and that of the Humean are very close indeed. (This is a claim which is also borne out of history. There are strong causal connections between Darwin's science and the philosophy of Hume, whereas the connections between Darwin's science and Kant's philosophy, although not entirely absent, are much less sturdy.)

But does this not thrust us right back into the worries of Stroud about conventionalism? I think not. The critique only holds if the evolutionary epistemologist is committed to the notion that possi-ble rational beings might think in ways contradictory to those ways that we ourselves think today. If it were the case that today we think that $5 + 7 = 12$ is a necessary claim (which indeed is so), but that other beings elsewhere in the universe might think that $5 + 7$ does not equal 12, or that $5 + 7$ necessarily does not equal 12, then the evolutionary epistemologist's philosophy would be in trouble for the kinds of reasons that Stroud details. But, as we have seen just above, this is not the type of claim that the evolutionary epistemologist wants to make. Rather than claiming that rational beings elsewhere in the universe would deny the necessary truths that we hold dear, he or she claims that perhaps a rational being elsewhere just might not think in the same terms as we.

In other words, it is not that such a being would think that $5 + 7$ does not equal 12, but that such a being would not even think in numerical terms at all – and the same goes for other of our necessary statements like the causal claims, as I tried to demon-strate with my little example about the fire and burning. The extraterrestrial does not explicitly think that fire does not cause burning, but rather the extra-terrestrial never really thinks in terms of the causal connection at all. It is not that fire does not cause burning, whereas tepid water does. That, it seems to me, would be in conflict with our kind of thought. Rather, one does not think in terms of fires, or tepid water, or chili peppers, or anything causing burning. The cause is not part of the constraints of the extraterrestrial's thinking.

This is all a bit hypothetical, by necessity! These sorts of dis-cussions are wont to be. At this point, all I can do is refer you to the general background of neo-Darwinian thinking against which I work. In order to get from A to B, birds fly. It is not necessary, or at least not normally necessary, to fly in order to go from A to

B. One can walk, one can run, if one is a snake one can slither, one can swing through the trees, one can perhaps swim, one can ride on the back of another organism, one can float through the air – or many other things. Flying, using wings, is not a necessity (Gould 1977a). That is the crux of the evolutionary epistemologist's case. It is true that what one cannot do – although this is what Stroud's example is intended to force upon us – is go from *A* to *B* by flying with a birdlike body but with no wings whatsoever (and no cheating like being thrown by a catapult). If one is going to fly and one is a bird, then one needs wings. To deny this is indeed an impossibility, but this is not what the neo-Darwinian is claiming when one says that wings are not necessary to go from *A* to *B*. Likewise, it is not necessary to have our principles of reasoning in order to be rational, but if you do think in our sort of way then you cannot deny the truths that we believe. To deny our truths is to think in our way, but incorrectly.

I argue, therefore, that Stroud's critique of the conventionalist does not affect the evolutionary epistemologist. It may well be – in fact, it seems to me that it certainly is – that the conventionalist of the type Stroud characterizes does indeed fall prey to Stroud's criticism. If one simply said that necessity is a matter of convention or choice, then presumably one could equally as well have chosen another way. However, the evolutionary epistemologist does not want to argue that his or her beliefs are just a matter of choice and that our genes could have taken us in an entirely contradictory way. There is therefore no barrier yet demonstrated against the possibility of evolutionary epistemology, although I agree fully that not all the things which have been claimed under the name of evolutionary epistemology can legitimately be sustained.

THE PROBLEM OF REALISM

I do not want to go on indefinitely, taking on all comers, so I shall begin to draw my discussion towards a close. I shall consider but one further writer on evolutionary epistemology, and this time it is with one whose conclusions I agree entirely. I choose such a person, not that I might go out in a blaze of confirmatory glory, but because I believe he draws attention to a matter on which, to date, I fear there has been altogether too much sloppy and inadequate thought.

The philosopher Andrew J. Clark (1986) adopts a position very

similar to mine with respect to our reasoning ability and its implications for the nature of science. He even goes so far as to suggest,
as do I, that extra-terrestrial thinkers will produce a very different
picture of reality than we.

> One interesting consequence of this analysis is that we must
> accept the possibility of alien epistemologists (perhaps even
> alien evolutionary epistemologists) working successfully with
> a different model of the 'common reality' to our own! Such
> epistemologists may even diagnose man's models as a natural
> and explicable outcome of our biological nature as it appears
> to their science. We, of course, might do the same for them!
> Each scientific model would therefore be sufficiently power-
> ful to embrace the working of the other. The question as to
> which model is the correct one would never be raised.
>
> (Clark 1986: 158)

But this then leads Clark to ask questions about one of the
most contentious issues in philosophy today. What implications
does an evolutionary philosophy have for our thinking about ultimate reality? Is the evolutionary epistemologist committed to a
belief in some sort of real world, that is to say, the world which
exists independent of our knowing it: the world of the tree
which makes a sound in the forest when it falls when no one is
around? Or is the evolutionary epistemologist a non-realist of
some kind, believing that all knowledge is dependent upon our
abilities to sense and think, and that once you take these abilities
away, then there really is no reality beyond? Is the evolutionary
epistemologist (although this is not a term that Clark uses) an
'idealist' of some kind?

It can be stated with vigour that the general opinion of evolutionary epistemologists is that their philosophy demands a
realistic picture of the world (see, for instance, Popper 1972).
After all, there is something intuitively implausible about a person
suggesting that we are the end products of a long and arduous
process of struggle and selection, all occurring before we got on
this earth, and then that person turning right around and suggesting also that none of this history occurred except in the minds of
humans. Perhaps 'arrogant' is a better term than 'implausible'.

Of course all agree that one cannot simply adopt such a robust
conception of reality without some qualification. It is all very well
to talk about reality, but it is clear – it is especially clear to the

evolutionary epistemologist – that this reality is mediated as it were through our own perception and thought. Moreover, if you accept – as again the evolutionary epistemologist must accept – that there is something contingent about this perception and thinking, then even if the real world does exist it is at least one step removed from us. Nevertheless, the realism must be maintained. Towards such an end, the usual move of evolutionary epistemologists is to acknowledge the distance between themselves and the external world by speaking, not of 'realism' *simpliciter*, but of 'hypothetical realism'. It is said that we cannot know absolutely that there is a real world, or what its true nature is. However, we can and must postulate that such a reality does obtain and we note this by speaking of 'hypothetical' reality – although it may well be that the course of our investigations is to chip away at the 'hypothesis', perhaps never removing it but making it more secure.

A typical exponent of this position is the German philosopher, Gerhard Vollmer. He writes:

> Evolutionary epistemology is inseparably connected with hypothetical realism. This is a modest form of critical realism.
>
> Its main tenets are: All knowledge is hypothetical, i.e. conjectural, fallible, preliminary. There exists a real world, independent of our consciousness; it is structured, coherent, and quasi-continuous; it is at least partially knowable and explainable by perception, experience, and intersubjective science.
>
> (Vollmer 1987: 188)

Clark takes an entirely contrary position, arguing that far from being a realist, hypothetical or otherwise, the evolutionary epistemologist is properly driven towards non-realism. Clark writes:

> To adopt the quasi-realistic notion of science as aiming to produce tolerated models is to invite the philosopher's retort 'models of what?' Two courses are open to the evolutionary epistemologist here. He may allow that all such models are models of the one (alas indescribable) objective, mind-independent reality to which all beings are variously adapted. Or he may dig in his heels and refuse to countenance any conception of reality save that of whatever is said to exist by some successful model (be it a human or non-human one). So either we give up the very idea of the world-in-itself (as

191

Rorty and Davidson urge us to do) and replace it with the notion of multiple valid species-specific descriptions whose objects are determined by the descriptions themselves, or we retain the idea of the world-in-itself as a bare noumenal something = X which somehow supervenes (or maybe transcends) the totality of possible descriptions of it. Whichever we choose, the divorce of science from the description of noumenal reality is ratified.

Of the two options suggested, I find myself attracted to the more austere alternative of dropping the notion of the world-in-itself entirely.

(Clark 1986: 158–9)

Why would one want to take so drastic a step? Basically, suggests Clark, because on the one hand, the notion of the real world, the thing in itself, has now become redundant. On the other hand – and here Clark is influenced by the analysis of meaning provided by the philosopher Michael Dummet (1978) – because the notion is no longer comprehensible. What sense can we give to the idea of a reality that lies beyond our ken, and that necessarily must remain so? The answer seems to be that no sense at all can be given: to speak of a reality, we must in some way specify what it would be like to meet with this reality and, on the evolutionary epistemological position, this is precisely what we cannot do.

Let me state flatly that I agree entirely with Clark's position and have in fact elsewhere (in my book *Taking Darwin Seriously*) independently arrived at exactly his conclusion. You might have expected this, given how you have now seen that I adopt a Humean perspective on evolutionary epistemology. Hume likewise always had trouble with the notion of a world beyond us. It was precisely this gap that Kant's *Ding-an-sich* was intended to fill, but as is well known this Kantian notion has brought at least as many problems as it was intended to solve. Thus with Hume and Clark, I am led to reject the notion of a reality beyond our experience.

Does this not plunge us into a world of subjectivity where anything goes, where there are simply no constraints on knowledge? Other evolutionary epistemologists fear so – and, today, in this they would probably be backed by various radical pragmatists like Richard Rorty (1979). He likewise would see subjectivity and relativism, even though he would welcome such a consequence rather than reject it! However, Hume did not think that he was plunged into such a quicksand and neither do I. We still have the real world, but it is the world as we interpret it. What is being rejected is not reality in any meaningful sense. No one is saying, for instance, that dinosaurs did not exist, or that if you see a fierce tiger, you can simply put your hand through it and wish it out of existence. It is simply to acknowledge that reality and thinking about it are inseparable and that the belief in something beyond this is meaningless and redundant.

Hillary Putnam (1981) argues that although ultimate reality is chimerical, it does seem to be part of human nature to believe in it. I think that this is a perceptive statement, which, given what I have already said about the human mind's propensity to project into reality, can readily be given an evolutionary explanation. Putnam (1982) himself, incidentally, rejects evolutionary epistemology but this is because (mistakenly) he, like most evolutionary epistemologists, believes the philosophy commits one to realism. Whereas the evolutionary epistemologists welcome this conclusion, Putnam takes it to be a refutation of the whole position. I argue that he is right in his refutation but wrong in thinking it the whole position.

My conclusion, therefore, is that evolutionary epistemology has some fairly fundamental and far-reaching implications about ontology. What I also conclude is that these are not implications yet properly appreciated by the majority of evolutionary epistemologists.

THREE QUESTIONS – AND A BONUS

I have written this paper in a spirit of inquiry. Subject to the various qualifications that I have made, I believe that essentially my philosophy is correct. Yet, although I hope to convince you of my position, in a way I have been more concerned with laying out basic themes and illustrating points of controversy, dissent and concern. Let me therefore end my discussion by gathering together the threads and raising three questions which I think must be tackled by all evolutionary epistemologists if we are to carry the philosophy on further.

First, let me reiterate something about the cultural type of evolutionary epistemology, the kind espoused by David Hull, against which I have had some critical comments to make in this paper.

Although I have been negative, I have acknowledged that I have not offered a definitive and case-closing refutation. I think, despite virtues, there are severe problems with the approach. Hull and others think that, despite problems, there are great virtues in the approach. Here we differ. Can we carry inquiry further other than by shouting at each other across the trenches? I believe we can, but that what is needed in this case is not more conceptual analysis. We have had that for twenty years or more now. Rather, the Hull-type epistemologist must put his money where his mouth is – or, in less vulgar terms, he or she must show that his or her approach yields rich dividends. If it can, then my criticisms will seem less pressing. If it cannot, then to be honest, my criticisms will be unnecessary, for this approach will wither and die of its own accord.

How is one to put the approach to work? Fairly obviously, as Hull and others recognize, by applying it to actual science and seeing if fresh insights can be obtained. We must look in depth at episodes in the history of science, or ongoing disputes and movements in contemporary science, and see if fresh and valuable perspectives can be gained by employing the evolutionary model. If they can (and I readily conceive that to a certain extent they can) then the model will be worth implementing. If they cannot, or if we can gain the insights just as readily by using other models, then this particular evolutionary epistemology will destruct of its own accord. At this point, therefore, all I can urge is that the enthusiasts stop talking and get to work. This, of course, was written before the appearance of Hull 1988a, b, as well as Richards 1987. As I agreed in the introduction to this section, the enthusiasts have now carried the game to the doubters' part of the court. See also Adams 1979; Bechtel 1984.

My second and third questions, or rather suggestions, concern the kind of evolutionary epistemology I endorse. They both come out of earlier discussion. Second, I argue that we must – simply must – carry forward our empirical understanding of human evolution, especially as it related to thinking and behaviour. We must learn more of the brain and of its functioning, of the dispositions of the mind and of how these translate into explicit thoughts and actions (Churchland 1986). At the same time, we must look at questions to do with cultural variability and the extent to which biology constrains culture and how culture can, if at all, overcome such constraints. Likewise in the realms of psychology and sociology, we must look at already-mentioned questions about the actual functioning of thinking and how big a gap there is between reality and the ideal. All these and more questions must be explored by the evolutionary epistemologist.

At the same time, working the other way from the philosophical end of things, it is necessary for the evolutionary epistemologist to dig further into the nature of science, exploring the kind of constraints and rules that make the scientific endeavour the success that it is. Here it might be the case that the two evolutionary epistemologies come together, for one might feel that in uncovering the processes governing the development of science one uses the evolutionary model, which then is given a biological underpinning. Obviously, the purely empirical scientist and the philosopher will not be working independently on their problems, hoping that perhaps their results will coincide. I would think that one looks for a fairly keen feedback process, with the philosopher responding to the discoveries of science and conversely. However, although much work has been done it is clear that much work remains to be done in this field. Indeed, we are at present barely scratching at the surface.

Third and finally, I believe that evolutionary epistemologists must start turning with more care, if not enthusiasm, to the writings of non-evolutionary philosophers. I realize that this is sometimes difficult to do. One is frequently contemptuous of the bulk of philosophers for being so blind about our evolutionary origins and at the same time irritated when they do make comments about biology, for so often these comments are based on prejudice and/or misconceptions. Nagel is a good case in point. Quite brazenly, he admits that he knows virtually no biology and yet presumes to rush in and dictate. For example, at the most basic level, he shows his ignorance by critiquing the evolutionary epistemologist on the grounds that modern science seems to have no survival value. In fact, did Thomas Nagel but know, evolutionary biology looks much more to reproductive virtues than survival virtues. (This I realize is perhaps a small and trivial point, but it is symptomatic. What philosopher would presume to write on Plato without reading the *Republic*? Why therefore should philosophers write on biology, without reading the *Origin*?)

Contemptuous, irritated, or whatever, we evolutionary epistemologists must recognize that we need help and that conventional philosophy can offer this. This point, I believe, has been brought out very clearly in the discussion of the last section. I do not at the moment ask you to agree that Clark and I are right on the realism/non-realism issue. All I hope to have done is to have convinced you that the natural inclinations that one might have are not necessarily the correct ones, and that some reading in the work of epistemologists who have been troubling themselves about the realism/non-realism issue might yield great dividends (Dancy 1986). I fear that if we evolutionary epistemologists do not engage with other philosophers, then not only will they ignore us, but we will decline into an inwardly looking circle. This has been the fate of other movements, like orthodox psychoanalysis. It could also be the fate of evolutionary epistemology – indeed, I sense symptoms of this already, given the enthusiasm of Popperians for evolutionary epistemology and their somewhat paranoid attitudes towards all who dissent from their views.

These then are some of the suggestions I make for further work, and I am confident that if they are taken up we shall see evolutionary epistemology bloom and take its rightful place in our understanding of human nature. I have promised you three questions; now let me conclude with a fourth as a bonus. This discussion has been concerned exclusively with epistemology, but as you will all know, epistemology is but one of the great questions of philosophy. The other centres on right behaviour, that is to say, on our understanding of morality or ethics. I believe that the evolutionist has an obligation to turn his or her attention also in this direction, and I believe that the rewards will be just as great as in the epistemological realm (Ruse 1986; Ruse and Wilson 1986). I think also that this will lead to some interesting questions about the relationships between epistemology and ethics, which will have to be explored. But this is obviously the subject for another paper. So, with this thought, let me bring this discussion to an end. It is enough to say that mine is a view from somewhere. Still around me are many clouds. Only time and work will clear them, and only then shall I be able to say whether I am standing on a peak or a tussock.

Part III

EVOLUTIONARY ETHICS

INTRODUCTION

If I were pressed, I would confess that this is the section of the collection which is closest to my heart, partly because values do interest me most, and partly because (as I explained in the Introduction) evolutionary ethics has such a dreadful reputation. The gamble that one might turn around the way that people think would surely appeal to less inflated egos than mine. Perhaps here is a chance to break from normal science and to be a bit of a revolutionary!

The first essay of the section bridges what has gone before with what is to come. Certainly, in Part I of this collection I was grappling with the value-impregnated nature of science, and in Part II I was working towards a philosophy which would accept these and related findings. Now I am trying to take the argument a little further, as well as saying more about the historical relationship between evolution and progress, something which has already been the theme of earlier essays. Reverting back somewhat to the case study approach of the first section, my aim now is to make even stronger the conclusion that science must be seen as a delicate balancing act between the demands of objective knowledge of reality and the culture within which it emerges and within which it remains always.

But, as I have said repeatedly, the fact that science reflects culture does not mean that it cannot be turned back to explain that very culture. The arguments may be circular, but it is the circularity of a feedback mechanism and is not vicious – so long as you are prepared to give up a God's eye view of knowledge, where truth is the correspondence between what you believe and ultimate reality. And since this is so, in the second essay of this section I am encouraged to look at the most significant aspect of human culture, the fact that – wars and strifes notwithstanding – there is more to human existence than stark conflict and selfishness. An important aspect of human nature – I would argue, *the* most important aspect of human nature – is that we are social animals and that the key to this sociality is that we believe that there are certain ways in which we ought to behave and that there are certain ways in which we ought not behave.

In short, we are moral beings. We have an ethics, an appreciation of right and wrong, which guides our actions, even though we may not always obey the perceived rules of right and wrong. Like evolutionary epistemology there are two general approaches to evolutionary ethics, and as in evolutionary epistemology I have fairly strong convictions that one way is right and the other way is not. (In fact, I would argue that the epistemology and ethics are not so very far apart and that what makes for success in the one case is what makes for success in the other, and conversely.)

The most important thing is that just as I believe that advances in science are making a real difference to the emergent epistemology, so also this is true of ethics. Given modern biological understanding of the nature and reasons for sociality, we can now hope to make real progress on the understanding of the traditional problems of ethics – what should I do, and why should I do it? This then is the claim that I make in the second essay of this section, and as with my discussions of epistemology, I candidly admit that what I have to say at the empirical level may well soon prove dated. The important thing is the structure of the argument, which can then be updated in the light of ongoing research.

Finally, concluding the section, I take the opportunity of turning to my critics. For nearly ten years now, I have been editor of the journal *Biology and Philosophy*. Nothing has been more encouraging for me as an enthusiast for evolutionary ethics than the fact that submissions to the journal on the topic have probably been twice that of any other topic. It is true that most have been critical, but as I said earlier, that is a significant step above silence and indifference. Before I die, I confidently expect that people will be telling us that 'they have known it all along'!

However, with a delicacy which my friends will agree is not usual, as editor of my journal I have been reluctant to join the discussion within the covers, even when my own work has been discussed and criticized. Every rule is made to be broken, but the prohibition on editors occupying the refereed pages of their own journals is about as close as one can get. Hence I seize now the opportunity to reply to critics, less in the spirit of controversy for its own sake – although I would be a hypocrite if I said that this motive is entirely absent – and more as an opportunity to further the approach to moral philosophy which I believe to be correct.

7

EVOLUTIONARY BIOLOGY AND CULTURAL VALUES

Is it irremediably corrupt?

In recent years, philosophers have come to realize that the relationship between sciences and values raises questions which are both important and not readily answered. It is true that the major figures in that tradition known as 'logical empiricism' appreciated that science always exceeds its empirical grasp and that it is necessary for scientists to be guided and constrained by so-called 'epistemic values', these being values (in the words of one supporter) 'presumed to promote the truth-like character of science, its character as the most secure knowledge available to us of the world we seek to understand' (McMullin 1983: 18). However, these values – such things as internal and external consistency, simplicity, predictive accuracy and fertility, unificatory power (consilience) – were considered special. Inasmuch as they could not be reduced to basic principles of logic – and there were attempts to do this – they were still thought of, in some sense, as beyond the vagaries of human emotion. Their importance was not a function of the individual's personal inclinations, nor of those of the group, whether this group be understood as a closely knit band of researchers or even up to a complete society.

Epistemic values transcend culture. If you will forgive the use of such a term for a group of thinkers who were almost exclusively non-believers, epistemic values are God's values rather than human values. (Actually, this is not such a bad metaphor. Remember that when Einstein was trying to articulate his problems with quantum mechanics, he complained that 'God does not play dice'.) Despite the epistemic values – or, rather, because of the epistemic values – the integrity of science is not compromised. It continues as the paradigm of human intellectual achievement. It is objective, above culture, inter-personal. It is, as Karl Popper (1970) has said in one

202

of those felicitous phrases for which he is justly famous: 'Knowledge without a knower'.

But is it? In recent years, this vision of science has been under heavy attack. It is argued by Marxists (Young 1985), by sociologists (Barnes 1977), by historians (Desmond 1989), by feminists (Fausto-Sterling 1985), by those who dislike the pretensions of science (Rifkin 1984), and even by some philosophers (Longino 1990), that human values – cultural, non-epistemic values – are as rife in science, including the best science, as they are elsewhere in human activity and thought. Literature, religion, politics, medicine, all show human values; so does science. Indeed, the very belief that science does not show such values is itself a value-laden activity, pointing to the fact that science is a tool of the establishment. (More charitably, one might say that philosophers like Popper argued for the value-free nature of science because they, observers and victims of the repressions of the totalitarian states of this century, wanted to find an anchor of stability in this dreadful world – an anchor that would replace the rusting relic of religion.)

Of course, to make a case like this, you need some examples, and it seems fair to say that there is barely an area of modern science (or past science) which has not come under scrutiny (Graham 1981). For fairly obvious reasons, the social sciences have tended to come in for more critical treatment than (say) the theory of relativity. But nothing has been exempt. And I think it is fair to say that, *prima facie* at least, the would-be finders of human values have indeed found such values. Indeed, I am not sure that a hardened logical empiricist would want to deny some success, although no doubt their conclusion would be that such success shows only that much that masquerades as science – psychoanalytic theory, for instance – is not genuine science at all.

For various reasons, evolutionary theory (past and present) has been a much-cited example of a non-epistemically value-laden science (Ruse 1989). Moreover, the treatment it has received has not been gentle. General opinion – stated and restated – is that if you can name a morally or ideologically offensive cultural value, you can be sure that it has been incorporated into evolutionary thought at some point. Indeed, it is a safe bet that such values are still residing in the work of evolutionists, sometimes more or less subtly disguised, but ready to spring forth at any moment. These values disguise themselves as objective fact, but are truly no more than the hopes and wishes of scientists, being built in at the point of conception of theories. Racism, sexism, capitalism, heterosexism, and more. You name it. It will be there (Levins and Lewontin 1985; Gould 1981; Hubbard 1983).

Can this be true? Ten years ago, those of us who love and cherish evolutionary thought – and I want to be quite candid in saying that I believe it to be one of the greatest testaments to human intellectual achievement – had to fight off the attacks of the religious right (Ruse 1988c). We even had to stand up in court against the fundamentalists, who would have introduced so-called 'Creation science' alongside evolution in the biology classes of state-supported schools. We won that time; but were we mere tools of the conservative side of society, even if unwittingly? (At least, I was!) Were we truly propping up one of the chief ideological supports of all that decent people today find morally offensive?

In a spirit of inquiry, rather than that of mere polemic, I want to go back over this issue of values in evolutionary biology. My own personal commitment is to Darwinism, that theory which sees natural selection as the chief driving mechanism and adaptation as the chief problem posed by the organic world (Ruse 1982). But, for the purposes of this discussion, I will open up the field to all that has been said in the name of evolution. And my questions are whether there are (have been) cultural or human values expressed in evolutionary theorizing; whether these values are an essential, unremovable part of such theorizing; and whether the conclusion must be that there is something irremediably corrupt about evolutionary thought. Were the Creationists right for the wrong reasons? We would be better off without evolution.

CULTURAL VALUES

Let us start with the clearest of facts. There is no doubt that, through the ages, evolutionists (and here I include Darwinians and non-Darwinians) have held cultural values and have put such values into their science. Moreover, these values have certainly included those very values that critics highlight (with good reason) as morally and socially objectionable, at least by our standards today. Most obviously, sexism and racism have been a feature – at times a prominent feature – of evolutionary thought. One can start right away with Darwin (1871), who had very conventional views on the relative statuses and potentialities of men and women. The former are the strong masculine types, who do the thinking and the hard and dangerous work. The latter are the soft feminine types, who care for the children and generally by nature are best fitted for matters of the heart. Similarly, Darwin held fairly stereotypical views about the races. Whites are up there at the top and blacks hold their traditional lower-rung places, concerned as they are more about choosing the ripest females as mates than in improving their lots in life's struggles.

Like many others, Darwin worried mightily about the Irish, who are clearly an inferior people but who yet bide fair to outbreed more worthy people (the Scots!). Fortunately, he was able to console himself that although the Irish may have more children than their more prudent and deserving contemporaries, by the time of offspring-reproduction – thanks to their inability to provide decent care – their numbers have fallen way off, down below those of the more civilized. (In modern terminology, Darwin decided that the Irish are r-selectionists, preferring reproduction over follow-up attention, whereas the Scots are K-selectionists, going the other way. For humans, the second strategy is the right one.)

Views like these, made in the name of evolutionary biology, repeat again and again through the century after Darwin, as indeed they could be found in the writings of those (incidently, both for and against evolution) in the decades before Darwin. We all know about the claims of the so-called 'Social Darwinians' who argued for a stern *laissez-faire* political economy in the name of evolution (Hofstadter 1959); and we know equally about the dreadful story of Darwinism in Germany, where it ended up in the service of the most vile ideology that humankind has yet devised. Haeckel, the prophet of evolutionism in the years after the *Origin*, was appallingly anti-Semitic; and I am afraid that this was a tradition that continued among evolutionists long after his death (Gasman 1971).

Thus the critics' charges. Even now, I would counsel some caution, apart from pointing out that although the recognition of the values of earlier evolutionists may have been highlighted by the modern critics, this is not their exclusive discovery. Earlier, more traditional students had discovered much that was going on (Ruse 1979c). More significantly, it is often the case that a more detailed historical analysis shows that the relationship between a scientist with his or her values and society's reactions is more complex than an initial reading would suggest. I have no desire to exonerate German evolutionists entirely – after all, *something* had to lead to National Socialism – but it is certainly the case that there is no easy isomorphism between the thought of Haeckel and someone like Hitler. Apart from anything else, the evolutionists were arguing that we are all descended from monkeys and that Jews and Aryans are siblings under the skin. This was not a cherished item in Nazi ideology (Kelley 1981).

But I am not really arguing at this point. Evolutionary biology has been used to carry horrible beliefs, and these have been promoted in the name of Darwinism as well as alternative evolutionary theories. Moreover, I would agree that this is a legacy which persists. If we jump to the present, or at least to the immediately past present, we find similar sorts of values alive and well there also. I am certainly not saying that people today are open racists in quite the way that someone like Darwin would be if he were writing today. At least, I am certainly not saying that the bulk of respected evolutionists wear their prejudices in quite the open way that one finds among the Victorians, although around the fringes one can certainly find such thinkers.

Yet I would say that even among the respected and respectable, the sentiments are often unchanged. Consider, for example, Richard Dawkins' well-known book, *The Selfish Gene* (1976). In talking about the sexual strategies open to females in the course of reproduction, he distinguishes the 'he man' strategy from the 'domestic bliss' strategy. Without commenting on the full extent to which Dawkins is pointing to real aspects of the living world, it surely requires little argument to see that his use of these terms is insulting to women. I for one would not like to be a member of the sex whose options apparently are either attracting Tarzan or staying home with the kids.

Alternatively, if you want some fairly stereotypical thinking about the races, consider the speculations of the well-known theoreticians Paul Harvey and Robert May (1989), writing in *Nature* no less, on the reasons for different testicle sizes among human beings. Apparently, the Danes are well-hung because their ancestors were into a bit of rape and pillage. The Chinese, on the other hand, come from a long line of home-bodies, and their genitalia suffered accordingly. This is about on a par with Darwin (1871) quoting, with approval, the explorer Richard Burton, to the effect that the Hottentots set up their women in a straight line, and then the bravest warrior gets to choose she who protrudes farthest *a tergo*. Bottoms or bollocks, take your choice. Or, at least, take your choice if you are top dog in the pack.

THE OTHER SIDE OF EVOLUTION

So much for the case against evolutionary thought. Usually the discussion stops here, showing (I suspect) the value-systems of those who make these points, and (I know) a regrettable insensitivity to the niceties of historical research. In saying this, I do not want to deny the points just made – I have made them myself. But they must be set in context, and when this is done, the impact is at least shifted, if not changed. For a start, one must surely look at people's work against the mores and beliefs of the culture within which they were writing. This does not deny cultural values in science; it affirms them. But it does go some way towards defusing the suspicion that there is something inherently and above-average distasteful about evolutionary thought.

Take Darwin. He was a Victorian. He was a rich Victorian, with many of the convictions of his class – about women, about race, about capitalism (Desmond and Moore 1992). But he was a liberal Victorian, as were most of the evolutionists at the cutting edge. At a time when it was really open to serious debate, he was affirming the universality of the family of humankind. It was because of Darwin and his fellows that, although he may have condescended towards other peoples, the Nazis in their own age could be seen unequivocally as brutal murderers.

Likewise within his own society, although Darwin saw and approved of the differences between the classes and the sexes, he affirmed (in the name of evolution) the existential worth of the differences. We may think he was demeaning to women. He would have replied indignantly that he saw women as having unique essential attributes. No second-class men, they. We may feel that we have the upper hand – which of course we do, because we are alive and he is not – but in important respects, it is simply not very helpful to think of Darwin as a male chauvinist pig. If you want male chauvinist pigs, turn to some of the doctors of the age. Or the churchmen.

And much the same point goes for other evolutionists of Darwin's time and later. Thomas Henry Huxley, Darwin's great supporter, held Darwin-like views on women and Blacks; but because his evolutionism committed him to the unity of human-kind he was led to work for women's educational liberation and for the well-being of other races. With John Stuart Mill, he was one of the leading voices against Governor Eyre of Jamaica, who had without trial hanged the ringleader of a rebellion. (For details of Huxley's social views see the *Life and Letters* edited by his son Leonard 1902.)

I do not want to say that every evolutionist has always har-boured liberal views, or that these have readily been translated on to the science – the thinking of Darwin's friend the botanist Joseph Hooker on the subject of Negroes would have brought comfort to an Arab slave trader. Nor do I want to say that today's evol-utionists always stand for liberal values – I suspect that even as he wrote and published, many within and without the evolutionary community thought Richard Dawkins, at best, a bit adolescent. But, if we are to avoid being unbearable prigs about our ancestors, we must always keep before us a sense of history.

So much for simple points of historical accuracy and charity. But the argument does not stop here. If you think about it, it would be very odd if there had never been an evolutionist – acting individually or because of the society in which he or she lived and worked – who had not subscribed to what then, and perhaps now, was considered a morally commendable position. A position which was, as it were, above and beyond its time – or, more prosaically, a position which was in tune with the thinking of today's most vocal critics of the perceived iniquities of evolution-ary thought. Moreover, given what we have seen thus far in this discussion, it would be even odder had none of these thinkers tried to incorporate their moral and social views into their science.

Such people did exist and they did try to do precisely that with their cultural values and their science – to put the former into the latter. Take Social Darwinism. Some businessmen took the reactionary position: they argued that life is a bloody struggle for existence and that this is the way that things should and must be in society (Hofstadter 1959). Supposedly, John D. Rockefeller, the founder of Standard Oil, argued that the law of survival is the law of God is the law of business, and that it is therefore right and proper that Standard Oil should have pushed all its competitors to the wall. But others (Andrew Carnegie the founder of US Steel was one) put more emphasis on the survival of the fittest rather than the non-survival of the non-fittest. As is well known, Carnegie gave away a great deal of his money to the founding of public libraries. This was all part and parcel of his Social Darwinism, which aimed at giving the poor but talented child a place where he or she could go and practise self-improvement (Russett 1976).

You may think – I am inclined to think – that Social Darwinism is not part of evolutionary biology proper: it is more something on the fringe, at best a matter of application of scientific ideas. But socio-political views did get right into the science, and some were as enlightened as one could possibly wish. Today, nigh on everyone would agree that the modern state must play some active role in the well-being of its members. At first, T. H. Huxley had been an enthusiast for a *laissez-faire* economic system (this was thanks to the influence of his good friend Herbert Spencer). Later, as he himself became a leading part of the middle-to-late Victorian move to a bureaucratic-run society, Huxley shifted to a more holistic view of society, justifying himself in evolutionary terms by arguing that life's tendency is towards a more integrated division of labour, where co-operation rather than combat is the overriding theme. By the end of Huxley's life, this was as much part of his biology as was anything – certainly more than natural selection, which always had a minor role in Huxley's work. (See the introduction by James Paradis to Huxley 1989.)

Huxley was one person. Russia was a whole society, with a deep and rich culture. Evolution caught the imagination of a great many Russian intellectuals. In the nineteenth century and right down into the twentieth century, before everything was twisted by the power of the Soviet state, Russian evolutionists always stressed what they saw as the essentially co-operative nature of the evolutionary process. We in the English-speaking world know of the work of Prince Peter Kropotkin (mainly because he was in exile in Britain and wrote and published in English). He argued that the *leitmotif* of evolution is 'mutual aid', whereby animals band together to help each other, primarily against the elements. He saw this as directly analogous to human society and conversely. For him, openly anarchistic as he was, formal society is an unnecessary perverting encumbrance, which acts only to stifle our natural benevolent dispositions. His biology reflected his values and in turn supported his philosophy (Kropotkin 1955).

But Kropotkin was only an extreme and visible aspect of the whole national approach to evolution. To the Russians, living in a vast land which was essentially pre-industrialized, without the teeming cities of Western Europe, the idea of a struggle for existence between organisms seemed remote and unconvincing. What made sense to them, far more, was the need to struggle against the harsh elements, and in this struggle mutual aid was a necessity, let alone a desired value. Russian evolutionary biology, therefore, simply did not incorporate a sense of individualistic Malthusian struggle leading to selection (Todes 1989). Their values lay elsewhere and so did their science.

Others, in America for example, thought in analogous ways, if not always for the same reasons. In Chicago, in the 1930s, there was a whole school of evolutionary ecology which stressed co-operation as fundamental. Their motive was hardly a lack of awareness of the troubles of industrialized society, but was apparently more a function of a shared sympathy with the beliefs and ideals of Quakerism. The doctrine of the 'inner light' was translated straight into biological terms (Mitman 1992).

What about sex and race? Here also we find that, whereas some evolutionists were pretty conventional in their beliefs, others took stances that even the most politically correct of today's thinkers would find acceptable. Natural selection's co-discoverer Alfred Russel Wallace thought that blacks and other non-European peoples have abilities which quite outstrip their jungle needs (Wallace 1870a). He was so impressed by this fact that he even invoked non-evolutionary processes to explain them! As far as sex is concerned, much impressed by Edward Bellamy's futuristic novel, *Looking Backward* ([1889] 1951), Wallace argued that society will and must evolve to such a point where all the sexual selection of mates is done by females, who will raise us all up by their wise and sensitive choices. Not only will self-centred males no longer have control over the destinies of females; before long, they will be selected out of existence (Wallace 1905).

If you move to the present, you find a variant of such views alive and well in feminist biological circles today. There are many pop-scientific accounts of human evolution which make females the essential driving forces of the evolutionary process (Morgan 1972); but in serious circles also one finds scenarios which reflect values running counter to those that the critics of evolutionary theory always parade. Sarah Blaffer Hrdy (1981) has argued that human females conceal their points of ovulation: they do not come into heat, as do other mammals. This means that females exercise all sorts of sexual and social control over males, who simply do not know whether they are coming or going.

I could go on in this manner, so let me just stay in the present and conclude with the recent work of the Harvard entomologist Edward O. Wilson. I choose him deliberately, because he is better known as a student of the biology of people, as a human sociobiologist, than as a student of ants. With some reason, Wilson has been taken as an exemplar of the insensitive white male, reading into his evolutionary biology the values of his society. ('With some reason', yet with never an acknowledgement of how far he has transcended his pre-War Alabama childhood.) Yet, in recent years, Wilson has been much involved in the conservation movement, and this concern is reflected in and supported by his reading of evolution (Wilson 1984; Wilson and Peter 1988). In particular, Wilson believes strongly that humans have evolved in such a way that we are symbiotically dependent on the rest of organic creation. Both physically and at some level emotionally, we humans need nature. A world of plastics would be stunting, in all senses of the word. Hence for our continued survival, let alone our forward movement, Wilson argues that we must have diverse nature around us. Else, we wither and die.

If all this is not culturally value laden, then I do not know what is. And the values are as respectable, as acceptable to today's critics of evolutionary theory, as anything. Hence I simply have to conclude that the direct argument about the unambiguous moral corruption of evolutionary thought, Darwinian or otherwise, is just not well taken. I have not counted heads. I do not know which cultural values have made the biggest appearance in evolutionary theorizing since evolutionary theorizers first made an appearance on the scene. Perhaps the nasties have it. But I will say that it is historically inaccurate to present evolutionary theorizing past and present as one long story of morally and culturally offensive proselytizing.

EPISTEMIC VALUES TRIUMPHANT?

I suspect that at this point the denigrators of evolutionary thought will have an objection. Even though they might quibble about details, they will agree that there have been people in the past, perhaps even in the present, whose hearts have been in the right place and who have been influenced by cultural values of a worthwhile and commendable nature. Indeed, some might even point to the fact that they themselves have tried to produce an ideologically acceptable evolutionism. I think, for example, of the work of the Marxist biologists Richard Lewontin and Richard Levins. By their own admission, they have openly attempted to put their philosophy into their science, explicitly endorsing holistic approaches, trying to analyse nature in a hierarchical manner, standing against the 'reductionism' which is the mark of so much of modern science (Levins and Lewontin 1985).

Yet, so the objection will run, not even evolution's most ardent defenders could deny that much (most) of the work done by those who have tried to put a gentle face on evolution was based on very thin evidence indeed. Often such evidence as there was, certainly as there is now, points the other way. But, unfortunately, science shows no charity. There is little merit in having your heart in the right place if all of your supporting facts are false!

Alfred Russel Wallace was a wonderful, lovable man, but does anyone seriously think that, now or ever, young girls are going to choose just those mates with the highest moral qualities? If they do, they must be as divorced from reality as he was – or that fuzzy-minded Chicago Quakerism of the 1930s. It is all very well to put forward holistic views of nature's processes: if they find no true correspondence in the real world – and, by the 1950s, supporters as well as critics were forced to conclude precisely that – your science belongs on the dustbin of history, along with astrology and phlogiston theory.

Even Wilson's musings about biodiversity are suspect, quite apart from the very questionable status of his motives. After the rightful battering he received in the 1970s, because of his ill-advised excursions into sociobiology, it must be nice to bask in the praise of those very people who once attacked him. But, this aside, perhaps people do have a biologically ingrained need for nature. Perhaps our genes do make us dependent on natural beauty. The trouble is that there is not the slightest empirical evidence to make the hypothesis plausible.

Indeed, in respects, Wilson seems to be playing precisely those tricks for which he was criticized earlier. Think of a gene, double it, and there you have a homozygote for precisely that aspect of human nature you are trying to explain. Then it was genes for aggression, now it is genes for conservation. The variation is different. The tune is the same. To be honest, I think there is much truth in this criticism. Admittedly, one might point out that if so much of the soft side of evolutionary thought is based on scanty evidence, this might possibly be true also of the reformulations of the critics themselves. I think particularly of the Lewontin-Levins work – although given the general woes of Marxism today, it is a little mean to kick a dog when it is down. (Stephen Jay Gould is one who is extremely good at locating and faulting the value–evidence relationship in the work of others, but who gets a little touchy when it is done to his own work (Ruse 1989).)

However, to carp for the sake of making a point is to miss the truth of the general criticism. Take Kropotkin's mutual aid. Study after study shows that it is a very simplistic notion. Without at all denying that there is co-operation among the beasts of the field, we now know that there is masses of aggression, quite incompatible with Kropotkin's idealized picture of nature (Wilson 1975). The same is true of so much else. Even a friendly observer of Wilson's work – and I am proud to count myself as such – has to admit that his vision of the organic world pushes out beyond the bounds of hard data. Indeed, I suspect that he himself might admit as much: Wilson takes pride in subscribing to a philosophy of scientific research that puts a premium on bold conjectures, to use another of Popper's happy terms (Segerstrale 1985).

Of course, the argument does not stop here. If one may legitimately critique the one side of evolutionary thought *qua* cultural values and the evidence, one may surely also critique the other side. Wallace's views on women fall because they do not match the evidence, but then so also do Darwin's! Consider one of the concerns that Darwin had, namely about the way in which the Irish were out-breeding the Scots. He worried that this would lead to a degeneration of humankind. (Obviously he could not put it in genetic terms, but that is what he would have done if he could have done.) I assume that today no one takes that kind of concern seriously, simply because we now know that there is essentially no biological difference between the Irish and the Scots. Despite all of the troubles of recent years, I have never seen it suggested that membership of the IRA is a consequence of a malfunctioning gene.

Similar points could be made about much else that the critics find offensive. I am not saying that modern evolutionary thought has now been purged of all that the morally sensitive finds offensive. We have seen, indeed, that it has not. But much that passed for commonplace in the nineteenth century has no more a place in modern evolutionary thought than it has in modern political or religious or social thought. Some change really is progress. It really is quite unfair to condemn modern evolutionary theory for the sins of the past. Nor am I much impressed if you complain that the sins were of the very recent past. The last two decades have seen a sea-change in such things as the use of language demeaning to women and people whose skin is not lily white. Evolutionary theorizing has responded as fast as anything.

So what conclusion are we being pointed to? It seems as though what I am arguing is that evolutionary thought, Darwinian or otherwise, is little more than a hanger on which to drape the value-laden clothes of the culture within which an evolutionist lives – or even just the part of the culture within which the evolutionist lives. You take your values and you just drop them right into the work that you are doing.

And, at one level, I think there is truth in this, certainly when evolutionists are writing at a semi-popular level – an activity which happens a great deal in a subject like evolution and which is often not as far from the professional cutting-edge as evolutionists like to admit. Indeed, I would go so far as to say that, in one sense and at one level, evolution from the time of Thomas Henry Huxley on has functioned as a kind of secular religion – what Popper (1976) has called a 'metaphysical research programme' – into which people have poured their hopes and on which they have hung their values.

Nor has this era come to an end. If you doubt me, look at the comments about the status of evolutionary theorizing by Edward O. Wilson in his bestselling book *On Human Nature*:

> The evolutionary epic is mythology in the sense that the laws it adduces here and now are believed but can never be definitely proved to form a cause-and-effect continuum from physics to the social sciences, from this world to all other worlds in the visible universe, and backward through time to the beginning of the universe.
>
> (192)

But this is not the end of the story. I have not admitted the existence of cultural values in evolutionary biology simply to conclude that it is at best semi-science, and not the real thing at all. You have only to look at one of the professional publications of evolutionists, the journal *Evolution* for instance, to realize that there is a very great deal more to modern evolutionary thought than mere value-mongering. It is a travesty to say that today's theory is no more than a coat for cultural hopes and personal desires. There is a large body of subtle theory backed by sophisticated experimentation.

The point I would endorse – a point which I have already made in passing – is that over time evolutionists have improved their work, if by 'improvement' you mean getting rid of overt reference to cultural values. (As you will see, I am not sure that I would use 'improvement' in this context. But it is enough for me here that scientists would, when they are thinking self-consciously.) Things like Darwin's blatant racism and sexism (judged by our standards) are simply no longer acceptable. The same goes for the warm glow brought on by Kropotkin's mutual aid.

How has this cleansing or expulsion taken place? Here I think one might usefully refer to an analysis by Ernan McMullin (1983). He argues that, although young immature science is laden both with epistemic and non-epistemic values, over the course of time, as scientists theorize and gather data and experiment, the epistemic values slowly but surely thrust the non-epistemic values out of the nest. Copernicus may have put the sun at the centre of the universe because he was a Platonist, but the heliocentric theory today stands on its predictive-unificatory power (Kuhn 1957). Likewise, Lyell's geological theory of uniformitarianism may once have appealed because of its natural theological virtues (Ruse 1979c); but today we have no need or desire for such religious underpinning. Uniformitarianism succeeds on its epistemic merits.

A philosophy like this surely fits our ticket perfectly. Once upon a time, evolutionary theorizing was a mixture of the epistemic and the non-epistemic. Then the epistemic values started to shine through and to gain the upper hand. Now they are well on the way to total victory, with the exception of antediluvian places like Oxford, the home of Richard Dawkins. Take, for example, the various kinds of holistic approach to evolution, which see organisms working together in happy harmony – society founded on Kropotkin's mutual aid, for instance, or the super-organismic ecological picture of the Chicago school. These fell, quite simply, because they failed to exhibit the right epistemic virtues. They proved not to be predictively fertile or unificatory or whatever. The alternatives won out.

Let me reinforce this point. In recent years, one of the most lauded triumphs in evolutionary thought has been the theory of kin selection launched by William Hamilton (1964a, b). He argues, in direct opposition to holism, that organisms co-operate because they serve their own 'selfish' ends. In particular, Hamilton has shown that close relatives, who as a consequence of their relatedness share many of the same genes, can often further their own reproductive ends most efficiently by aiding the reproduction of these very relatives. Inasmuch as copies of the relative's genes are transmitted, copies of one's own genes are transmitted. Reproduction by proxy, as it were!

Applying this insight to the *hymenoptera* – the ants, the bees, and the wasps – Hamilton thereby solved one of the most famous problems in the evolutionist's book, namely why it is that these insects have developed sterile castes of females, who forgo their own reproduction apparently for the good of the nest. To the contrary, argues Hamilton, since the *hymenoptera* are haplodiploid – the females have two parents and a complete chromosome set, whereas males have only mothers and a half chromosome set – females further their own reproductive ends more efficiently inasmuch as they raise fertile sisters rather than fertile daughters. Paradoxically, the algebra of the case shows that this is the way to maximize one's own gene output.

An explanation like this simply leaves all of the old holistic explanations standing when it comes to the manifestation of the epistemic values. It is fully consistent with genetical theory, requiring no *ad hoc* explanations. It possesses major predictive power, enabling evolutionists to think of and test all sorts of subsidiary hypotheses about what to expect in special circumstances. Above all, it has an elegance, a simplicity, equal to that of the very best hypotheses of physics. As Wilson (1975) has said, something as beautiful as this simply could not be false.

The full story, therefore, seems to be that cultural values have certainly ridden high in evolutionary biology. Whether they have been more abundant and whether taken individually they have been worse than other branches of science, I really do not know. They have not been unmitigatedly bad, but then they certainly have not been uniformly good. The main point is that, as time has gone by, they have been washed out by the epistemic values, as evolutionists strove to achieve the closest thing one can get to an objectively true scientific theory in this vale of tears.

Hence, judged historically, even if you repudiate any sense of charity you can allow that the critics may have had a point. They have a point no longer: evolutionary theorizing is no longer the sort of thing which could be morally objectionable.

THE PROBLEM OF PROGRESS

This is a comforting conclusion to a sometime positivist like myself. One shows sensitivity to the arguments of the critics, both in the general sense of acknowledging the significance of cultural values in science and in the specific sense of agreeing that evolutionary biology has (at the very least) reflected the often less than edifying values of cultures past and present. At the same time, apart from pointing out that not all the values reflected into evolutionary biology were that bad, one can argue that, in the end, the cultural values were merely transient. Ultimately, the objectivity of science – of evolutionary biology – has been maintained.

Unfortunately, this is not all to be said on the matter, quite apart from the fact that I have surely been jumping the gun somewhat on the extent to which cultural values have been expelled from evolutionary biology. Perhaps the kind of values that I have been talking about can be completely cleansed from evolutionary studies. In real life, they are still a long way from being so cleansed. Leave, without prejudice, questions to do with sexism and racism and the like. What about a notion like equilibrium? It is deeply ingrained in much of modern evolutionary thought. Model after model studies conditions under equilibrium – starting with all those systems which take as their starting point the basic premise of population genetics, the Hardy-Weinberg law (Ruse 1973a; Sober 1984).

I would agree that much of the time when equilibrium is being invoked it is because the mathematics is thereby rendered more manageable. But there is little doubt that, over and above the pragmatic questions, equilibrium is a deeply satisfying emotional value to many people. Indeed, it has roots back in the theological notion of a 'balance of nature' (Gale 1972). There is a feeling that if things are in equilibrium then all is right with the world. Even though it is certainly true that most of today's very secular evolutionists would probably deny indignantly that any such old-fashioned factors influence them in their work, the simple fact is that this deeply cultural value is the dog wagging the tail of much that they produce.

Yet you might still argue that the remaining sexism, the remaining racism, the latent capitalism, these will pass. Yes, even the love affair with equilibrium, it too will go. Given enough time, the epistemic values will triumph. Which counter leads me to ask, as a final question, whether there are any cultural values, if not in science generally then in evolutionary biology in particular, which will never fade completely. Are there values that will persist in evolutionary thought, so long as there is such thought? And if so, what are they and what implications do they have? Are they forces for good or are they forces for bad?

I cannot give a general answer; but I believe that there is one such cultural value that has persisted – which shows reason to suggest it will go on persisting. This is the idea of *progress*, the belief that things are getting better thanks to human effort and that they will continue to improve. This is certainly a value of long standing. Indeed, it is a well-documented fact that evolution is the child of progress (Ruse 1995). It came into being on the back of eighteenth-century hopes for social and intellectual advance, and incorporated such values firmly in its body. For people like Erasmus Darwin that was what evolution was all about – an upward progression from monad to man (to use what became a popular catch-phrase).

It is often thought that evolution and progress exemplify beautifully McMullin's thesis about the expulsion of the non-epistemic by the epistemic. Supposedly, the death blows were struck first by Darwin's natural selection which allows only the survival of the fittest, where what is 'fittest' is a very relativistic notion; and second by Mendelian genetics, which postulates that the raw building-blocks of evolution, the 'mutations', are random and non-directed towards organisms' needs. Hence evolutionary thought today is progress free, at least in any objectionable sense (Hesse and Arbib 1986).

But this is just not true. Whatever Darwin did, he did not expel progress – at least, not in his own mind and writings. Just read the closing lines of the *Origin*. And the same non-event is true of the coming of Mendelism. He who did more than any to integrate the new genetics into evolutionary thought was R. A. Fisher. Yet his seminal *The Genetical Theory of Natural Selection* is a peon to upward advance, supported most crucially by Fisher's progressionist and central 'fundamental theorem of natural selection'. And today likewise, progressionism rides triumphant in evolution. Look at Wilson's *Sociobiology: The New Synthesis*. It is progressionist through and through, from the insects to the humans. And it is explicit:

> We should first note that social systems have originated repeatedly in one major group of organisms after another, achieving widely different degrees of specialization and complexity. Four groups occupy pinnacles high above the others: the colonial invertebrates, the social insects, the nonhuman mammals, and man.
>
> (379)

I do not want to say that every evolutionist is a progressionist. The thing about values is that some people reject them. Those who work on micro-studies usually have neither need for nor interest in long-term patterns. And I agree fully that evolutionists often feel discomfort about so blatant a cultural value-commitment as progress, and try to conceal their beliefs from others as well as themselves. But I do say that progress is there in modern evolutionary thought, as it was in the past, and that it is a cultural value.

Moreover, I do claim that the removal of progress would be no easy matter, if indeed possible at all. Or rather, I claim that there are reasons to think that evolutionists as evolutionists are less than full-hearted in wanting to remove progress, and that theirs is a situation likely to persist. Evolutionists, like most scientists, are very visual people: they love graphs and diagrams and photographs and pictures. Imagine how they would feel if you took away from them all their lovely pictures of trees of life, with evolution thrusting ever-upwards. Imagine further how they would feel if you followed by removing the most popular metaphor/picture of this century, Sewall Wright's (1932) so-called 'adaptive landscape'. Perhaps logically this idea need not be shown in a progressionist manner. But it always is. The peaks are never put at the same height, nor is there much evidence of these peaks sinking. Rather, peaks are shown as firmly fixed, just like those in the real world, and one or a number of peaks are always shown as those to be scaled above all others. No prizes for guessing whose peak won the overall competition (Ruse 1993).

There is something deeply progressionist about the very fabric of evolutionary thought. But the pictures and all the associated language apart, there are the motives of the evolutionists themselves. I can think of at least three reasons why they (many, much of the time) will go on pushing progress, as they have in the past.

First, as scientists, they have a faith in the continued progress of their work. As Mendel was above Darwin and Morgan was above Mendel and Jim Watson was above Morgan, so science progresses as it has in genetics. There is therefore a natural tendency to read this faith in scientific progress into the world of organisms. At least, evolutionists have been doing it since Lamarck and they are still doing it. Nor are they much impressed by philosophers who argue that perhaps the progress of scientific knowledge is an illusion. This is not how scientists feel, genuine illusion or not. There are good reasons why Popper (1970), the philosopher of scientific progress, is the philosopher of the practising scientist.

Second, there is at work a version of what the physicists call the 'anthropic principle' – the world seems as it is because of the way that we view the world. In evolution, we have a built-in tendency to read the record in a progressivist manner, because in asking about the existence of progress in evolution we thereby stress our abilities to ask about progress, not to mention the fact that we must be at the end of the evolutionary process – else we would not be around to ask about progress! To inquire about progress is to hint that we are Number One (Simpson 1950).

Third, quite simply, there is self-selection at work. People who are interested in evolution often are so precisely because they are seeking a secular meaning to life – they are after a modern-day substitute for religion. This is a fact in the biography of evolutionist after evolutionist. No wonder such people find progress! (See Dobzhansky 1967.)

I stress that I do not claim that logically these reasons mean that progress must be forever ingrained in evolutionary thought, nor do I claim that every evolutionist is a progressionist. But they do suggest to me that progress is one cultural value that we shall not soon see vanish.

CONCLUSION

I confess that I simply do not know how typical progress, as a cultural value, is of evolutionary thought or of science in general.

Perhaps, in evolution, equilibrium is at least one other idea which shares the same status as progress. Interestingly, from Herbert Spencer onward, there has been a tendency of evolutionists to combine progress and equilibrium in one grand synthesis – 'dynamic equilibrium' (Russett 1966). What I do say is that in evolutionary studies one cultural value persists, and bids fair to persist. This is not instead of the epistemic values. Nothing I have just said denies their ever-greater manifestation. It is just that here is one case where the epistemic values are not going to expel one non-epistemic value.

Which brings me full circle back to my original point of entry. Is the persistence of a non-epistemic value as such a bad thing, and is the persistence of this one non-epistemic value itself a bad thing? Are we back with the corrupt nature of evolutionary thought? As far as any value as such is concerned, I am not sure that this is necessarily a bad thing. It is true that the world of culture-free objective science seems further away than ever; but this is perhaps not the ultimate tragedy. No one is now saying that science is pure culture – at least, no one who has followed my argument: the epistemic values still guarantee standards and a sense of scientific progress, cast in terms of their ever-greater manifestation.

The question of progress itself is more tricky. One of today's most vocal evolutionists – Stephen Jay Gould (1989) – argues strongly against biological progress. He does this primarily on the grounds that, paradoxically, beliefs in evolutionary progression are inimical to social progress. Once you start thinking in terms of upward advance, you start leaving some people behind on the lower branches of the tree, and before you know where you are, you are back to old-fashioned racism.

To be frank, I am not sure that matters are quite this simple. There is some historical truth in what Gould claims; but, equally, some of the people discussed in this essay were ardent progression-ists, and used their progressionism to the highest moral ends. This is quite apart from the fact that some people want to use their biological progressionism for a justification of morality itself. One thinks here of E. O. Wilson, whose progressionism is a crucial plank in his case for a biologically based ethics. (Humans, at the peak of the evolutionary process, represent moral worth, and therefore their well-being – including their dependence on nature – must be cherished.)

221

As it happens, in the past I have criticized Wilson's logic (Ruse 1986), just as I have cast a dubious eye on some of Gould's claims, within and without his science (Ruse 1982, 1989). I am still not sure about progress. So perhaps it is best if I end here, on a somewhat unresolved note. I think evolution is a wonderful idea. And I think modern evolutionary thought is a wonderful testament to the power of human thought and imagination. But it is not to be taken without caution. *Caveat emptor*!

8

EVOLUTION AND ETHICS
The sociobiological approach

Evolutionary ethics is one of those subjects with a bad philosophical smell. Everybody knows (or 'knows') that it has been the excuse for some of the worst kinds of fallacious arguments in the philosophical workbook, and that in addition it has been used as support for socio-economic policies of the most grotesque and hateful nature, all the way from cruel nineteenth-century capitalism to twentieth-century concentration camps (Jones 1980; Richards 1987; Russett 1976; Ruse 1986). It has been enough for the student to murmur the magical phrase 'naturalistic fallacy', and then he or she can move on to the next question, confident of having gained full marks thus far on the exam (Flew 1967; Raphael 1958; Singer 1981).

Having once felt precisely this way myself, I now see that I was wrong – wrong about science, wrong about history, and wrong about philosophy. It is true that my newfound enthusiasm is connected with exciting developments in modern evolutionary biology, especially that part which deals with social behaviour ('sociobiology'), and it is true also that much that has been written in the past does not bear full critical philosophical scrutiny; but evolutionary ethics has rarely if ever had the awful nature of legend. The simple fact of the matter is that, like everyone else, philosophers have been only too happy to have had a convenient Aunt Sally, against which they can hurl their critical coconuts and demonstrate their own intellectual purity, before they go on to develop an alternative position of their own. (For a critique by me, see Ruse 1979a. For other, more positive assessments by me, see Ruse 1986; Ruse 1989; Ruse 1990.)

In this essay, I shall put the case for an adequate, up-to-date evolutionary ethics. I shall do this partly historically, starting with

223

the roots of the philosophy in the middle of the nineteenth century when it first began to attract attention and support, and going down to the most recent and still enthusiastic proponents. I shall do this partly analytically, arguing that modern advances in science enable one to appreciate the convictions of those that have gone before – that it really has to matter that we humans are the product of a long, slow, natural process of evolution rather than the miraculous products of a Good God on the Sixth Day – and yet arguing that we can produce a moral philosophy which is no less sensitive to important issues than it is to crucial insights grasped by past students of ethics.

As I set out on my task, however, let me remind you of a distinction which it is always useful to make when talking theoretically of moral matters, and which will certainly prove its worth to us. This is the distinction between prescriptions or exhortations about what one ought to do, and the justification which might be offered for such norms of conduct. The former level of discussion is generally known as *normative* or *prescriptive* ethics and the latter level as *metaethics* (Taylor 1978).

Simply to illustrate this distinction, let me take Christianity, which is nothing if not a religion with a strong moral basis. At the normative level, we find the believer instructed to obey the Love Commandment: 'Love your neighbour as yourself'. At the metaethical level, we frequently find invocation of some version of the Divine Command Theory: 'That which is good is that which is the will of God'. As it happens, there are sincere Christians who would challenge both of these ideas – some think faith more important than works, and, long before Christ, Plato was showing the problems with an appeal to God's Will (Could He really will us to do something that we now consider to be truly bad?) – but I am not going to argue these matters here. For me, it is enough that you can now surely see how, when you are thinking about moral matters, there are these two levels of inquiry.

'SOCIAL DARWINISM'

In 1859, the English scientist Charles Robert Darwin published his great book, *On the Origin of Species*. Before this, evolution had at best been a half-idea, at the realm of pseudo-science. After this, educated people the world over accepted that all organisms, including ourselves, have natural, developmental origins (Ruse

1979b; Bowler 1984). It is therefore not surprising that it was from about this time that many people began turning from traditional sources of wisdom, especially religion, to science (evolution in particular) for help and guidance in what we should do and what we should think (Moore 1979).

It would be a mistake, however, to think that Darwin single-handedly pushed conventional belief to one side. If anything, the crisis in nineteenth-century Christianity came more from within, as scholars wrestled with the historical accuracy of their beliefs, and theologians with the contemporary relevance of their faith in a world of rapid industrialization. It would be a mistake also to think that Darwin himself was the chief spokesperson for the new evolutionary ethics, even though it was his work which inspired and gave confidence.

For all that the position was labelled 'Social Darwinism' – scholars debate to this day whether Darwin was really a genuine Social Darwinian – the chief enthusiast ('proselytizer' is not too strong a word) was Darwin's fellow Englishman Herbert Spencer (Jones 1980; Russett 1976). It was he who spent his life – and it was very long – writing a series of books – and it and they were likewise very long – promoting evolution, not just as a science but as a whole way of life, including a way of moral life (Spencer 1904; Duncan 1908).

Like many people who write at great length, Spencer did not overly cherish the attribute of consistency – although perhaps a kinder verdict would be to say that, manifesting his own world philosophy, like all else, his own thinking evolved. But, thinking now first at the normative level, we find what seems to be a fairly straightforward connection between Spencer's evolutionary beliefs and his prescriptions for moral conduct (Ruse 1986). Consider for a moment the theory or mechanism for evolution that Darwin proposed in the *Origin*. He argued that more organisms are always being born than can possibly survive and reproduce. There will thus be a 'struggle for existence'; only some will survive and reproduce; and because success in the struggle will (on average) be a function of superior qualities, there will be an ongoing process of 'natural selection' or (to use a phrase that Spencer invented and Darwin adopted) the 'survival of the fittest'. Given enough time, this will all add up to evolution, with the development of 'adaptations', that is to say, features which help in life's battles.

It was Spencer's contention that, generally speaking, evolution is a good thing – a very good thing. Therefore, he argued simply and directly, what we humans ought to do is promote the forces of evolution – or, at least, not stand in the way of their natural execution and consequences (Spencer 1892). How does this cash out as a social or moral philosophy? We have to face the fact that for humans, as for the rest of the living world, life is a struggle, and it always will and must be. In the world of business, as well as every other dimension of human existence, there will be those that succeed and those that fail. We therefore should do nothing to impede this natural process, and indeed we should do all that we can to promote it.

Simply put, in the words of the economists, we should promote a *laissez-faire* philosophy of life, where there is an absolute minimum of state interference in the running of daily affairs. Private charity may come to the aid of widows and children who stand in danger of going to the wall, but government has no right to interfere, let the chips fall where they may. Spencer (1851) even went so far as to argue that the state ought not to provide lighthouses to guide ships at sea. If the owners want them badly enough, they will provide them!

As it happens, recent scholarship has started to suggest that the connection between Spencer's evolutionism and his ethicizing is more complex than appears at first sight (Peel 1971; Wiltshire 1978; Richards 1987). For a start, although Spencer certainly believed in natural selection, for him it was never the main force of evolutionary change (Spencer 1864). That role was always given to so-called 'Lamarckism', the inheritance of acquired characters. For Spencer, the giraffe's neck was long because of ancestral stretching rather than because those would-be ancestors with longer necks succeeded in life's struggles. For a second, Spencer endorsed *laissez-faire* before he became an evolutionist (see Spencer 1851). Paradoxically, he who was often taken as promoting a major challenge to Christianity probably owed his greatest intellectual debts to his early training in Methodist principles of self-help (Richards 1987). (Another who shares his philosophy and who comes from an almost identical background is Britain's former Prime Minister, Margaret Thatcher.)

But, whatever the true connections in Spencer's mind, there is little doubt that his philosophy was widely popular, especially when it was transported to the New World. Spencer's books far out-sold those of Darwin, though the fate of his philosophy in that land illustrates a point we should keep always in mind when looking at sweeping moral philosophies. As with Christianity, very different normative consequences can supposedly be drawn from the same premises.

Some barons of industry and their supporters went the whole hog on a philosophy of individualism and minimal state interference. Supposedly, John D. Rockerfeller I told a Sunday School class (no less!) that the law of big business is the law of God and that it is right and proper that Standard Oil (which he founded and from which he made his wealth) should have crushed its competitors, whatever the economic and social consequences. Others, however, no less ardent in their Spencerianism, felt quite differently. One was the Scottish immigrant Andrew Carnegie, as successful as Rockerfeller, for it was he who founded US Steel in Pittsburgh. In mid-life, he took to the founding of public libraries, explicitly using the evolutionary justification that through such institutions the poor but gifted child would be able to practise self-improvement. Survival of the fittest, as opposed to non-survival of the non-fittest! (Russett 1976 is most informative on Spencer in the New World.)

Spencerianism went East also. At the turn of this century, the Chinese were his followers to the man(darin) (Pusey 1983). It was Germany, however, which saw the greatest flowering of evolutionary ethics, part in consequence and part in parallel with the thinking of Spencer himself. The greatest proponent (of what came to be known as 'Darwinismus') was the biologist Ernst Haeckel (1866). Yet, once again showing how ideas can change and be moulded, we find that far from promoting individualism, Haeckel argued that one ought to endorse strong state controls, particularly as enforced through a trained and powerful civil service (Haeckel 1868). This was a philosophy admirably suited to his society, for it was just at this time that Bismarck was extending Prussian rule – which did incorporate tight state control – to the rest of Germany.

To Haeckel, however, there was nothing artificial or forced about his moral thinking for, unlike Spencer (and, as we shall learn, unlike Darwin), Haeckel located the centre of life's struggles as occurring not between individuals, but between groups or societies. To him, therefore – remember, this was just the time when Prussian virtues apparently triumphed through a massive defeat of France – evolutionary success demanded that one promote harmony and control within the group, for the betterment of all within against those without.

Many people think that, as we came into this century, traditional evolutionary ethics declined and vanished; or should have done, since it was transformed into an apology for some of the most vile social systems that humankind has ever known. In fact, as with perceptions of the nineteenth century, these claims are likewise somewhat mythical; although it is certainly true that Spencer's personal reputation sank to depths rarely before fathomed – apart from anything else, as a scientific theory Lamarckism was shown to be completely and utterly wrong – and perhaps, because of the bad reputation (brought on by excesses in the name of Darwin), people generally sought to avoid the label 'Social Darwinian'.

But there were still many evolutionary ethicists, even if drawn mainly from the ranks of biologists themselves. The most voluble and effective was probably Julian Huxley (1948), brother of the novelist Aldous, and grandson of Darwin's famous supporter, Thomas Henry Huxley. He thought the way to promote evolution lies in the spread of knowledge, especially scientific knowledge. In this fashion will humankind be able to conquer life's problems like disease and poverty and war, and ensure a happier future. He was able to further his ends when, after the Second World War, with the founding of the United Nations, he was appointed first Director General of UNESCO. (Fairness compels me to add that his evolutionary philosophy so upset his staid sponsors that they denied him a full term of office. See Huxley 1948.) (Others endorsing an evolutionary ethics include Dobzhansky 1967 and Mayr 1988.)

The connection between Social Darwinism and the dreadful social philosophies of this century has been a topic much discussed by historians and students of political theory (Gasman 1971; Kelley 1981). Something had to cause the worst of them all, National Socialism, and I would not hold Haeckel entirely blameless. There was both fervent nationalism and a strong streak of anti-Semitism, for instance. But historically, the Nazis did not much like Haeckel or his ideas, and one can see why: at the heart of his philosophy is the belief that we are all interrelated, including the Jews, and that our ancestors were monkeys!

Concluding this brief survey of normative exhortations by traditional evolutionary ethicists, and switching now from the past to the present, let me simply tell you that the philosophy is far from moribund. Most widely published in recent years has been the Harvard entomologist and sociobiologist Edward O. Wilson (1978). A great admirer of Spencer, Wilson believes that we humans live in symbiotic relationship with the rest of the living world, and that by our very natures, without a diverse range of flora and fauna surrounding us, we would literally wither and die (Wilson 1984). Life in an all-plastic world would be impossible. Hence Wilson would have us promote biodiversity, and as a student of tropical ants, he himself is much concerned with movements to save the rain forests of South America. And all in the name of evolution! (See also Wilson 1992.)

EVOLUTION AND PROGRESS

But now, guided by our distinction, let us turn to the question of metaethics. Even if you agree with me that evolutionary ethics has been nothing like as crude and offensive as legend would tell, there is still the matter of justification. Why should we promote *laissez-faire* and free enterprise? Why should we found public libraries? Why should we favour an efficient civil service, a world body for science and culture, the preservation of the rain forests?

It is at this point that, traditionally, philosophers swing into critical action. Inspired by a devastating critique of Spencer by G. E. Moore, in his *Principia Ethica* published in 1903, it is complained that admirable though any (or at least most) of these various directives may be, their supposed derivation stands in flat violation of the supposed 'naturalistic fallacy' (Flew 1967; Waddington 1960). In Moore's language, goodness is a non-natural property, and one simply cannot define or explicate it in terms of natural properties, like happiness or the course of evolution.

Another way of putting the point, reaching back to an older and more venerable philosophy, that of David Hume (1978), is to say that there is a logical difference between claims about matters of fact ('is' statements) and claims about morality ('ought' statements), and that traditional evolutionary ethics violates this distinction (Hudson 1983; Ruse 1979a). One is deriving claims about the way one ought to behave ('found public libraries'; 'preserve the rain forests'), from claims about the way that things are ('Evolution works to preserve the fittest, to make humans dependent upon nature').

As it happens, I have considerable sympathy for these criticisms, and not simply because I am a professional philosopher. Indeed, as you will learn, I think David Hume was absolutely right to draw a distinction of kind between claims about matters of fact and claims about matters of obligation. This will be a key element in the evolutionary ethics that I myself will propose. But my experience is that those who endorse a traditional form of evolutionary ethics tend to find these arguments profoundly unconvincing – and not simply because they are not trained philosophers. Why should one claim that goodness is a non-natural property? Surely that is to presuppose the very point at issue?

And why should one declare *a priori* that there is ever a gap between 'is' and 'ought'? Perhaps there is usually, but what makes evolution exceptional – or so claim the enthusiasts – is that here uniquely one can bridge the gap. If it is all a question of personal intuition, then the traditional evolutionary ethicists beg to differ with respect to their intuitions. One cannot simply point to the difference in language. Deductions from talk of one kind to talk of another kind are meat and drink to scientists (Nagel 1961). There is surely at least as much a gap between talk of molecules and talk of pendulums as there is between talk of fact and talk of morality.

I suggest therefore that, although it may bring relief to an undergraduate in the middle of writing an exam, simply invoking a label like 'naturalistic fallacy' is no substitute for detailed philosophical argument. We must dig more deeply, and to do this we must turn back to the evolutionary ethicists and see precisely what they thought were the metaethical (although they probably never used this term) foundations of their moral theorizing. Once this is done, we shall be better able to critique them. (In fairness to Moore himself, I must report that he never thought that Spencer could be vanquished simply with the incantation 'naturalistic fallacy'. In *Principia Ethica*, Moore offers detailed argument, much in the spirit of that which I am about to offer, to refute the evolutionist.)

In fact, although I am insisting on doing the job properly, in truth this is very easy. To a person, the traditional evolutionary ethicist makes justificatory appeal to one thing, and one thing only. This is quite irrespective of the norm being prescribed. It is claimed simply that the process and pattern of evolution make sense. Change may be slow and seemingly meaningless; but when looked at as a whole, one sees that evolution is essentially *progressive*. It is not a meandering path, going nowhere. Rather, for all the undoubted backsliding, it is upward climb, from simplicity to complexity, from the single-celled organism to the multi-celled organism, from that which is a Jack-of-all-trades to that which incorporates an efficient division of labour, from the diffuse to the organized, from the homogenous to the heterogeneous. In short, from the monad to the man. (This last phrase is a term of Darwin's, although I do not think it was original to him. In the nineteenth century, 'man' was what people said and man was generally what people meant. See Darwin himself, especially his *Descent of Man* (1871), for confirmation of this point. Or, more quickly, see Ruse 1979b.)

For Spencer, for Rockerfeller, for Carnegie, for Haeckel, for Huxley, for Wilson, it is this progressiveness, this upward thrust, which is the defining mark of evolution.

> Whether it be in the development of the Earth, in the development of Life upon its surface, in the development of Society, of Government, of Manufactures, of Commerce, Language, Literature, Science, Art, this same evolution of the simple into the complex, through successive differentiations, holds throughout.
>
> (Spencer 1857, reprinted in Spencer 1868: 3)

And since this pattern is that which generates us humans as its unique, triumphant end point, we see that evolution is a process which, in itself, generates value. (For details, see Ruse 1988a, 1993.)

At once we have our metaethical justification. No one likes the fact that widows and children go to the wall – Spencer himself would have been horrified were any actions of his to lead directly to such a result – but unless we let the forces of nature have full reign, progress will stop, and (even worse) degeneration will set in. Short-term kindness may well lead to long-term disaster. Likewise for Haeckel. Unless we promote an efficient state, run by a trained bureaucracy, we could all decline to the flabby level of the French. Or Wilson. For him, sociality is everything, and thus judged he sees humans as the very pinnacle of the evolutionary process. His oft-expressed fear is that, if biodiversity be lost, then so also will go humankind. At best we will survive as stunted half-beings, if at all. (Wilson's progressionism comes through very clearly in his well-known *Sociobiology: The New Synthesis* (1975).

He links his biology to his ethics in the intensely personal *Biophilia* (1984).)

I will not labour this firmly established point about people's reading of evolution. What is fascinating historically is how much more powerful was Spencer's message of progress than his immediate prescriptions for social action. At the end of the last century in America we find, along with Rockerfeller and Carnegie, that the socialists and Marxists were putting themselves under the banner of Spencer in the name of progress (see Pittenger 1993)!

But, history notwithstanding, will it do? Let me say flatly at this point that I side with Julian Huxley's grandfather, Thomas Henry ([1894] 1989). He too felt the attractions of progressiveness – so do we all, for we are human and come out at the top – but, for the life of him, he could not see any justification for the belief. He valued humans more than others – his life was dedicated to the improvement of their lot – but he could not see that this was something to be read from the fact and processes of evolution.

The contrary, if anything, seems to be the case. To use examples in tune with our own time, why should we say that humans are the great success story of evolution? However you classify us, we humans have had a pathetically short life-span compared to the 150 million years that the dinosaurs ruled the globe; and, given our weapons of mass destruction, who would dare say that we will last into the future to outstrip the success of those extinct brutes? Or, if you insist on taking organisms still alive and well, can one honestly say that – from an evolutionary perspective – humans are that much more successful than, say, the AIDS virus? Of course, humans are more intelligent and more social and more in many other things that we humans value. But that is not quite the point. Anyone can set up their own criteria and then declare us the winners, especially if the criteria are 'humanlike' by another name. The point is whether in looking at evolution and its record, as it is, we see progress and an increase in value. And this is another matter. Bluntly, the answer is: 'No, we do not!' (An eloquent recent critique of progression in biology is to be found in Stephen Jay Gould's *Wonderful Life* (1989).)

What I conclude therefore is that, although traditional evolutionary ethics has far more variety and interest than one would suppose from the usual caricature, and although the usual dismissals of its metaethical foundations are (at the very least) more satisfying than convincing, ultimately it is deeply flawed. Indeed, to return once again to religion, my suspicion is that the progressionist reading of evolution is more a function of submerged Christian thoughts of redemption and ultimate salvation than it is of anything to be found in the fossil record. This is not necessarily to say that Christianity is wrong, but it is to say that it is not a true foundation for an adequate evolutionary ethics. (I do not draw the connection between progressionism and Christianity whimsically. Just take a look at E. O. Wilson's *On Human Nature*, a book authored by a man who has, by his own admission, moved from born-again Christianity to the theology of Darwinism. Spadefora (1990) discusses in detail the Christian roots of British progressionism.)

SOCIOBIOLOGY

Having refuted my case before I have begun, what can I possibly hope to do for an encore? Is this all there is to be said on the subject of evolution and ethics? I rather think not. There has always been an as yet undiscussed kind of sub-theme to writings on evolution and ethics, a sub-theme which I shall suggest leads to a far more satisfactory melding of the insights of the evolutionist with the demands of the ethicist.

Since it is only human to try to burnish one's thinking with the glory of the past – that is, when one is not taking the alternative strategy of claiming total originality – it would be nice to say that other way of bringing evolution to ethics is that which is truly Darwinian, as opposed to the more common approach, which we have seen is truly Spencerian. There is some truth to this, although to be candid, Darwin himself never really committed himself to one way of thinking about evolution and ethics. (Going the other way, the same should really be said of Spencer, who may not have been altogether inconsistent but who was nobody's fool. Darwin's most detailed discussion of ethics is in his *Descent of Man*. See also Murphy (1982) for discussion of Darwin's views. Spencer's most detailed discussion of ethics is in his *Principles of Ethics*. See Richards (1987) for a sympathetic discussion.)

What I will say is that with recent advances in evolutionary biology, advances which I will also say were certainly implicit in Darwin although not developed by him, the proper way to develop this sub-theme is now a great deal more obvious. Not that I want to take credit from those who have gone before me in travelling this path, most notably the Australian philosopher, the late John

Mackie (1978, 1979). (It was the fact that his efforts attracted almost hysterical animosity from those who fear the power of science, including the most unpleasant review I have ever seen penned in a philosophical journal (Midgley 1979), that first suggested to me that Mackie might be saying something of importance. See also Midgley 1985.)

First, then, let me talk about the science. When I have done that, I will turn to the concerns of moral philosophers, and as I have done for others, I will structure my discussion around the distinction between normative ethics and metaethics. I should say that as I begin – and here I speak as critically of my former self as I do of others – I intend what I have to say now to be taken a lot more literally than one usually takes discussions of fact in philosophical writings. It is our stock in trade to think up fanciful examples to illustrate philosophical points, and no one really thinks the worse if it be pointed out that the example could never really obtain. What I have to say now is at the cutting edge of science and requires a certain amount of projection and faith. But if the science be not essentially true, then my philosophy fails. I mean my evolutionary ethics to be genuinely evolutionary.

The advances to which I am referring come under the heading of 'sociobiology'. If life really is a struggle, and the race goes to the swift – less metaphorically, only some survive and (more importantly) reproduce – then, as Darwin (1859) pointed out, behaviour is just as important as physique. Adaptation is required in the world of action as well as that of form. It is no use having the build of Tarzan (or Jane), if your only interest in life is philosophy. If you are not prepared to make the effort and act on it, then your chances of reproduction and adding to the evolutionary line are minimal.

Of course, no one who takes natural selection seriously would ever want to deny this. The antelope fleeing the lion, the battle of the male walruses for mates, the mosquito in search of its feast of blood, these are the commonplaces of evolution. What is not quite so commonplace, or rather what is apparently just as commonplace but not quite so obvious, is the fact that behaviour is not exclusively a question of combat, hand raised against hand. As Darwin always stressed, the 'struggle' for existence must not be interpreted too literally. Often in this life, you can get far more by co-operating than by going at once into attack mode. *Social* behaviour can be a good biological strategy, as much or even more than blind antagonism.

Darwin thought much on these matters and discussed them extensively in the *Origin*. I have noted how he always favoured an interpretation of natural selection which focused on the individual, and this led to an intense interest in the social insects, especially the *hymenoptera* – ants, bees, wasps – where one seemingly has individuals (sterile 'workers') devoting their whole lives to the reproductive benefits of others. Primarily because he possessed no adequate theory of heredity, he was unable adequately to resolve what seemed to him to be in flat contradiction to his basic premises (see Ruse 1980).

However, some thirty years ago the breakthrough occurred when the then graduate student William Hamilton (1964a, b) saw that social co-operation is possible – can indeed be a direct result of natural selection – so long as the individual giving aid benefits biologically, *even if this benefit comes about vicariously*. Close relatives share the same units of heredity (genes), and so inasmuch as one's relatives succeed in life's struggles and reproduce, one is oneself reproducing, by proxy as it were. Hamilton pointed out that the social insects are just an extreme case of such co-operation, and that even they are no exception to selection's rule. (Anecdotally, for those who feel that their virtues go unappreciated by their teachers, I might say that his supervisor was so unimpressed with his work that it was only under extreme pressure that Hamilton was allowed to present his thesis – containing *the* major breakthrough in evolutionary thought in the past fifty years – for examination.)

This theory of 'kin selection', and related models, spurred massive interest in the evolution of social behaviour, both at the theoretical and at the observational levels. And with such interest came one overwhelming conclusion: although the social insects may be an extreme, co-operation is virtually the norm in the animal world rather than the exception. As soon as one gets into detailed study of just about any species – reptile, mammal, bird, invertebrate – one finds individuals working together. Most often this is between mates and relatives, parents and children for instance, but it can even occur between strangers and possibly across species. (Non-relative co-operation is usually thought to be a form of enlightened self-interest, and is revealingly ascribed to 'reciprocal altruism'. See Trivers 1971. If you are interested in the science then Wilson's

Sociobiology: The New Synthesis is still very informative. The writings of Richard Dawkins, especially his *The Blind Watchmaker* and his updated *The Selfish Gene* (second edition 1989) are most helpful, as is Helena Cronin's *The Ant and the Peacock*. A good collection, giving some indication of the technical side to the work is J. Krebs and N. Davies' *Behavioural Ecology: An Evolutionary Approach*. The review journal *Trends in Evolution and Ecology* has clearly written, pertinent discussions in almost every issue.)

Now, without wanting to seem tendentious, let me pause for a moment, and – putting on my philosophical hat – make a terminological point. Famously, notoriously, the theory about which I am talking, a theory which shows how even the most giving of actions can be related back to self-interest, has been labelled the 'selfish gene' view of evolution (Dawkins 1976). As it happens, I think this is a terrific term – it is a brilliant use of language to hammer home a basic point – but note that it is a metaphor. Genes are not selfish – nor are their possessors as such. Selfishness is a human attribute, something which results of thinking only of yourself and not of others. I have no reason to believe that ants or bees or wasps ever think, so literally speaking neither they nor their genes are selfish. The point of using the term 'selfish' is to draw attention to the fact that the units of inheritance work in such a way as to benefit their possessor's biological ends, whatever the behaviour.

Some philosophers (most notably the very same who was so rude about Mackie) have objected that one should never use such a metaphor as selfish gene (Midgley 1979, 1985). But this is just plain silly. I doubt if you could even open your mouth without using a metaphor, certainly not express a coherent thought. (Where do you think the word 'express' comes from?) Scientists use them all the time – 'work', 'force', 'attraction', and all the rest. The point, however, is that you should be careful with your metaphors, and should not kid yourself that they prove more than they do. As I have just said, genes may be selfish: that is no warrant for thinking the same may be true of ants.

Which brings me to the nub of what I want to say, speaking philosophically. The flip side to the selfish gene is the co-operating organism. The term that biologists use here is 'altruism', and they thus speak happily of the widespread altruism that they have discovered through the animal world (Trivers 1971; West Eberhard 1975). But I want to stress that this is no less metaphorical. 'Altruism', like 'selfishness', is a human term. It means not thinking of yourself but thinking of others. Mother Teresa is an altruist, as she bathes the brow of the dying poor of Calcutta. Just as I have no reason to think that ants are selfish, so in this sense I have no reason to think that ants are altruists.

My point, then, is simply that we should remember that the biologists' term 'atruist' is a technical term, with only a metaphorical connection to the literal human term. It speaks not of intentions or thinking or anything like that, but rather is used simply to designate social behaviour which one has reason to think occurs because ultimately it benefits the biological ends of the performer. A bird which helps to raise its siblings is (most probably) this kind of 'altruist'. Hence, although it would be somewhat precious were biologists to insist on putting their word in quotation marks, for this discussion I shall show its metaphorical nature by always so doing.

'HOMO SAPIENS': FROM 'ALTRUISM' TO ALTRUISM

Animal 'altruism' is a fact of nature, and we now have a good theoretical understanding of its existence. Let me therefore move straight to the organism which interests me, namely *Homo sapiens*. In the technical biological sense I have just been discussing, we humans are 'altruists' *par excellence*. People often say that our defining characteristic is our use of language. I rather would almost say that it is our 'altruism'; although I am cheating a bit because I would count language as one of our chief means for effecting such 'altruism'. The point is that we co-operate flat out and because we do co-operate we succeed mightily in surviving and reproducing.

Of course, I am not saying that we humans never quarrel and fight, even unto the death. I am hardly that insensitive to the dreadful events of this century. But even if you take into account the carnage of the two world wars, not forgetting the deaths of six million Jews and twenty million Russians, the human species still comes low on the scale of mammalian intra-specific carnage. The murder rate in a pride of lions is far higher than that in the slums of Detroit. And without forgetting the counter-evidence, all that pop-talk about humans being the killer apes, with the mark of Cain forever on their foreheads, is just plain nonsense.

Humans did not simply wake up one morning and decide to be

'altruists'. Their evolution has clearly been one of feedback, with social success promoting the evolution of yet more efficient tools of co-operation, be these positive like speech, or negative like our low excitability levels. (Try putting a troop of chimpanzees together in a philosophy class for an hour, especially if one of the females is in heat.) Obviously the evolution of the brain has been important, but so also have other things like the hand with its opposable thumb. At the same time, we have failed to acquire or have lost other features possessed by many mammals: for instance, the large teeth which can be used for attack or to tear apart and digest large chunks of raw meat.

I will not spend time here giving a detailed discussion of the ways in which palaeoanthropologists (students of human evolution) think that we have actually evolved (see Isaac 1983; Pilbeam 1984). Probably at some crucial point, coming from our ape ancestors, we were scavengers, stealing the kills of fiercer animals. This would obviously put a major premium on 'altruism', as would another suggested factor, namely the threat that roving bands of humans would pose towards their fellow bands. At the risk of sounding desperately politically incorrect, male strife for mates may well have been significant here, especially if contemporary anthropological evidence is any judge (see Ruse 1989a, especially Chapter 7); combined, if my own experience is any measure, with whacking great doses of female choice. (In his book on our species, *The Descent of Man*, Darwin argued that a sexual selection of partners is very important.)

We humans are 'altruists', meaning that we co-operate for the biological ends of survival and reproduction. The next question is how exactly our 'altruism' gets put into action. To use an Aristotelian term, what are the proximate causes of our 'altruism'? How do we set about being 'altruists'? I can think of at least three possible ways, and in respects I suspect that we humans have taken all three.

The first is the way of the ants (Hölldobler and Wilson 1990). They are, to make heavy use of metaphor, hardwired to work together. They do not have to learn to co-operate. The instructions are burned into their brains by their genes. Their 'altruism' is innate, in the strongest possible sense. And clearly, this kind of 'altruism' is to be found among humans in many ways. Anybody who has seen the care and affection shown by a mother towards her young child has to be moved by its basic animal nature. It is not something for which one strives or has to learn. It is there. (This is not to deny that there are 'freaks' who do not have this instinct any more than that there are people born without two legs. Although, given the realization in recent years of just how strong is the need of biological parents to find their adopted-away children, and conversely, I suspect that these emotions run much deeper than any of us used to imagine.)

Of course, I am not saying that this kind of innate 'altruism' is everything to humans. We are not ants. Much that we do socially requires learning, and – a point to which I shall return – we seem to have a dimension of freedom, of flexibility, not possessed by the ants – which is just as well, biologically speaking. Genetic hard-wiring is just fine and dandy, so long as nothing goes wrong. But when there are new challenges, it is powerless to pull back and reconsider. Ants, for instance, do much of their travelling outside the nest guided by chemical ('pheromone') trails. Generally this is incredibly efficient: there is no need to buy a map or a guide to find your way. But a major disturbance like a thunderstorm can spell disaster, with the loss of literally hundreds of insects.

Ants can afford this loss. (I speak now in universal terms, but you can put the point in terms of individual selection.) Mother ant has millions of offspring. What is the loss of a few hundred? Humans, to the contrary, in major part because of the kind of social strategy we have taken, cannot afford such a loss. Rather than having many offspring in which we invest relatively little care, we have but a few offspring in which we invest much care. One cannot risk losing a kid in a shower of rain every time it goes to McDonald's. Hence, ubiquitous genetic innateness is not for us. We need an 'altruism' which allows for problem solving. (I cannot go into the details here, but there is a major biological literature on the comparative benefits of adopting high/low off-spring parental investment strategies. Generally humans are very high investment strategists; but, it is thought that there may be biological reasons why some societies or religions encourage large families and why others do not. Any good ecology textbook will discuss the question of investment strategies. A quick introduction can be found in *Evolution: A Biological and Palaeontological Approach* edited by Peter Skelton. Reynolds and Tanner (1983) talks about humans and the biology of their religion.)

The need for problem-solving ability points very clearly to the second way of effecting 'altruism'. Why not simply have very

239

efficient on-board computers (call them 'brains', if you will) that allow us to negotiate with our fellows, and if a certain course of social action is in our biological self-interests we will decide to act positively on it, and not otherwise? Co-operation will come about simply because it is the rational thing to do. Note that there is no morality involved here, but neither is there immorality. Beings with super-brains are often portrayed in fiction as being like Darth Vader – evil and wanting to conquer the world. However, if everyone were similarly endowed, I see no reason why there should be constant strife. To me, the intelligent moves would seem to go the other way.

Again, I think we humans have taken this strategy to some extent. Much of our lives we do spend in negotiation and bargaining, without much more being involved than self-interest. I buy a loaf of bread from the baker: he gives me the bread, I give him the money. Neither is doing the other a favour, but neither is doing the other down. We have a happy division of labour, where I do my thing and he does his, and everybody else does theirs, and then (through the monetary system) we get together to swap the fruits of our efforts. From an overall evolutionary perspective, taking home one loaf of bread may seem a bit far from having more children; but, ultimately, this is what it all adds up to. (See Axelrod 1984 for a very clear and informative discussion of these issues.)

However, again this is not all that there is to human 'altruism' and again there are good biological reasons why it is not. Apart from the fact that there may be biological constraints on producing humans with mega-brains – how wide a pelvis did you want your mother to have? – negotiating towards a perfect solution has its costs too. Most obviously, it can take a great deal of time, and time in evolutionary terms is money. Often what one wants in biology is a quick and dirty solution – something which works pretty well, pretty cheaply, most of the time – rather than perfection with its attendant price. It is not much use working out if it is in your biological interests to save your chum from the tiger if, by the time you have finished your sums, you are both in the tiger's belly.

This points us towards the third strategy for achieving human 'altruism', something which can be more readily grasped by means of an analogy. The second way, just discussed, highlights a problem much akin to that faced by the people who built the first generation of chess-playing computers. They programmed in all of the right moves and then discovered that the computers were virtually useless because, after a couple of moves, they were paralysed. Time stood still as they ran through all the possible options, seeking the best. But, unfortunately, in this real world, we just do not have the luxury of infinite time.

Now, however, we have chess-playing computers which are very good indeed. They do not always win against the top competition; but, even the best of human players are now firmly in their sights. How is this possible? Simply because the computers are programmed to recognize (say 'recognize' if you dislike the anthropomorphism) certain situations, and to act then according to predetermined strategies. Sometimes the strategies fail the computers, and they lose. But generally the strategies, built on past experience, prove reliable and the computers can win within specified times.

I would argue that humans are much like the new breed of chess machines: we have certain built-in strategies, hard-wired into our brains if you like, which we bring into play and which guide our actions when we are faced with certain social situations. Sometimes things do not work out – I will talk more about this in a moment – but generally these strategies provide just the kind of quick and dirty solution that we super-'altruists' require.

One more step is needed to complete my argument, and you can probably guess what it is going to be. How do these strategies present themselves to us in our consciousness? In a word, they are the rules of moral conduct! We think that we ought to do certain things and that we ought not to do other things, because this is our biology's way of making us break from our usual selfish or self-interested attitudes and to get on with the job of co-operating with others. In short, what I am arguing is that in order to make us 'altruists' in the metaphorical biological sense, biology has made us altruists in the literal, moral sense.

In the language of the evolutionist, therefore, morality is no more – although certainly no less – than an adaptation, and as such has the same status as such things as teeth and eyes and noses. And, as I come to the end of this part of my discussion, let me stress, as I stressed earlier, I mean this claim to be a literal matter of biological fact. I am pushing out somewhat from firmly established truth. But, although here I simply do not have room to go into empirical details – I must nevertheless mention that we

241

now have knowledge of what, at the very least, can be described as quasi-morality from the ape world (De Waal 1982; Goodall 1986) – if I am wrong, then I am afraid that you are wasting your time as you read on. (In my *Taking Darwin Seriously* (1986) I do talk more about the empirical evidence.)

SUBSTANTIVE QUESTIONS

Let us return to the philosophical questions, and being guided (as promised) by our twofold distinction, let us ask first about the substantive ethics that I am proposing. In truth, a point which might rather disappoint you, I do not have anything very surprising to say at this stage. In fact, I am rather pleased because I am always very wary of sweeping claims to originality – they are usually wrong or have been said by somebody before. More seriously, it would seem to me to be profoundly implausible if no one before Darwin had ever grasped the essence of substantive ethics properly understood, and profoundly depressing to me as a professional philosopher if no philosopher before Darwin had ever had things of importance to say on such matters.

Indeed, let me speak more strongly that this. As one who is trying to bring ethics into tune with modern science, in the strong sense of wanting to show how ethics can be grounded (I use this word without prejudice to what I shall be arguing shortly about justification) in evolutionary thought, I am clearly what is known as a philosophical 'naturalist' (Ruse 1995). And this being so, my crucial intent is to do justice to the way that things are – how people feel about morality and how it has evolved – rather than how some idealist would like them to be. I would be deeply worried if what I wanted to say was not, at some level, general knowledge. The astronomer tries to explain why the sun rises above the horizon. He or she does not deny this is what we see.

(Is this not to admit that I shall fail to tackle the real problem of the moral philosopher – prescription of the true nature of morality? I think not, for this is to confuse the preacher with the teacher. The job of the moral philosopher is not to prescribe some new morality, but to explain and justify the nature of morality as we know it. This, of course, may involve showing that our present beliefs are inconsistent, and on the basis of such a conclusion the philosopher may urge us to rethink some of our beliefs. The point is that, from the pre-Socratics on, no philosopher *qua* philosopher has tried to spin substantive ethics out of thin air. Think of how Plato, a master at telling us what we should do, was forever getting his circle to reflect on its experiences and feelings.)

What I want to say, therefore, is that the kind of being on whose evolution I was speculating in the last section, that is to say ourselves, is one whose prescriptive morality is going to be fairly commonplace – 'commonplace' in the sense of familiar, and not at all in the sense of trivial or unimportant (Mackie 1977). One is going to feel an obligation to help people, especially those in need, like children, the old, the sick. One will feel that one ought to give up one's seat to a mother with a young child, or to an old man bent over with arthritis – one should not need asking. One will feel that one ought to try to be fair, and not to be influenced by favouritism. Therefore, a male professor should not give a higher mark to a pretty young woman because she is pretty, nor, if she has earned it, should he withhold one because she is a woman – conversely for female professors and their male students. One will feel that one should not be wantonly cruel, or thought-less. Leaving your children at home to go on holiday might make a good movie, but in real life it is wrong because it is unkind and irresponsible.

If you complain to me that moral prescriptions ought to be about sterner things, like murder and stealing and the like, I shall agree that morality should cover these. Let me assure you that, as an evolutionary ethicist, I am against them. But I would also point out that most moral decisions are much more low key for most of us most of the time. I have never felt the urge to rob a bank and if I did I would not know how to set about it. I have had a lot of pretty young women in my classes. This is part of what I mean by saying that morality (in the sense of normative ethics) is commonplace.

If you complain to me that this all starts to sound like warmed-over Christianity, I shall agree again. 'Love your neighbour as yourself,' sounds like a pretty good guide to life to me, and I gather it has also to many other people in non-Christian cultures. I take it that a major reason why Christianity was such a raging success was that it did speak to fairly basic feelings that humans had about themselves and their fellow humans. But I do not want to give all the glory to religion. Secular thinkers have grasped the major insights of morality (prescriptively speaking) also. Immanuel Kant (1959), for instance, put tremendous emphasis on respecting people for their own sake, as persons. Is this not a major basis of co-operation?

Actually, speaking of Kantians, you will have noticed that I claim one major part of morality is the urge towards fairness. In fact, I would say that this is a very major part; although perhaps I am prejudiced as one who is the father of five children and who has spent his whole adult life as a teacher. Humans spend incredible amounts of time worrying about getting their fair share. I am convinced that we would all happily accept another dime on the dollar in taxes if we knew at last that the filthy rich would pay their dues.

Today's most eminent neo-Kantian moral philosopher has made a whole system out of fairness, and it is just the sort of system favoured and expected by the evolutionist. In particular, John Rawls (1971) invites us to put ourselves in a 'position of ignorance'. If we knew beforehand what kind of place and talents we were to have in society, then we would (out of self-interest) rationally argue for a system which maximally rewarded such persons as us. Knowing that you were going to be female, intelligent and healthy, would make you argue for the benefits properly accruing to the female, intelligent and healthy.

But what if you end up as male, dumb and sick? Rawls suggests that, given our ignorance about our ticket in life's lottery, we should aim for a just society, where this is to be interpreted as a fair society, where everyone gets the best out of society that could possibly be arranged. (This does not mean total equality. If the only way you can get the best people to be doctors is by paying them twice as much as anyone else, then we all benefit by such an uneven distribution.)

It seems to me that this is just the kind of set-up that our genes would favour. If we are going to have to get along and everybody wants a share of the pie, then let us have some way of sharing it out as evenly as possible. In fact, as Rawls himself notes, the evolutionist nicely closes a gap that has always faced the Social Contract theorist, which is what Rawls (and Kant before him) exemplifies. It is all very well talking about positions of ignorance, but this is surely hypothetical. Hence, while it may do to give an analysis of morality, it hardly does to explain its origin. But if we put on the genes (as selected in life's struggles) the burden of explaining how actually morality came into play, there is no longer need to suppose some surely fictional bunch of proto-humans sitting around talking of 'positions of ignorance' and planning moral strategies.

Indeed, I would make the case even more strongly than this. One of the major weaknesses of any system of morality like Rawls' (or Kant's before him) that tries to derive moral rules from rational principles of self-interest is that it really cannot get at the true nature of morality. To pick up again on Hume's is/ought distinction, a defining mark of moral claims is that they really do seem to be different – there is a sense of obligation about them that is missing from a simple factual statement. Even if you think that the gap can be bridged, then it is surely up to you to show how this is to be done. And simply translating morality in terms of self-interest is not enough. The whole point is that Mother Teresa is not helping the sick and dying out of self-interest. She is doing it because it is right.

Here is a point of real strength in the evolutionist's approach. He or she argues that there is indeed something logically distinct about the nature of moral claims. The is/ought barrier is not to be jumped or ignored. The key point, never to be forgotten, is that we are in many respects self-centred. Nature has made us that way and it is just as well, or we would never survive and reproduce. Imagine if every time you got a piece of bread you gave it away! Imagine if every time you fell in love you denied your feelings so someone else could take your place! But because we have taken the route of sociality, we need a mechanism to make us break through that self-centred nature on many, many occasions. Evolution has given us this logically odd sense of oughtness to do precisely that. (Incidentally, I am not insensitive to the fact that there is little surprise that modern-day Social Contract theories and modern-day versions of Darwinism coincide, because they have shared roots in eighteenth-century political thought. But I do not take this coincidence to be refuting or weakening of either. The point is that they both work, in their respective domains.)

Two more points, and then I am done with the normative side to my case. You may be wondering if I am not a little bit too ecumenical in my attitude to other moral systems, religious and secular. Christianity, Kantianism, probably utilitarianism, and more. Should one not plump for one system and have done with it? After all, as moral philosophers delight in showing, there are certain crucial cases where one system succeeds and others fail. (Paradigm example: You are held prisoner by a vile regime. If you can escape, you have the knowledge and means to end this rule and save the lives and happiness of millions. But to do so, you must bribe the guard with your chocolate ration. Should you do so? Most systems cry out 'yes'. The Kantian regrets, however, that you are not treating the guard as a person in his own right.)

Again, I would claim a strength not a weakness for the evolutionist. The simple fact of the matter is that it is the philosopher's stock in trade to look for counter-examples to established moral systems. But most of the time, the well-known and tried systems agree on what one should do. Kantian, Christian and everyone else agrees that you should not hurt small children for fun, and that if you are blessed with plenty then you should help the poor person at your door. Standard moral systems do not urge you to do crazy moral things.

And where there are points of conflict, perhaps this tells us something about morality itself. Moral philosophers tend to think that their own favoured moral system can solve all the problems, so long as you push it long enough and hard enough – and perhaps this is a reasonable belief if you think that morality is backed by a good God or a Platonic form or some such thing. But, if you deny such a foundation, it could just be that there are some problems where there are no proper moral solutions. We may have to make a decision, because life must go on, but there is no uniquely compelling right answer. We are going to feel badly, whatever we do.

This, it seems to me, is precisely what the evolutionist would expect. Adaptations are rarely perfect. Big brains are a bright idea and so is bipedalism. Put them together and you have the agony of human childbirth. Biological life is a matter of compromise, building the best that you can with the materials that nature has dealt you. Ethics is a good adaptation, but sometimes it simply breaks down, and cannot function. The oddity is to think this a surprise rather than an expectation.

Yet, is there nothing that my kind of evolutionary ethicist would say that would give us pause to think? I believe there is one such thing – familiar and yet somewhat disturbing. This concerns the scope of (normative) ethics. 'Love your neighbour as yourself.' Yes, but who is my neighbour? And what should I do about those who are not my neighbour?

The Arabs have the answer: 'My brother and I against our cousin. My cousin and I against the stranger.' This was surely first spoken by a sociobiologist. Biologically, one is more closely related to one's siblings than to one's cousins, and to one's cousins than to strangers. One would certainly expect the emotions to grow more faint as the blood ties loosened. The obligations would loosen. This is not to say that they would vanish, nor is it to say that without blood ties there can be no morality. Where kin selection fails, reciprocal altruism provides a back-up. But again, as one grew more distant in one's social relationship, one would expect the feelings to decline.

I want to emphasize that I am not just talking about warm feelings of love here, but of morality. I believe that my kind of evolutionary ethicist expects the very call of morality to decline as one moves more and more out from one's immediate circle. Of course we love our children more than we do those of others; but, also, we have a stronger sense of morality towards them. And the same is true of our immediate neighbours and friends, as opposed to those more distant. I stress that, even towards strangers, the sociobiologist can see reason for some moral feelings – we are all here together on planet earth – but it is silly to pretend that our dealings across countries are going to be that intimate or driven much beyond self-interest.

As it happens, although this may seem a somewhat stern conse-quence – as a person with somewhat mushy left-wing sentiments, I confess that I myself felt somewhat uncomfortable when I first drew it – it is not really so much out of line with traditional thought. Historically, ethicists of all stripes have divided somewhat on this question, and how they have divided seems to have had little to do *per se* with whether they were religious or secular.

There are some who have said flatly that one has an equal obligation to everyone, whether they be your favourite child or a stranger in an unknown land. Everyone is my neighbour. That is precisely the moral to be drawn from the parable of the Good Samaritan. Others have argued for a more restricted morality, arguing that there is a falling away of the moral imperatives as one moves farther from oneself, one's family, one's friends, one's society and one's country. The whole point of the parable is that the Good Samaritan saw the man injured by the road. At that point they did become neighbours. Jesus did not suggest that the Samari-tan was in the general business of charity to strangers (Wallwork 1982).

Reporting on myself, I have found that, as one thinks about

these things, my intuitions start to fall in line with the evolutionary implications. Suppose you learnt that your philosophy professor, known to have a family dependent on him or her, was giving virtually all of his or her salary to some charity for African relief, and that as a result the family was living on hand-outs from the Salvation Army and the local soup kitchen. Would you think such a person a saint or a moral monster? Or what about yourself? Are you on a par with a child killer because you do not give every last penny to relief, even though you know full well that the money you could give probably would make a life and death difference to more than one person? (I am not saying that you should not give more than you do.)

I think it interesting that charities have come to realize that their advertising is much more effective if they show pictures of people in actual need. These, and in like fashion television reports of people in dire straits, bring the needy into our neighbourhood, just as effectively as if they had moved in. 'Charity begins at home' is the motto of the evolutionary ethicist.

FOUNDATIONS?

With good reason you may be wondering now about the meta-ethics of the position I am explaining and promoting. I have explained the problems of progress and the distinction between 'is' statements and 'ought' statements, carefully arguing that the distinction is a crucial piece of my overall picture. How then can I go on to talk about justification? Have I not undercut my own position? Even if you agree with me, more or less, about the normative claims I would make, and in fact I think there are many moral philosophers roughly sympathetic to something along the lines I have sketched, is not the metaethical position impossible? Or at least, does one not have to go outside the bounds of evolutionary biology for help and support?

I rather think not, although I am not sure that you will much like the answer I am now about to give – helpfully, I will give you biological reasons why you will not like the answer I am about to give. What I want to argue is that there are no foundations to normative ethics. If you think that to be true a claim has to refer to some particular thing or things, my claim is that in an important sense normative ethics is false. Although, to be frank, I prefer not to use the word 'false' here, for I have no intention of denying that a claim like 'Rape is wrong' is true.

What I want to argue is that the claims of normative ethics are like the rules of a game. In baseball, it is true that after three strikes the batter is out; but this claim does not have any reference or correspondence in absolute reality. Indeed, one can imagine a game where it took four strikes to get the batter out. Whether ethics has this kind of flexibility – could one imagine a case where rape is not always wrong? – is a matter I will raise in a moment. The point now is that normative ethics is indeed not justified by progress or anything else of a natural kind, for it is not justified in this way by anything!

The position I am endorsing is known technically as 'ethical scepticism', and I must stress that the scepticism is about the metaethical foundations, not the prescriptions of ethics (Mackie 1977). Alternatively, it is known as 'non-cognitivism', although I shall be at pains shortly to explain where I differ from other non-cognitivist positions like 'emotivism'. A major attraction to my position in my eyes is that one simply cannot be guilty of committing the naturalistic fallacy or violating the is/ought barrier, because one is simply not in the justification business at all. To use a sporting metaphor, instead of trying to drive through these things, one does an end run around them.

This is all very well, but am I not just stating my preferred position, rather than arguing for it? What right have I to say, *as an evolutionist*, that normative ethics has no foundation? I may not offer justification for normative ethics; but, surely, I must offer justification for the claim that normative ethics has no justification! In fact, this I think I can do, for (to use the language of causes and reasons) I believe that sometimes when one has given a causal analysis of why someone believes something, one has shown that the call for reasoned justification is inappropriate – there is none (Murphy 1982). I would argue that we have just such a case here. I have argued that normative ethics is a biological adaptation, and I would argue that as such it can be seen to have no being or reality beyond this. We believe normative ethics for our own (biological) good, and that is that. The causal account of why we believe makes inappropriate the inquiry into the justification of what we believe.

An analogy may help. In the First World War, on the death of their loved ones, many of the survivors back at home turned to spiritualism for solace. And sure enough, through the ouija board or whatever would come the comforting messages: 'It's alright Mum! Don't worry about me! I've gone to a better place. I'm just waiting for you and Dad.' Now, how do we explain these messages, other than through outright fraud, which may have happened sometimes but I am sure did not happen universally? The answer is surely not to offer the justification that the late Private Higgins, sitting on a cloud, dressed in a bedsheet, and holding a number four sized harp, was speaking to his mum and dad. Rather, one would say (truly) that the strain of the loss, combined with known facts about human nature, yield a causal explanation that make any further inquiry redundant.

The same is the case for normative ethics, except that – rather than an individual illusion – here we have a collective illusion of the genes, bringing us all in (except for the morally blind). We need to believe in morality, and so, thanks to our biology, we do believe in morality. There is no foundation 'out there', beyond human nature.

But can this truly be so? Is my analogy well taken? Consider another analogy. Our eyes are no less an adaptation than is our normative ethics. They have a more secure status in the opinion of some. They too help in the business of living: for instance, in the avoidance of danger as exemplified by the speeding train heading towards us. Would anyone seriously suggest that this means that the train does not have an objective existence, independent of us? Why then should we assume that our normative ethics fails to have an objective existence, independent of us? Why should our moral sense, if we can so call it, be a trickster in a way that is not true of our more conventional five senses (see Nozick 1981)?

Actually, I am not that sure that our regular senses never do deceive us for our own good. Sight is a pretty complex matter, with a fair amount of input by the looker. But leave this, for I fully agree that the train does have an independent existence. My counter is that I am not sure that the analogy between external objects like the train and substantive ethics holds true.

Think for the moment about the train. Why do we, as evolutionists, think it has an external existence, and is not just a figment of our senses? First, because there is no obvious reason why our senses would deceive us at this point. Why think there is an approaching train if there is no train? Second, because there are good reasons why we would think there is a train and why our senses would not deceive us. Trains kill. More than this: even if there were no need to think there was a train, we would think there is a train. Do I really need to think there is (say) a moon. Third, because, although we humans may have our distinctive ways of finding out about trains, it seems that (if necessary) other organisms likewise can find out about trains in their ways – through sounds or pheromones or whatever.

I am not sure that any of these points hold in the case of normative ethics. There are very good reasons why we would believe in normative ethics whether it has independent existence or not. We need it for 'altruism'. Perhaps if such ethics does exist, we would believe in it – let me be fair, I am sure we would – but if we did not need it, I cannot imagine it would be in evolution's interest to make us aware of it. And I simply cannot see how one would get at such ethics without the moral sense or something akin (which, I am happy to agree, may not be exclusively human).

Let me put my collective point another way. Do we really need an objectively existing normative ethics to believe in it? I can see nothing in the argument I have given for the existence of normative ethics which supposes that it exists 'out there', whatever that might mean. In fact, let me put things more strongly. An objective ethics strikes me as being redundant, which is a pretty funny state of affairs for an objective ethics. ('You should do this because God wants you to; but, anyway, whatever God wants, you will believe that you should do it.')

If there is no objective ethics, and if you do not believe in progress (as I do not), then you might think that nature could have had other ways of getting you to co-operate – after all, to get from A to B, humans walk, horses run, fish swim, birds fly, snakes slither, monkeys swing. But, far from taking this as an objection, my response is that this might well have been the case. In the 1950s, at the height of the Cold War, the American Secretary of State, John Foster Dulles, thought he had a moral obligation to hate (rather than love) the Russians. But he realized that they felt the same way about him. Therefore, we had a very successful system of reciprocation. Why should not nature have provided a Dulles morality rather than a Christian/Kantian/etc. morality?

We now seem to have the position that objective morality could exist but that it is quite other than anything we believe. 'God wants us to hate our neighbours, but because of our biology we think we should love them.' 'God is indifferent to rape, but because of our biology we think it is wrong.' This is even more of a paradox than before and yet one more reason why I want to drop the whole talk of objective foundations. I admit, of course, that my Dulles morality shares with our morality some kind of structuring according to formal rules of reciprocation; but as I have pointed out earlier, this in itself is simply not morality. 'I will help you if you will help me' is simply not normative ethics. Hence I feel confident in arguing that ethical scepticism is not only the answer to the evolutionist's needs, but the way pointed by evolution.

(Incidentally, before you accuse me of being needlessly and heretically offensive about rape, let me point out that the whole question of rape, biology and religion is very complex. Some sociobiologists think that there could be biological reasons why some men are rapists (Thornhill and Thornhill 1983). Some Christians think it is by no means top of the sin list. Aquinas put rape below homosexuality and masturbation, because the former only violates another human being whereas the latter violate God. See Ruse 1988b.)

OBJECTIONS AND CONSEQUENCES

There are all sorts of implications and questions that my position raises. Let me conclude my discussion by mentioning three of the most common.

First, there is the question of determinism. The most common charge against human sociobiology is that it is an exercise in biological or genetic 'determinism' (Allen *et al.* 1976; Burian 1981). It is not always made crystal clear what exactly this means, but whatever it is, it is not a good thing. Most obviously, in the present connection, if the charge be well taken, it throws serious doubt on the whole enterprise of articulating an evolutionary ethics. The most crucial presupposition of ethics, speaking now at the normative level, is that we have a dimension of freedom. You must be able to choose between right and wrong, otherwise there is no credit for good actions and equally no credit for bad ones.

However – drawing now as much on standard philosophical results as much as on biology – although one can see that this charge does point to some important aspects of my evolutionary ethics, it certainly does not point to unique or unanswerable problems. Perhaps, indeed, the contrary is the case. And to see this, consider for a moment the level at which my science does suppose that there is a direct genetic causal input. It is in the structuring of our thinking in such a way that we believe in moral norms. (I am not denying that a mad psychologist could probably rear a child to be morally blind. Hence, even here I am allowing – demanding – an environmental causal input. But I do want to argue for a strong sense of genetic determinism at this point.) However, did any moral thinker, except perhaps the French existentialists at their most bizarre and unconvincing, ever truly think that we choose the rules of moral action? This is what makes traditional Social Contract thinking so implausible. Moral choice comes into whether or not we obey the rules of morality, not whether we choose the rules themselves. We are not free to decide whether or not murder is wrong. It is! The freedom comes in deciding if we are going to kill, nevertheless.

My morality certainly allows for freedom at this level. Indeed, the whole point is that we humans are (not exclusively) like the ants, in being determined in all our actions. We have a dimension of flexibility. Although (and because) morality is an adaptation, I am not saying that we will always be moral – for biological or non-biological reasons we may break from it. The point is that we can break from it. To use an analogy, whereas ants are rather like simple (and cheap) rockets shot off at a target, we humans are like the more complex (and expensive) missiles which possess homing devices able to correct and change direction in mid-flight.

(This analogy does highlight the fact that I am committed to some sort of general causal determinism. But in line with other philosophers, notably David Hume (1978), I would argue that such determinism is a condition of moral choice rather than a barrier. Technically, I am a 'soft determinist' or 'compatibilist'. See Hudson 1983.)

Second, what about the question of relativism? Since I am a subjectivist, at least not an objectivist in believing in some sort of external foundation for morals, does not this mean that at some level 'anything goes'? Am I not reduced to the misguided therapist's: 'If it feels good to you, then that's OK'. Such a conclusion would indeed be the very refutation of my philosophy. I would immediately set about denying my premises! But, fortunately, I am able to argue that the very opposite is the case, for I am a subjectivist of a very distinctive kind. For a start, the whole point about having morality as an adaptation is that it has to be a *shared* adaptation. If I alone am moral and you are not, then you will win and I and my blood-line will soon be eliminated. Morality (in the sense of normative ethics) is a social phenomenon, and unless we all have it, it fails.

In this respect, morality is like speech where, without shared comprehension, it is pointless. Of course, language does vary across cultures and so does morality somewhat. But, just as Noam Chomsky (1957) has shown that language may yet share a (biologically based) 'deep structure', so I would argue that the same may well be true of morality. In line with conventional philosophical thought about ethical norms, it would seem to me that particular manifestations of the norms may vary according to circumstance, while the underlying structure remains constant.

Perhaps I must concede inter-galactic relativism (Ruse 1989a); but, for humans here on earth, given their shared evolutionary history, I am not much of a relativist. Yet there is another point about my subjectivism which is worth making. Although I am a non-cognitivist, in crucial respects, quite apart from the biology (or perhaps because of the biology), I differ from other non-cognitivists. For someone like the emotivist, normative ethics has to be translated out as a report on feelings, perhaps combined with a bit of exhortation. 'I don't like killing! Boo Hoo! Don't you do it either!' (See Ayer 1946; Hudson 1983.) For me, this is simply not strong enough. I believe that, if emotivism be the complete answer, genes for cheating would soon make a spectacular appearance in the human species – or rather, those genes already existing would make an immediate gain.

The way in which biology avoids this happening is by making moral claims seem *as if they were objective*! To use a useful if ugly word of Mackie (1979), we 'objectify' morality. We think that killing is wrong because it seems to us that killing *is* wrong. Somehow, whatever the truth may be, the foundation of morality does seem to be something 'out there', binding on us.

In other words, what I want to suggest is that – *contra* to the emotivists – the *meaning* of morality is that it is objective. Because it is not, it is in this sense that it is an illusion; although, because it is, this is a reason why it is not relative – not to mention why you are finding my arguments so implausible! (This is also a reason why I do not fear that my telling you all this will let you go away and sin with inpunity. Your genes are a lot stronger than my words. The truth does not always set you free.)

Third, what about predecessors? My rather gloomy experience, when I have made a successful argument, is that somebody will claim that it has all been made before. Although, actually, as with the science and with normative ethics, I am fairly happy to seek and acknowledge that others have been there before me. The most obvious pre-evolutionary predecessor is Immanuel Kant (1949, 1959), for not only did he have a form of Social Contract ethics but he (like me) argued that one should not seek the foundation of ethics in some sort of external reality, 'out there'. Rather, Kant argued that we find the basis for ethics in the interrelation of rational beings as they attempt to live and work together. Without ethics, in the normative sense, we run into 'contradictions', where these are to be understood as failures of social living rather than anything in a formal sort of way. (This is also the position of Rawls (1980).)

Yet, although I am quite sympathetic to the Kantian perspective – after all, I have spoken in a positive way of Rawls' system of moral philosophy – I believe that, in one crucial way, my system of evolutionary ethics can never be that of the Kantian. For Kant, the ethics we have is uniquely that possessed by rational beings, here on earth and anywhere else. This, to the Darwinian evolutionist, smacks altogether too much of a kind of progressionist upward drive to the one unique way of doing things. As I have argued, why should not the John Foster Dulles way of doing ethics have become the biologically fixed norm? (Perhaps it has, as a kind of minor sub-variety.) The Kantian wants to bar inter-galactic relativism, and this I am not prepared to do. (Although he finds Darwinism useful for explaining the origins of morality, explicitly Rawls (1971) denies that Darwinism can throw light on the foundations of morality.)

Rather, I would recommend to my readers the ethical system of David Hume (1978). As an eighteenth-century Scot, he was certainly not insensitive to the significance of reciprocation in human relationships. This meant that he was unwilling to see everything collapse into some kind of groupie-feelie relativism; even though, at the same time, he felt that ethics could be no more than a subjective phenomenon. Resolving this dilemma, like me, he saw the psychological phenomenon of objectification as being a major element in the ethical experience (Mackie 1979). (More truthfully, like Hume, I see the psychological phenomenon of objectification as being a major element in the ethical experience.)

255

There are other reasons why I think of my position as being essentially that of David Hume brought up to date by Charles Darwin. One is that Hume is the authority for the compatibilist approach that I have taken to the problem of free will and determinism. Another is that Hume, like me, sees morality as being a differential phenomenon, weakening as one moves away from one's relatives and friends. But most crucially, Hume is my mentor because he went before me in trying to provide a completely naturalist theory of ethics. He was no evolutionist, but he wanted to base his philosophy in tune with the best science of his day. And this is enough for me. (On philosophical antecedents, see also Ruse 1990.)

CONCLUSION

There are as many questions raised as answered in this discussion. This is no fault but the mark of a vital ongoing inquiry. A scientific 'paradigm' is something which gives you things to think about, and this is precisely what sells my position to me. I want to ask, for instance, about the relationship of my evolutionary ethics to conventional religion, especially Christianity (which is the one in my background). Can one be an evolutionist of my kind and yet still accept the central elements of the Christian faith? One certainly cannot do so if one is a fundamentalist, taking the Bible absolutely literally; but more sophisticated Christians have always prided themselves on being able to resolve the demands of faith with the findings of science. (See Ruse 1989a for some thoughts on this question.)

I want to know also if one can use the knowledge of evolution to work with one's ethical commitments, recognizing them for what they are and as not necessarily the ideal strategy for long-term survival and reproduction in an era of high technology. Could we possibly owe it to our children to be immoral – at least, in the short term for the long-term benefits? Even if we could see that this would make sense, would it be possible, or am I right in fearing that our biology will always be too strong for us to break from or around it?

There are these and many other questions which come to mind. If you are spurred to answer them, then my defence of an updated evolutionary ethics has not been in vain.

9

EVOLUTIONARY ETHICS
The debate continues

I believe that ethics is an adaptation, put in place by our genes as selected in the struggle for life, to aid each and every one of us individually. Because it is a social adaptation, I believe that essentially we (societies, but at some ultimate level the whole human species) share the same ethics, and that charges of relativism are ill-taken. I believe also that ethics is genuine in the sense that people really do do things because they think them right (and conversely), and connected with this I would argue that there is a real difference between the language of ethics and the language of other aspects of human life, specifically those about matters of fact. However, my claim is that ethics is without justification or foundation – in this sense, I am a non-cognitivist – although I do think that an essential component of ethics as an adaptation is that we believe that ethics does have a real foundation (we 'objectify').

I am not sure how many people would accept what I have to say, either in whole or in part. Many have felt the need to criticize, presenting alternative positions. I am gratified, nevertheless, that even the most severe critics have generally accepted my initial premise, namely that evolution *must* matter somehow to our thinking about morality, even if they cannot accept the ways in which I have tried to explore the consequences of this premise. Hence now, entirely (well, almost entirely) in the spirit of one who wants to advance our understanding, as opposed to one who wants merely to score points against opponents, I intend to consider some of the discussions which directly or indirectly impinge negatively on my position. This is not, therefore, intended to be a general discussion of recent work on evolution and ethics, but as it happens I suspect that we shall cover most of the ground.

In what follows, I shall deal first and very briefly with empirical issues, specifically those criticisms which touch on the science from which I make my case for an evolutionary ethics. Then, moving towards philosophy, I shall consider first those who take a position weaker than I take; next, those who take a position stronger than I take; and finally, those who take a middle position of some sort, although very much not the position that I take.

THE BIOLOGY OF ETHICS: DISAGREEMENT

My fellow evolutionary ethicist Robert J. Richards (of whom more later) deals robustly with those who would critique him on empirical grounds, complaining that his scenario for the supposed evolution of morality is mistaken. He responds that, frankly, he is unmoved because, as a philosopher, his concern is with the move from an evolved morality to the implications, and it is enough for his purposes that he has sketched a roughly plausible empirical picture, consistent with what we now know – what we now know being, as admitted by all, very far from the whole truth (Richards 1986a, b).

I am much tempted (for one of the very few times in my life) to follow in Richards' footsteps, for I agree that as philosophers our job truly is not that of trying to better the empirical scientists, the sociobiologists in this instance. But a naturalist cannot turn his or her back on the empirical science entirely – after all, the whole point of naturalism is that if the empirical science is wrong, you are wrong. Hence, in a careful and a reasonably modest spirit, let me say a few things. (In speaking thus of 'empirical science' I do not mean to imply that the philosophical naturalist is not an empirical scientist. Indeed, that is the name of the game. I am using a lexical rather than a prescriptive or even descriptive definition.)

The empirical comments fall into two categories, which I shall take in turn. First, there are those who argue that the kind of approach taken by one such as myself – claiming that the key to human moral belief and behaviour lies in the central models of sociobiology, kin selection, reciprocal altruism, and the like – is fundamentally mistaken, or at least mistaken in the strength of the conclusions that one such as myself would draw. Second, there are those who agree, or at least do not disagree, with one such as myself, but who feel charged to make some comments, amendments, qualifications, and so forth. I will take them in turn, dealing collectively with all, whether or not they direct their comments specifically at me.

Among those who are critical there are still some who subscribe to the traditional critique of the whole sociobiological enterprise – that it is racist, sexist and so forth, and that it is little more. One who argues this way is the Dutch philosopher Bart Voorzanger (1987), who writes:

> In a sense, I agree with the feminist critics of sociobiology who argue that its conception of man is not based on evolutionary theory at all, but that it is the image of man of western capitalist ideology, in a scientific garb.
>
> (265)

Against this, all I can argue is that while it may be true that much evolutionary thought has the same roots as much modern capitalistic thought (of course it does! Think of the influence on Malthus), it is simply not true that sociobiology, or its parent Darwinian theory, is necessarily and always value-laden in a vile way. In my own case, I would have thought that a much stronger case could be made for saying that my thinking about morality, with the explicit rejection of relativism, owes far more to my Quaker childhood than it does to the economics of Adam Smith (Ruse 1994).

Also unconvincing now is the other traditional argument that Voorzanger employs, namely that there is far too much variation between human cultures for one to aspire to a biological explanation of human nature, let alone morality.

> Of course, if you search long enough you may find values we have in common, we all have approximately two legs after all and we all like company at times. But I am afraid that the common moral human nature some ethicists look for will not be much more substantial than just that.
>
> (268)

To which again I can only say that this seems to me to be a criticism that both ethicists and sociobiologists have deflected, in fact making a point of weakness into a point of strength. No one denies that there is variation from society to society. The significance is that, biologically and ethically, we bring shared universal second-order principles to bear on particular situations – and as the situations differ, so the first-order principles will differ.

259

Monogamy may be a good biological strategy and morally sanctioned in a society like ours, but in a society like Tibet where many men must collaborate to work the scarce land resources, polyandry may be both a biological and moral imperative. (In fact, I happen to think that Western society is serially polygamous, and that if the biological truth were known, it is not really so very different from so-called 'primitive' societies.)

More worrisome than Voorzanger, if only because the critic is a leading evolutionist, is the claim by Francisco Ayala (1987) that morality has to be essentially cultural and not something fashioned by natural selection. Or, to spell things out, although 'ethical behavior is an attribute of the biological make-up of humans and, hence, is a product of biological evolution ... I see no evidence that ethical behavior developed because it was adaptive in itself' (239). Ayala is therefore led to reject the relevance to humans of all animal models of social behaviour – kin selection and so forth. (I suppose it is not unfair to note that although Ayala is an evolutionist, he is a population geneticist rather than a sociobiologist.)

The easiest and not unjust way of countering Ayala is to say that simply stating one's opinion is no substitute for argument. He allows that 'Certain animals exhibit behaviors analogous with those resulting from ethical actions in humans, such as the loyalty of dogs or the appearance of compunction when they are punished,' but he adds, 'But such behaviors are either genetically determined or elicited by training ("conditioned responses")' (241). To which I can only reply that if Ayala thinks that human behaviour is not elicited by training he has a very funny idea of moral education, and more seriously that such a response takes no account of the massive studies of ape behaviour which show a great deal more than mere 'conditioned responses', not to mention the equally massive studies of human behaviour which show a (sociobiologically fuelled) genetic component. The point is not whether or not behaviour is genetically determined, but what one might mean by this in a particular case, and specifically what the genetic component might be to moral thought and action. (See Ruse 1988a for my most detailed discussion of this topic, and Ruse 1986 and 1989a for empirical details.)

It would be easy to dismiss Ayala by making reference to his personal history, sneering that his thinking shows more allegiance to his previous incarnation as a Catholic priest than it does today to his incarnation as an evolutionary biologist. But it is more profitable to take this as less of a sneer and more as a way to highlight the kind of moral position I am endorsing and to contrast it with those of others. Ayala's training was as a Dominican, which means that his thinking about morality will be Aristotelian, and as such stressing very strongly the *rational* element to human decision-making, including human moral decision-making. Naturally, almost necessarily, therefore, he will be inclined to dismiss the moral status claims of those he considers beneath humans. (Remember, Ayala is an open enthusiast for biological progressionism.)

Conversely, one finds that Ayala's approach to human morality does indeed stress the intellectual element. He argues that there are three (necessary and sufficient) conditions for ethical behaviour. 'These conditions are: (i) the ability to anticipate the consequences of one's own actions; (ii) the ability to make value judgements; and (iii) the ability to choose between alternative courses of action' (237). These three conditions, taken together, lead to moral thought and action. But while it is most certainly the case that Ayala locates our abilities to satisfy these conditions as products of our evolutionary past, his point is that morality is a kind of epiphenomenon on the abilities – a sort of non-adaptive by-product. It is true that 'the acceptance and persistence of moral norms is facilitated whenever they are consistent with biologically conditioned human behaviors'. However, 'the moral norms are independent of such behaviors in the sense that some norms may not favor, and may hinder, the survival and reproduction of the individual and its genes, which survival and reproduction are the targets of biological evolution' (237).

The point I would stress here, however, is not simply one of disagreement with Ayala about biology, although there is certainly that. It seems to me remarkable that a Darwinian might argue that morality is no more than a non-adaptive by-product. More significant is a fundamental difference about the nature of morality. I suggest that Ayala himself gives the game away, showing that his position does not generate a genuine morality, when he writes: 'I find it hard to see how *evaluating* certain actions as either good or evil (not just choosing some actions rather than others, or evaluating them with respect to their practical consequences) would promote the reproductive fitness of their evaluators' (239). My point against Ayala is that morality is more than simply *evaluating* A against B; it is rather a question of *valuing* A over B. It is all very well to take seriously the Aristotelian stress on reason; but unless you have the gut feelings you simply do not have morality.

You might reply that this is precisely what one would expect from a Humean such as myself. My enthusiasm for something akin to a moral sense is no more than gut feelings by another name. And in a way this is true, and this is why I am glad to have Ayala as a foil to sharpen and clarify my own position. But I would also, vigorously, defend my position as the right one. Consider two men, one of whom unthinkingly shares his crust of bread with the starving child and the other who agonizes over the situation before sharing. Are we to say that only the second is the truly good? There are those who would say, and those with whom I would agree, that the first man is far closer to God.

(Actually, my suspicion – confirming my evolutionism and belief that morality is not in fact a creation of an all-wise God but the imperfectly adaptive product of natural selection – is that we might have a place here where basic intuitions conflict. Of course one gets moral credit for worrying and for triumphing over temptation. Of course one gets moral credit for doing good spontaneously. In real life though, we need both of these supports. Only occasionally do they come into conflict. Perhaps emotions keep you going most of the time, but every now and then you have to invoke reason. I would not think much of a bachelor who agonized over sharing his crust with a child, even if he finally did so. I would not think much of a man with a large family who readily gave away what he had to the first comer, without thinking and calculating the effects on and obligations to his own children. My point is that my position can appreciate this difference and that Ayala's position cannot.)

One final criticism, one which in a way builds on but goes beyond the kinds of feelings motivating Ayala. The most detailed (and negative) analysis of my position has come from the collaborating colleagues, philosopher William Rottschaeffer and biologist David Martinsen (1990). In the course of their biological critique, they accuse me of over-extending the true consequences of Darwinism, arguing that although biology yields the moral *sentiments* needed for immediate action, it does not produce the full-blown moral *dispositions* needed for full moral personhood.

Let us distinguish between ... a *bare disposition* and both a *cognitive/emotional disposition* and *moral disposition*. A cognitive/emotional disposition can manifest itself in subjective feelings and cognitive states and is reportable intersubjectively. A moral disposition has the features of the cognitive/emotional disposition as well as the features ascribed to moral sentiments by Ruse. If parents possess a moral disposition, they report that they feel morally obliged to care for their children and that by that intend that these feelings have the characteristics of full-fledged prescriptivity and universality proper to moral norms and principles. What Ruse, therefore, needs to make his case for the primacy of nature in the origin of moral sentiments is *evidence* that moral sentiments are moral dispositions and that such sentiments are included states. But Ruse has failed to provide this evidence.

(154–5)

Hence we learn that culture, in the form of moral education, must come into play, and only then will a person have the second-order dispositions through which he or she as a thinking being can attempt to order and control his or her basic sentiments (gut feelings, in my language).

To which criticism I want to say two things, although first let me express my entire agreement that moral reasoning will often (always?) involve the evaluation of first-order sentiments against second-order principles. This is the basis of my (Humean) free-will defence. Yet on the one hand, I am appalled that my writing is apparently so unclear that anyone could think that I deny the existence or importance of moral training. Humans are animals which develop through the interaction of their innate dispositions, as cultivated through their childhood training. Language is the paradigm, and I see no reason to make morality an exception. This is not to say that I think that any training whatsoever will lead to a moral being, or that I think that every moral lapse is due to inadequate training. (Rottschaeffer and Martinsen report on some empirical studies supposedly showing that, because of their training, some people have not internalized moral principles but act solely out of fear of punishment. To which I can only reply that these people have been turned into moral cripples.)

On the other hand – and here I want again to use critics to stress my own thinking, rather than simply to refute – I deny

263

that my morality does fail on the grounds of prescriptivity and universality, at least not in the sense that matters. Appearances to the contrary, prescriptivity and universality are not etherial absolutes, but are always context-dependent, relative to what one is wanting to claim. If, for instance, the claim is that one should at all times and all opportunities give everything that one has to the poor, then you are right that my ethics cannot generate this. Thank goodness! But my position is that ethics is a much more limited thing than this, being confined more or less to personal interactions and ready extensions. Beyond this scope and one is into relationships which may well be reciprocal but not necessarily very moral (or immoral). I see no reason at all why, at the level I postulate, one should not have all the prescriptivity and universality that is needed and is seemly. 'Love your neighbour as yourself.' That is an absolute for me, and I think it should be for you too.

THE BIOLOGY OF ETHICS: AGREEMENT

Let me switch now to those (staying still at the empirical level) who make claims that certainly do not threaten my position, and might indeed be used to augment it. I do want to stress again that, from an empirical point of view, I believe that we have taken only the first few steps. These were crucial, and they have set us in the right direction, but the journey ahead is long and will, no doubt, prove arduous. I should say also that I will have less to say now than in the earlier context of criticism, simply because, for furthering one's own thinking, opponents are much better tools than friends.

Some people have been making general points of clarification, with which I can only nod agreement. One is the biologist David S. Wilson (1992), who warns that we should take care in our use of such terms as 'selfish' and 'altruist'.

The fact that evolutionarily successful behaviors are not necessarily selfish, and that proximate mechanisms are designed to elicit evolutionarily successful behaviors regardless of whether they are selfish or altruistic, destroys any hope for a simple relationship between definitions based on fitness effects and definitions based on motives. Not only can altruistic behaviors (in the evolutionary sense) be selfishly motivated (in the psychological sense), but the reverse is also true; individuals that care truly for others can be selfish in the evolutionary sense. . . . These observations are elementary but they are not sufficiently appreciated by evolutionists or philosophers interested in the concept of altruism.

(63)

I can only agree with all of this, noting immodestly that I have been at the forefront of those who try to tease apart various meanings of such terms as 'altruism'. I bring this up now mainly because, as Wilson notes, it is all still not a point appreciated by evolutionary ethicists and their critics. In particular, the cry is still loud in the land from those who dislike or distrust science in general. Under the guise of a broad-minded critique saying (let us be fair) some needed things about the silly extensions that scientists would draw from their theorizing, they try to poison any kind of naturalistic enterprise as engages me and my fellows (Midgley 1979, 1992). Wilson is right that one ought to appreciate the problems when one extends metaphorically such terms as 'selfish' and 'altruist'. At the same time, one must appreciate that such extensions are the very life-blood of science – and of philosophy (Lakoff and Johnson 1983).

Related approval should also be given to Katherine Paxton George (1992) when she warns that those (like myself) who are engaged on the project of making ethics biological should remember that there is always more to ethical decisions than moral feelings, and that one must also treat adequately of one's general rules of reasoning:

> Any model which aims to identify the genetic component of moral behaviors or behaviors with moral import must provide not only a delineation of cultural causes but must also distinguish between those genetic causes which may have their origin in innate moral constraints or dispositions from others which are fundamentally non-moral; this is so because . . . the critical faculty necessary to higher level morality itself arises in part from innate constraints of an innate nonmoral type.
>
> (194)

Although, as it happens, George herself thinks that one can get morality out of biology, the point she is making is very much the point that I ascribed to Ayala. Unsurprisingly, George is open in her sympathy for an Aristotelian approach to ethics. 'Since Aristotle (and Plato before him) the importance of the agent's *knowing* and being able to reflect upon the value of his own acts has been a central aspect of ethical conduct being ethical at all' (191). Given that I have already taken the opportunity to explain why too heavy an emphasis on thought in morality worries me, let me now take this opportunity to agree again that morality does require thinking. Consequently, a thorough-going evolutionist like myself must also pay full attention to the non-moral elements in moral judgement and to their sources. As you know, I find these elements (as does George) much in the same way as I find morality – in the adaptive advantage of such beliefs for our ancestors – but this does not mean that they must not be thought about, and the same goes for their interactions with moral beliefs.

(Since I have sometimes heard it claimed that someone like myself does not appreciate the role of reason in moral thought – especially as one finds it working in philosophical argument – let me stress that although I do not think that everyday moral practice is particularly philosophical, I am as keen on philosophy as the next person! And when we are thinking this way – for instance, about whether it is reasonable for someone who is in favour of abortion to be against capital punishment – what really are going to count are the laws of logic and the like. Here George's point truly does have bite. Even more so when we are thinking about the kinds of cases I shall raise later, when we might be faced with the decision whether it is reasonable (not moral) for self-interest to take precedence over morality.)

There are other writers who want to augment the kind of empirical position I take with various suggestions and supposed improvements and so forth. Since to say a little means that one really must say much, I shall cut my discussion short. The biologist Patrick Bateson (1989), for instance, is concerned by the general criticism of human sociobiology that, if indeed such things as incest barriers are put in place to prevent close-inbreeding, why then can we not just get on with it (or rather not get on with it) like the animals? Why do we humans need the whole paraphernalia of explicit taboos? Bateson suggests that these might come about independently through language and pressures for conformity, and – without having studied the matter in any great detail – that seems to me to be a good idea and worth exploring further.

Passing reference might also be made to the suggestions of Gebhard Geiger (1993), who argues that charismatic authority is the fundamental legitimation of moral-cum-political systems. I must confess that, notwithstanding the fact that he takes his arguments back to Hobbes, I find Geiger's position depressingly Germanic, and not just because of the events of this century. One of the few things which make me sympathetic to Spencerian individualism is the reading of a page or two of Haeckel, when he is in full flight on the glories of the state. (He even wanted to award Bismarck the degree of Doctor of Phylogeny!)

However, given the way that Geiger ties in his thinking about morality and biology with the social sciences – particularly in relying heavily on the work of the sociologist Max Weber (1972), referring especially to the analysis of authority figures – Geiger does provide a useful reminder that, although the evolutionary ethicist may want to transcend the social scientist, he or she ignores this social scientist at his or her peril. There has been much tension between sociobiology and the social sciences. This is now starting to subside, in some quarters at least. It is good therefore to remind ourselves that the subtleties of human culture are the starting point for the social sciences, and that when and only when the fruits of such science are brought into the full picture can the evolutionary ethicist start to think that the work is in sight of finish.

To conclude this section, there is one other argument that I want to consider. In fact, it has been launched as a criticism against others who think that there might be something in the relevance of human sociobiology for ethics. But, I see now that, far from threatening me, it underpins a position which is crucial for my thinking. In a more formal working of points touched on by D. S. Wilson, Ishtiyaque Haji (1992) argues against people like Peter Singer who think that there is going to be a fairly direct and natural link between the biological drive to maximize fitness and feelings of genuine moral altruism. Considering the so-called 'Prisoner's Dilemma' (where two people, thinking independently, know that if they presuppose altruism by the other they will be better off if this proves true, and worse off if this proves false), Singer (1981) argues:

the existence of real-life Prisoner's Dilemma situations puts egoists at a disadvantage in situations where cooperation is advantageous. In these situations two genuine altruists will do better that two egoists, and a single egoist will not do as well as an altruist if her egoism is apparent to others. So at least within the sphere of personal relationships, genuine altruism could have come about consistent with the theory of evolution.

(163)

Looking at various Prisoner's Dilemma situations, Haji concludes against Singer that it is always compatible with one's biological interests that one behave from purely selfish motives. The fact that co-operation might be a paying strategy does not entail that one will always think that one ought to co-operate for good moral reasons.

But, however worrisome this conclusion may be for Singer (frankly, I do not read Singer's 'consistent with' as meaning 'necessitating'), it is very comforting for one of my line of thought. Crucial to my position is the claim that the morality that we have is not necessary – not necessary even if we have the same formal rules of reasoning and the genes are doing their best to follow them. That is the point of my John Foster Dulles example. It is precisely because morality is not necessary and it could have been other than it is – we might have had no morality at all – that I want to argue that, in the end, it is all a collective illusion of the genes.

Hence I celebrate the fact that the empirical criticisms end by supporting my thinking against those would beg to differ. And this is therefore a good point to end this part of the discussion and move on.

THE NATURALISTIC FALLACY AND BEYOND

I move now to philosophy, starting with those for whom a position like mine is altogether too much. The traditional criticism is that any attempt at an evolutionary ethics falls on the naturalistic fallacy, or on an illicit move from 'is' to 'ought'. This charge is certainly not absent from the recent literature, although it is perhaps surprising that this is the main complaint of Ayala (1987), given that he above all others has made so much of his enthusiasm for biological progress (Ayala 1974, 1988).

Because evolution has proceeded in a particular way, it does not follow that that course is morally right or desirable. The justification of ethical norms on biological evolution, or on any other natural process, can only be achieved by introducing value judgments, human choices that prefer one rather than other object or process. Biological nature is in itself morally neutral.

(245)

To which I can only reply that this may be a problem that troubles the positions of others (in fact, you know that I think it is), and it may be a problem which should trouble me (in fact, others will argue that it is), but it is certainly not a problem to which I am insensitive. Seeing a difference between 'is' and 'ought' is where I start, not where I end, nor what I ignore. So unless someone makes a reasoned case against me, I shall slough off the traditional criticism – not because I think it without force, but precisely because I think I am using that force to my own ends.

As it happens, there are those who have made the argument in a more subtle fashion, tailoring their case to the position I have fashioned, so (although at this point I shall be going beyond the pages of my own journal) let me turn now to one particularly forceful version – that made by today's leading philosopher of biology, Elliott Sober (1994). What makes his case particularly striking is that, unlike many critics, Sober does not advocate a blanket criticism against any and all attempts (as is mine) to go from the causes of why someone holds a position to the reasons as to whether or not it is reasonable to accept the position as true or false. (In other words, he does not think the 'genetic fallacy' always a fallacy.)

However, in my case – and indeed, more generally for any attempt to get ethics from biology – Sober thinks there is an unjustified slide from the facts to the values.

> My suspicion is that evolutionary ethics will always find itself in this [unhappy] situation. It may turn out that evolutionary findings do sometimes help us answer normative questions, although the proof of this pudding will be entirely in the eating. Just as hedonistic utilitarianism makes it possible for psychologists to provide information that helps decide what is right and what is wrong, this and other ethical theories may provide a similar opening for evolutionary biologists. This cannot be ruled out in advance. However, evolutionary findings will be able to achieve this result only when they

269

are informed by ethical ideas that are not themselves supplied by evolutionary theory. Evolutionary theory cannot, all by itself, tell us whether there are any ethical facts. Nor, if ethical facts exist, can evolutionary theory tell us, all by itself, what some of those facts are. For better or worse, ethics will retain a certain degree of autonomy from the natural sciences. This doesn't mean that they are mutually irrelevant, of course. But it does mean that evolutionary ethicists who try to do too much will end up doing too little.

(19)

Why this harsh verdict? Consider two arguments where Sober argues (correctly in my opinion) it is proper to go from the way in which a belief was gained to the truth value of that belief.

A   Ben decided that there are 78 people in the room by drawing the number 78 at random from an urn (which contains the natural numbers up to a 100)

There are 78 people in the room

B   Cathy carefully counted the people in her class and consequently believed that 34 people were present

---

34 people were present in Cathy's class

Why do we think that the conclusion to the second argument is probably true and the first false? Simply because in the first case the cause of the belief was independent of the facts of the case, and in the second case it was not: 'Because the process of belief formation was influenced in the right way by how many people were actually in the room, we are prepared to grant that a description of the context of *discovery* provides a *justification* of the resulting belief' (14).

But now, what about the ethical argument? The kind of case that someone like myself is trying to make goes somewhat as follows:

C   We believe the ethical statements we do because of our evolution and because of facts about our socialization

---

No ethical statement is true

(Actually, note that I only want to claim that ethics is untrue – 'a collective fallacy' – in one sense, namely that of having an objective human-independent existence. I most certainly claim that within the ethical system one can speak of 'true' and 'false'. I reject entirely the gripes of those like Woolcock 1993 who complain that this is not an option open to me; that in some way I am trying to have what I have given away. Within baseball, when three players are out, the team must step down. This is true, even though there is no objective reality to which this rule corresponds. It is not true in cricket, for instance. Likewise in ethics. Murder is wrong, whatever the objective facts of the case.)

As Sober (rightly) notes, this argument only works if something like the following is true:

D   The processes that determine what moral beliefs people
     have are entirely independent of which moral statements
     (if any) are true.

But his complaint is that everybody (including the likes of me) simply assumes this hidden premise, and hence any derivation of the desired conclusion is simply question-begging.

To which line of argument I respond that I certainly do assume that something like D is true – this was the very point to my analogy from spiritualism. But I would argue that I do not simply assume D as a hidden premise. The spiritualism analogy shows why. Even if Private Higgins is up there with God in His heaven, people do not believe this because of that. The case of those thought dead but not really (as Robert Graves described in *Goodbye to All That*), and yet contacted, suggests that there are more than adequate natural causes for the belief.

Analogously, my point (as was stressed again in the last section) was that we could quite well believe something completely different about ethics. One cannot compare a belief in the Love Commandment in precise analogy with a belief in the existence of a downward-bearing speeding truck. John Foster Dulles may never have accepted the Love Commandment (I am sure he did in personal relationships), but evolution would have given him short shrift had he been cavalier about the truck. Only if you believe in some sort of teleological progressive direction to evolution can you assume that we humans have hit upon the true objective ethics – an ethics which, in an almost Leibnizian way, corresponds to our subjective beliefs. Going back to Statement D, I argue that the radical contingency of moral belief – we could have believed, systematically, that one ought to hate one's neighbour – does indeed point to the independence of moral beliefs from moral truths.

At which point Sober might pounce, pointing out that I am not denying the existence of moral truths as such – only that they may be somewhat hidden from us. In other words, the conclusion to their non-existence requires another argument, using something like Occam's Razor ('It is reasonable to postulate the existence of ethical facts only if that postulate is needed to explain why people have the ethical beliefs they do'), a mode of argument about which Sober is positively sniffy. After all, he points out, most people spend most of their time making mistakes about statistical reasoning, but this does not deny the truth of statistics.

In reply, all I can say is 'fair enough', although the analogy with statistics is not well taken. The point about statistics is that we all (well, virtually all) can be made to realize the truth of statistics with appropriate training. This is because at some fundamental level the logic of statistics is not essentially alien. The point about alternative ethics is they could be just that – systems with no real point of connection. And it is precisely because there is this distance between what is believed by us and what it is logically possible that there might be, that I am not terribly worried by my concession to Sober.

Indeed, as I have said before, I am not really sure that it is that much of a concession. Suppose an objective ethics does exist, making a body of claims X. There is no guarantee that we will ever believe or know X, or that what we believe might not be radically different from X. That is the whole point about the non-directedness of evolution. And all this, it seems to me, is getting pretty close to making X a contradiction in terms. 'We ought truly to do x, y and z; but our evolution, which has kept this from us, makes us think that we ought to do a, b and c. Although, fortunately, we shall never be the wiser for it!' G. E. Moore must be spinning in his grave.

DEFENDING JUSTIFICATION

I turn next to one whose position is stronger than mine, for he talks confidently of 'justification' and of driving through (rather than round) the naturalistic fallacy. I confess that I do somewhat dread the task of giving a fair and acceptable-to-the-author account of the position, for apparently it is a universal fault of hitherto fairminded commentators that their expositions fail to do the position justice – a fact which may, of course, be due to the position's subtlety and innovation rather than to the fact that the author changes his thinking, on the jogging shoe as it were. But given that the author has shown an Indiana Jones enthusiasm for defending impossible positions against all comers, extricating himself from certain philosophical death when any reasonable person would have started to work on his or her own obituary, I feel certain that any misreadings of mine will be justly censured, to the edification of all and the amusement of many.

Like me, Robert J. Richards (1986a, b, 1987, 1989) has a two-pronged argument, directly empirical (that is, drawing on the work of empirical scientists) and subsequently philosophical. It is probably fair to say that, at the empirical level, in line with a general liking for group selection-type arguments at his home base of the University of Chicago (Wade 1978), Richards is inclined to a more holistic account of human evolution than I am. In particular, in what he truly notes is probably a position more closely Darwinian (in the sense of what Darwin actually held, rather than what Darwin should have held) than mine, Richards sees human morality as having emerged from a kind of selection between bands of proto-humans, generally although not necessarily closely related. But, although I would probably give a greater role to reciprocal altruism, I think it fair to say that viewed from a distance, at this level, even friends would say that our points of overlap are closer than our points of difference. (Actually, if we are going to slug it out on the minutiae of Darwin scholarship, I would suggest that in major respects, my position is more in the spirit of Darwin. See Ruse 1980, 1986.)

What is significant is that, having given what he thinks is a plausible empirical account of the evolution of human morality, Richards is disinclined to elaborate or defend himself further, feeling that it is not here that he can make a proper contribution. Although let me say on his behalf that where people have criticized him in this respect, my feeling is that he has perfectly adequate lines of reply. For instance, one oft-voiced complaint is that, as a matter of fact, human nature is not particularly good and that some pretty dreadful things get done, even by the most well-intentioned people. The Christian philosopher Roger Trigg (1986) complains of Richards' thinking that:

273

many serious moral theories start with the assumption that man is inclined towards evil, in that he is basically selfish and unconcerned with the welfare of others. The Christian conception of original sin, for example, takes human self-centredness seriously. This doctrine is based on a total misconception about human inclinations, if Richards is right.

(334)

Richards' response is that he is not denying that people do wrong, but that such wrongdoing generally stems from a mistake about the empirical facts of the case and not moral blindness. His favourite example is of the Inca priest making a monthly sacrifice of a virgin, to ensure the well-being of the harvest. This, in Richards' opinion, is a function of an inadequate grasp of the facts of agriculture rather than a D. H. Lawrence manifestation of misogyny. The priest could be no less high minded than the rest of us. To this, Richards adds an argument (used also by me, as I have used the previous one) that it is naive to suppose that evolution simply promotes benevolence. The interesting point is that it does support such benevolence, despite the general background of selfishness. 'The Christian doctrine of original sin finds ample empirical support in the evolutionary depictions of man the warrior and man (also woman) the sexual commando. But the Christian doctrine of redemption can also be given secular translation by our natural drive toward altruism' (350–1). I should add, however, that I find more emphasis on this last point in Richards' writings than in my own. This could simply be a function of his more loving nature and that he emerged from his Christian childhood at a more mature stage than I. However, given the necessitarian flavour of Richards' words, the difference may be significant.

Turning now to the philosophy, there is first the dismissal of the naturalistic fallacy, considered as a bar to an evolutionary ethics. Summarizing his position, Richards (1989) writes:

My strategy is to reveal that any ethical framework that might be urged upon us depends on a variety of empirical assumptions. I attempt to show, for instance, that philosophers who argue for the adoption of any normative framework – even that of modern logic – employ a common strategy, namely to justify the adoption by showing that the framework sanctions certain empirical descriptions that are deemed well confirmed. This leads me to reject the common belief that inferring values from facts is *ipso facto* fallacious.

(337)

Backing this, Richards then offers a number of arguments to support his belief that one ought to act for the common good. He stresses that these 'justifications' (his word) do not include the self-serving argument that help given ensures help received, which he claims is not true morality. (He ascribes this argument to me. Let me say that I agree fully that giving simply to get a return is no true morality. I may have held it once, although I incline to think not, but it is certainly not my position now. However, perhaps unlike Richards, I believe that a genetic mechanism of reciprocal altruism which is properly albeit metaphorically described in such self-serving terms, can yield a genuine morality.)

Two arguments for the necessity of morality are particularly important. The first, modelled on the metaethical theory of the neo-Kantian Alan Gewirth (1986), attempts to get 'ought' statements from factual 'is' statements, a move which is apparently allowed when one has something 'necessitated or required by reasons stemming from some structured context' (Richards 1987: 287). From this, Richards argues:

> Evolution provides the structured context of moral action: it has constituted men not only to be moved to act for the community good, but also to approve, endorse, and encourage others to do so as well. This particular formation of human nature does not impose an individual need, not something that will be directly harmful if not satisfied; hence, the question of a logical transition from an individual (or generic) need to a right does not arise. Rather, the constructive forces of evolution impose a practical necessity on each man to promote the community good. We must, we are obliged to heed this imperative. We might attempt to ignore the demand of our nature by refusing to act altruistically, but this does not diminish its reality. The inability of men to harden their consciences completely to basic principles of morality means that sinners can be redeemed. Hence, just as the context of physical nature allows us to argue 'Since lightening has struck, thunder ought to follow,' so the structured context of human evolution allows us to argue '*Since each*

275

man has evolved to advance the community good, each ought
to act altruistically.'

(288)

Frankly, this all looks a bit on a par with John Stuart Mill's notorious 'proof' of the Greatest Happiness Principle – we all like to be happy, so we ought to promote it for all – although I think that in a sense Richards would not take this analogy as a criticism. One of his more subsidiary arguments is that fundamentally he is not doing anything different from that which any metaethicist does, and he stresses again and again that ultimately the only proof that you have for morality is that which (as mentioned above) you offer for logic, namely that people accept it.

In conjunction with this point, Richards is keen to point out that although his argument depends on a move from factual premises to moral conclusions, this is not done in ignorance but is licensed by an inference rule along the lines of 'Given a certain factual situation, then certain moral imperatives will obtain'. He notes that if one is to avoid an infinite regress in one's argumentation, then (as Lewis Carroll showed) one has to stop the demand for justification at some point. And ultimately, this means ending 'in what are regarded as acceptable beliefs or practices' (285). That is: 'All meta-level discussions, all attempts to justify ethical frameworks depend on such inference rules, whose ultimate justification can only be their acceptance by rational and moral creatures' (289).

However, in the specific case we are dealing with, Richards does seem to feel that he escapes the usual objections (centring on the Naturalistic Fallacy) because of the peculiarity of the situation, namely that we are dealing with matters of human evolution, and that these have been matters leading to specific facts about morality, most importantly that we humans endorse them! 'Moral "ought"-propositions are not sanctioned by the mere fact of evolutionary formation of human nature, but by the fact of the peculiar formation of human nature we call 'moral,' which has been accomplished by evolution' (288).

Backing this first argument, Richards offers a second major argument:

> *the evidence shows that evolution has, as a matter of fact,*
> *constructed human beings to act for the community good; but*
> *to act for the community good is what we mean by being*
> *moral. Since, therefore, human beings are moral beings – an*

*unavoidable condition produced by evolution – each ought
act for the community good.*

(289, his italics)

The critic might feel that this simply restates the first argument
and indeed Richards does claim that it 'amplifies' the first. But,
apart from the reiteration of the importance of the empirical backing, there is a stress on the fact 'that the logical movement of the
justification is from – (a) the empirical evidence and theory of
evolution, to (b) man's constitution as an altruist, to (c) identifying
being an altruist with being moral, to (d) concluding that since
men so constituted are moral, they morally ought to promote the
community good' (289).

From the various criticisms launched against Richards at the
philosophical level, let me identify two as especially significant.
Or rather, let me say on my own authority that I think that there
are two which must be answered, although I would not deny that
these are criticisms often launched against any naturalistic attack
on ethics. (To his great credit, Richards has invited and relished in
criticism, feeling – as do I – that this is the way that the truth
emerges. I am more interested now in the spirit of the attacks,
than provision of a detailed catalogue of the counter-arguments.
See Cela-Conde 1986; Gewirth 1986; Hughes 1986; Thomas 1986;
Trigg 1986; Voorzanger 1987; Ball 1988; Williams 1990.)

First, even if we allow that an 'ought' has been derived from
factual premises (whether straight from the premises or via some
special rule of inference), there are serious questions about whether
this is a 'moral ought'. In the language of the philosophers, it
looks much more like an 'instrumental ought', as when one might
say 'If you want to win this chess game, then you ought to move
your queen'. Moreover, if it is indeed an instrumental ought, then
(as in the case of Gewirth) one might well conclude that (as is
always the case for Kantians) it has been derived somewhat for-
mally without any need of or genuine reference to the facts of the
case, including the evolutionary facts of the case.

Second, for all the talk of 'justification', at best Richards has
achieved some form of 'conventionalism' (to use another word of
the philosophers). By appealing to what people believe, one is
making no reference to the facts of the case 'out there', as it
were. One is making truth dependent upon belief and, once again,
although it is certainly true that what we believe may well be a

277

function of our biology, there is little evolutionary content to the fact that we believe what we believe and that this is taken as the criterion of truth. Indeed, Richards' subsidiary 'justificatory' claim for his position, that his approach to justification is akin to that taken by any metaethical thinker, might be taken as confirmation of this very point. (In this context, it may be significant that Gewirth took Richards as arguing merely for an evolutionary origin for ethics, without real regard for justification. I think this was a mistaken reading, but it would identify Richards' evolutionism in its limited functional place.)

Richards is not insensitive to charges such as these, and his responses draw us closer to what I think is the heart of his thought, although you will see that I shall start to speculate somewhat. Essentially, his is the response of every traditional evolutionary ethicist at this point, namely that while these charges may be well taken as a general rule, because, and precisely because, one is dealing with an evolutionary situation, one can argue legitimately as does he. The 'ought' is a moral ought, and the appeal to general opinion – 'intuitively clear and commonly made judgments' (Richards 1989: 334) – is genuinely justificatory. Comparing his derivation of ought with that which occurs when one concludes that, given lightning, it ought to thunder, Richards writes:

> The 'ought' is a moral 'ought', not because of its logical character, but because of the nature of the causal context to which it is applied – namely, man's moral nature (i.e. his altruistically disposed nature). The case of thunder is precisely the same: it is the physical process of 'lightning-producing-thunder' that makes the 'ought' a physical-process ought. So the moral process of acting according to the evolutionarily derived disposition to altruism makes the 'ought' a moral ought.
>
> (340)

This is still not enough, at least not in my eyes and (I suspect) those of Richards' other critics. Why should our judgements about morality be so special? Why should they have the authority that they do? Why should the way that we have evolved have its special force? One solution, the traditional solution, would be because evolution has added up to something. It is progressive. And, if this be so, then humans and their morality presumably have a special status. In appealing to 'intuitively clear' judgements, one is appealing to something with more than mere contingent status (as I or any other Humean would hold); one is appealing to the truth in some way, whether this truth be a function of a Moore-like independently existent non-natural property or a Kantian-like necessary condition of human existence.

At this point, I think it appropriate to remind ourselves that Richards is not just a philosopher, but also a brilliant historian – one who nevertheless sees sufficient connection between his history and his philosophy that he has appended essays on his epistemology and ethics to his major historical treatise, a work which was very much intended to refurbish the reputations of those like Spencer and Haeckel who argued for progressionism and for an ethics based on evolution (Richards 1987; see also Richards 1992). And the speculations to which this connection gives rise are strengthened, even as Richards (1986b) defends himself against critics, for he does make it clear that he sees evolution as having been more than totally random or (even more importantly) negative. Considering the possibility that evolution might have gone wrong, he writes:

> But it might also happen that most people begin to take seriously the Southern California 'moral' code. That is, the last vestige of altruism might atrophy and people commonly might not only act according to the principle 'if it feels good, do it' but they might also learn to call that 'the highest moral principle.' I believe this latter occurrence would be as probable as people generally and upon due consideration adopting as logically valid the principle 'if A, then B, but B, therefore A.' We would, I think, regard these as cases in which men have become rational and moral in name only. I certainly believe that early in our evolutionary history, those proto-men, our ancestors, were neither moral nor rational in our sense (which is to say, they simply were not moral or rational at all). The future course of evolution – perhaps punctuated by the bomb – may lead us back to our past condition. Who knows? I am warmed however, by the wisdom of natural selection, which will likely forestall the evolution of homo californensis.
>
> (346)

This is perhaps not an enthusiastic endorsement of progressionism, – I too hope not to evolve into Californian Man – but when people start talking of the 'wisdom of natural selection', my built-in progress-detecting geiger-counter starts to click. And it clicks even louder when people start to tell me that our ethics is uniquely necessary in some ways, like logic.

In short, my suspicion is that behind Richards' new-fangled ethics lies some old-fashioned biology. And my objections to this have been expressed at length elsewhere. It is either this, or (with his other critics) I argue that there is something radically incomplete about Richards' position. He may get his conclusions, but they are not coming from his premises and rules of inference.

NEW ETHICAL PRINCIPLES?

I come to the final part of my discussion, where I look at those who are fundamentally sympathetic to a position such as mine, but who feel that they can do the job better than I. There are two critiques or advances of or on my work that I shall consider; but to prepare the way, let me first take up a criticism, advanced by Philip Kitcher (1993) and endorsed by Elliott Sober (1994), which they apparently think shows the implausibility of a position such as mine.

The point of dispute revolves around two possible claims, with respect to ethics, that one might advance on behalf of biology:

1 Sociobiology can teach us facts about human beings that, in conjunction with moral principles that we already accept, can be used to derive normative principles that we have not yet appreciated.
2 Sociobiology can lead us to revise our system of ethical principles, not simply by leading us to accept new derivative statements – as in (1) – but by teaching us new fundamental normative principles.

Kitcher and Sober are happy to accept (1), but reject (2) – which I am supposed to accept – as too strong.

But is this a consequence, implicit or explicit, of my position? I rather think not. Let us take an example of where sociobiology might lead us to revise our thinking about human moral behaviour, namely that centring on the relationship between step-parents and step-children. In a society which is basically ignorant of the significance of the biological bond – I speak now with some experience and feeling when I thus characterize England in the 1950s –

a huge amount of guilt can ensue when step-parents and children do not mimic exactly the close relationships that one expects and generally finds between natural parents and their children. However, now – thanks to a much deeper understanding of human relationships, an understanding to which sociobiology has contributed – we realize that social relationships can rarely if ever replace biological relationships, and that to effect such social relationships as well as we can we need understanding and sympathy rather than condemnation and guilt.

However, I am not sure that any of this has involved the teaching of new ethical principles as such. Rather, as happens in moral discourse, new facts have been unearthed which allow us better to apply those moral principles we have had all along. Now we know that step-parents and step-children will have no natural affection, and so we realize that moral condemnation for its absence is inappropriate, whereas support and understanding above that which one might give for a natural relationship is appropriate. (Do not misunderstand me. I am not now saying that morality is lifted in such relationships, especially when the adult has knowingly entered into such a relationship. Most especially, I am not excusing the family violence which is much more common in such relationships than in natural families. I say this, even though one of the most dramatic findings of the human sociobiologists is that violence of parents to children is orders of magnitude higher when one has a step relationship (Daly and Wilson 1988). The whole point of what I am saying is that that does not make for new moral principles.)

However, before I turn to my critics, let me admit that there are senses in which I do want to go beyond proposition (1), even if not as far as proposition (2). For a start, and not particularly contentiously, I can well imagine that a better understanding of biology might make us more sensitive to and appreciative of moral feelings that we have already, just as psychoanalysis was supposed to make us aware of general feelings that are already there. In my own case, to give a real example, my understanding of biology has helped me to realize how insincere I was when I used to mouth conventional platitudes about obligations to the Third World. It is not that I am now less moral in my attitudes to life's unfortunates – in fact, I am inclined to think that from the point of view of action, I am if anything more moral – but I no longer claim what I do not believe.

For a second, perhaps more contentiously, I have always admitted that biology might make us realize that we have to treat certain moral principles more warily, perhaps even rejecting them. My point is that I am not sure that one does this in the name of normative principles, and certainly not 'new fundamental normative principles'. Let me explain my point through an example, based on a film which I once saw (which may indeed have had a true life basis).

A man was recruited, by the English in the Second World War, to go into enemy territory as a secret agent. Unfortunately he was betrayed and even more unfortunately the poison tooth which he had been given proved defective and he was unable to commit suicide. After several weeks' torture at the hands of the Gestapo he cracked and gave away vital secrets. But what he did not know, and what the Germans certainly did not know, was that this was all intentional! He had been recruited on the basis of a psychological profile suggesting that he would crack, the poison tooth was deliberately left harmless, and his betrayal was planned. The point of this exercise being that the information he gave to the Germans was seriously misleading, although because of the circumstances in which it was obtained they took it to be absolutely authentic.

I take it that the behaviour of the English was a gross violation of the Categorical Imperative, and just about any other moral rule that you can think of. (What made the story more poignant and thrilling was that the agent, because of his bravery and dedication to his country, took very much longer to crack than the English had expected and hoped.) However, one could justify the actions in terms of self-interest. If Hitler were not deceived, then immediately more of our soldiers would be killed and in the long run we would lose the war. (Perhaps a similar argument could be used of the dropping of bombs on Japan.)

My point is that I do not see the self-interest as being necessarily a normative principle – certainly not a new one – and even if you do claim it as a normative principle, it is certainly not a moral principle. It is true that one might dress it up as a moral principle (although not a new one) and perhaps this is what one tends always to do, given the tension of going deliberately against morality. 'The agent's spymasters were trying to save democracy from the threat of the Nazis, etc., etc.'. But generally, I think this is a gloss. The British in 1940 were not fighting Hitler to save the Jews. They were fighting to save themselves.

And bringing this tale round to sociobiology and ethics, my point is that a better understanding of biology might incline us to go against morality – especially if, as I do, you think of morality very much as something working at the immediate, personal level. We would go against morality for the sake of long-term goals, which I suspect will often centre on personal (including descendant) survival. The sort of example I have in mind is the forcible prevention of people from having children, especially as many as I have had, for the sake of world population. If world population is not limited, I and my descendants will probably suffer. My position is unfair. The attitude of the Chinese authorities, preventing more than one child per couple, seems morally repugnant. I am not sure, however, that I, or they, are unreasonable. (Of course, human nature being what it is, we find excuses – in my case that five well-educated children will be a benefit to the world, outweighing the actual addition of numbers. But it is a gloss.)

Do note that I am not now saying that the intellectual appreciation that it is not always in our best interests to be moral means that we shall give up on morality – that we shall escape it in some way, where 'escape' means 'sloughing it off', or eliminating it. A criticism which is commonly made against me, most recently by Peter Woolcock (1993), is that, once you buy my claim that morality is just an illusion of the genes, the jag is up: you can and might as well slip out from under morality and do entirely what is in your own best interests. But this is about as close as you can get to a moral contradiction in terms. Hence my moral philosophy is truly that of Thrasymachus, and about as edifying.

My response is that, generally, I think that morality is in our own best interests. We humans are social animals. Why go through life trying to cheat on those whose company and friendship we need as much as we need food and drink? Or, rather, why go through life trying to cheat on people more than we do? And where there is a real conflict between morality and self-interest, I just do not think that we can simply suppress our feelings at the dictate of our reason. That is why I am given to referring at this point to *Crime and Punishment*, for through his character Raskolnikov, Dostoevski shows quite brilliantly that human nature has a nasty (he would say 'good'!) way of making little of fancy philosophical theories.

Nor is my thinking at this point much changed when people

airily tell me that a little retraining is all that is needed to get around this point. If this is indeed true, then although it will certainly make for much more drastic consequences than I now suspect, remember that it will not make my general non-cognitivist position false. But as a sociobiologist, my empirical position (which, Richards-like, I now state and no longer defend) is that morality is embedded in the genes, and that although training is certainly very significant, it will take more than a few good philosophical theories to talk us out of it. At that kind of level, I expect my thinking to have about as much effect as my headmaster's quite fearsome sermons against 'self-abuse', and for much the same reasons.

This is not to say that I think what I am saying (*qua* philosopher) can and will have no effect; but the effect will not come by eliminating morality. Rather, the effect will come by recognizing it for what it is and trying to work around or through it. It is the same as for religion. I am afraid that handing out free copies of Hume's *Dialogues* is not going to solve the problems in Northern Ireland or in the Holy Land; but, thanks to Hume (among others), we can start to get some appreciation of religion for what it is, and without pretending that we can ever eliminate it – or even wanting to eliminate it – we can begin on the path of reducing religious conflict.

One final word on the Kitcher criticism. Whether it truly applies to others, you should see that, given my commitment to a Humean-type morality, essentially it must fail in my case. The very heart of Hume's philosophy is that 'reason must be a slave to the passions'. There is no possible way in which knowledge gleaned from an intellectual theory as such could change my thinking about right and wrong. The only way in which reason can interfere is by showing me how right and wrong come out on certain empirical facts of the case, or, as in the examples I have discussed above, how other passions, not particularly moral, might come into play and make me decide, rationally, to go against morality. But never could one such as I – so wary of scientism – argue for more.

DARWIN'S SERIOUS TAKERS

Now with these clarifications made, I can move rapidly to face and counter my fellow middle-of-the-road naturalistic critics. First, there are John Collier and Michael Stingl (1993) who argue very much for a position like (2) above, something which they believe gives them a reason for speaking legitimately of an 'objective morality' (in the Kantian sense of necessary conditions for human moral behaviour, rather than the Plato/Moore sense of values 'out there'). Essentially, their position seems to be that, biologically speaking, there is one perfect form of moral behaviour – one which, I take it, works at a kind of 'selfish gene' level of maximizing the benefits of social interaction for any particular individual in a group, but that since we are all in the group is going to benefit each and every one of us. This is their objective ethics.

Unfortunately, since evolution (as brought on by natural selection) is imperfect, we humans have not achieved this state. But we have evolved as thinking beings. Hence we can work out this optimal state, and once articulated we have reason (a morally driven reason) to work to achieve this state. Morality, thus, is both biologically based and culturally improvable.

> The capacity for articulating our moral intuitions in thought and language allows us to discover the meaning of moral value, and to formulate moral principles which are theories about the consequences of our innate moral sense. Knowledge of evolutionary theory and adaptive processes allows us to speculate about what our moral instincts might have been had our morality evolved more optimally. This, in turn, allows us to formulate (still as a process of empirical discovery) what general moral principles might apply to optimally evolved, intelligent, social creatures. On our proposal, moral theory is empirical, objective, correctable, provides both individual motives for compliance which are, in addition, objective moral obligations.
>
> (55–6)

I can deal with this argument quickly, noting in passing that, although I am an ardent Darwinian seeing adaptation everywhere, I am certainly not wedded to the belief that our moral system represents the apotheosis of adaptive perfection (and that this is the reason why I missed taking the route of Collier and Stingl). Indeed, I have admitted that I do not believe our moral system to be perfect and that this is why I think we sometimes get irresolvable moral conflicts. Like everything, particularly like human childbirth, morality is a matter of compromise.

As far as the central claim is concerned, with Kitcher and Sober I simply doubt that there are *moral* principles 'out there', waiting to be discovered (as apparently, Fermat's last theorem was waiting for the right moment). I am prepared to concede (more for the sake of argument than because I am enthusiastically convinced) that perhaps there is an ideal formal situation or system for inter-acting humans – a system that would (in a John Rawls fashion) give us everything that we could desire, from the perspective of fairness or justice or happiness. I am prepared to concede (again more for the sake of argument than because I am enthusiastically convinced) that we humans are significantly far from this state. (Perhaps I should be more enthusiastic here. After all, many of us are pretty lousy logicians.)

My worry is whether that formal system would be moral, as our real and actualized system is moral. As I and other Humeans have stressed again and again (as against the Kantians) a purely formal system in itself is not moral – you have to have something else, a sense of moral oughtness, added. In terms of the sorts of arguments that I have given, I see a purely formal system, however optimal, as being compatible with all sorts of moral systems (ours, the John Foster Dulles system, and more). How can you guarantee that one of these, uniquely, is the right one?

Of course, you might try to project from our morality, deciding that the optimal system ought to be actualized. But it is our morality which is motivating you, and the possibility of an ideal formal system does not make for objectivity. You have given me no reason to reject my reasons for thinking my morality subjective. Or, as I have suggested above as more likely, you might decide that it is simply in your own interests to go for a more optimal formal system. But then, even less do you have reason to think of an objective morality waiting to be discovered and actualized.

The worst kind of case I can imagine is that someone might be able to show that in order to achieve the optimal formal system, one needs a motivational system entirely different from ours – after all, if we are agreed that evolution does not necessarily do the best job, why should our system of morality be the right one, imperfectly realized? In this case, we are back to the kind of nightmare scenarios envisioned earlier in this paper, where there is an objective morality, but it is something totally alien to us. This surely makes a mockery of the proud claim of Collier and Stingl that 'The study of evolutionary theory allows a Copernican shift away from our imperfectly evolved (non-optimal) moral instincts to a more general and optimal moral theory' (56). As I remember, the last person to make the claim that his work represented a Copernican revolution in these matters was our old friend Herbert Spencer.

Finally, I return to the critique of Rottschaefer and Martinsen (1990). Their empirical criticisms of my position are but a prolegomenon to their philosophical criticisms. They argue that I have sold Darwinism altogether short, and like Collier and Stingl (although for different reasons) they too think that an evolutionary naturalistic position makes the way for objectivity in ethics – perhaps of a more 'robust' (their term) kind than Collier and Stingl, for Rottschaefer and Martinsen seem to think that one can go beyond mere formal conditions to a morality involving properties and entities with real existence (although they do agree that this may well be an existence which does involve, crucially, the perceiving subject). Moreover, they think that, my fears to the contrary, there is no fear that such a robust evolutionary ethics commits the naturalistic fallacy.

Basically, the move taken by Rottschaefer and Martinsen is to pick up on my claim (taken from Hume, via Mackie) that in respects moral properties are like colours. By this I mean that moral properties do not really exist 'out there' in the physical world, however real they may seem to us. They are rather, in some crucial sense, a part of our perceptual apparatus. But, just as we project colours out into real existence, so also we do the same of moral properties. The sky really is blue. Killing really is wrong. About this, my critics argue:

> In the case of colors, the realist can argue not only that there are objective sources for, but also objective referents of, the perception of colors. Micro-physical surface characteristics and electromagnetic radiation are the realities with which our visual perceptual system indirectly puts us in contact. Objectivity has not been abandoned; rather, naive realism has been replaced by scientific realism. Similarly, in the case of moral properties, a Darwinian can argue not only that there are objective sources for, but also objective referents of, the perception of values. But she need not claim that the moral sentiments are directly revelatory of the nature of the value properties of, for instance, food or companionship. Scientific

accounts of these objective value properties and their causal sources may supplement or replace common-sense assessments. But their objectivity need not be denied.

(160)

Given this view of moral properties, it seems to be the position of Rottschaefer and Martinsen that, rather than morality being in some sense a creation of human nature (I would say by the genes, rather than by conscious intention), morality in some sense exists as part of the environment in which we humans evolved. 'They [moral properties] are the properties of the natural and social environment to which the person is adapted and in terms of which one can claim that the person is fit' (160).

As such, it would seem that we might evolve to fit with this morality more closely, or – somewhat analogously to the position of Collier and Stingl – we might direct our social evolution, including moral education, to a tighter fit. Remember from earlier how I was criticized for belittling the role of culture in moral development.

> In our view, moral sentiments possess only a proto-prescriptivity and universality, deriving ultimately from their association with fitness and reproductive success, and of the same sort that attaches to any genetically based cognitive and behavioural disposition. The full-fledged prescriptivity and universality that Ruse ascribes to the moral sentiments belong rather to something like the Darwinian moral sense and are primarily the result of social/cultural learning.
>
> (157)

I am not quite sure where a deeper knowledge of biology would fit into all of this, but it seems to me plausible that one might suggest that such knowledge might lead to a revision of one's moral aims, which could then be achieved through education. Certainly, if the supposed objectivity of morality is to have any bite, it would surely allow for an external goal beyond any I would allow.

Finally, what of the naturalistic fallacy? Apparently my fears on this score are over-blown. Certainly, if one tried to *deduce* moral properties from non-moral properties, one would be in trouble, as one would be in equal trouble if one tried to deduce moral claims from non-moral claims. But neither of these things is occurring in the Rottschaefer–Martinsen world. Rather, moral properties in some sense sit upon non-moral properties, just as colour properties sit upon non-colour properties. There is a constant conjunction, and the underlying set in some way is responsible for the set above, but there is no reduction.

In a way, one has a kind of emergence, although (again we have the language of the philosophers) Rottschaefer and Martinsen prefer to talk of 'supervenience'. Discussing the property of substance like clay being malleable, they write:

> Similarly, moral goodness and rightness can be said to super-vene on natural characteristics. Such diverse properties and states as pleasure, happiness, knowledge, and friendship can all be characterized as morally good and the action right that they might prompt or from which they might result. But no one of these natural properties can be identified with good-ness and rightness. For each in proper circumstances can be both a source and a result of moral goodness and rightness. And each could, when associated with another property, pleasure with maliciousness, for instance, be morally evil and morally wrong. Thus there seems to be good reason for not identifying moral goodness and rightness with any particular natural quality. Yet we have a way to understand them as objective properties of persons and things.
>
> (162)

Let me pick up on just one major point of disagreement with Rottschaefer and Martinsen, although in passing let me suggest that one ought not to over-stress the differences between their position and mine. In speaking of ethics as 'illusory', I am clearly not intending to say that it does not exist in any sense at all, just as I would not want to say that Macbeth's dagger did not exist in any sense at all. The key to the illusions is that ethics and the dagger do have some kind of existence, otherwise they would not have the effect that they do. My point is that ethics is 'in the mind' in some sense, as is the dagger – although even this gives an impression of being somewhat stronger than I want to say, for as an internal realist I think that everything is in the mind in some sense, although (like Putnam whom I follow at this point) I really want to get away from the whole metaphor of 'in the mind/out of the mind'.

However – and here I candidly admit that Rottschaefer and

Martinsen have helped me to think through that which hitherto was not thought through – I would suggest that the analogy between morality and colour, helpful though it is in some respects, fails in one crucial respect. And this makes all the difference! In particular, with colours, given the appropriate underlying conditions, you are going to get one colour uniquely. It is true that how we perceive this will depend in part on our visual apparatus – the colour blind will see just greys and shades – but there is going to be no switching from one end of the spectrum to the other. One person will not see green and another red, and conversely. (At least, I think not. If what I am saying is wrong, then I suspect that what I shall now say about morality applies equally to colour.)

But the point about morality, as I have characterized it and tried to demonstrate in my supporting arguments, is that there is going to be flexibility and a range (perhaps unlimited) of possibilities. If what I have said about the possibility of alternative moralities is correct, then you are not going to get 'good' corresponding to 'red' and 'bad' to 'blue' and so forth, because depending on the way that evolution has gone, good and bad could be different according to the circumstances of the case – in a way that would not be so of red and blue. Put it this way. I can imagine it being true that one ought to hate and try to cheat neighbours. I cannot imagine that the sky be red and the grass blue. (And as I have said, if you can give me physico-chemical reasons why I am wrong, I argue for the increased subjectivity of colour rather than the objectivity of morality.)

But if what I am saying is true, then it is simply not the case that there is in any sense an objective morality, waiting for selection to mould our natures around it – nor will culture be able to complete the task that biology has begun. Morality comes with us, and it comes with us by courtesy of our biology. The problem as I see it is that, for all their claim that it is I who have not taken Darwinism truly seriously, Rottschaefer and Martinsen are the ones who have not absorbed the true message of sociobiology. Evolution works not just between individuals and the outside world, that is the world of things, but it works equally between individuals and individuals, considered as individuals. Morality is a creation of the genes to help us get on with our fellows, not to help us get on with physical creation. As such, we should not expect to find, as indeed we do not find, that morality has any existence beyond the relationships between individuals. And as always in evolution, although we may skin the cat pretty well, there are probably many other ways in which the job might have been done.

CONCLUSION

Like Father William, I have answered three questions. Indeed, I have answered a great deal more The urge to throw you all downstairs is strong, although I am not sure if it is biologically caused. As I said when I started, what impresses me is the general quality of the debate. We really have moved the level of discussion significantly higher than it was when we began. I do not feel that anyone has changed my thinking in a drastic way, but I do admit that I now think a lot more sharply about some important issues than I did hitherto. That, for me, justifies the exercise. No doubt, my critics will feel equally satisfied, if only for the pleasure one derives from seeing others squirming at the end of one's barbs.

If asked, I suppose my main reaction to my critics would be one of surprise at the strength of feeling that there is in favour of some form of moral realism. I suppose that I should not really be surprised, since for many years I felt exactly the same way myself; although, since I entered professional philosophy around 1960 when non-cognitivism still flourished, in many respects I have now the feeling of having come home. All I can say to my critics is that their genes are deceiving them and, as is usual, they are doing a good job. But it just ain't so, folks. Sorry!

BIBLIOGRAPHY

Achinstein, P. (1968) *Concepts of Science*, Baltimore: Johns Hopkins University Press.

Adams, M. (1979) 'From "gene fund" to "gene pool": On the evolution of evolutionary language', in *Studies in History of Biology*, W. Coleman and C. Limoges, Baltimore: Johns Hopkins University Press, 241–85.

Agassiz, E. C. (ed.) (1885) *Louis Agassiz: His Life and Correspondence*, Boston: Houghton Mifflin.

Agassiz, L. (1842) 'On the success and development of organized beings at the surface of the terrestrial globe, being a discourse delivered at the inauguration of the Academy of Neuchatel', *Edinburgh New Philosophical Journal* 23: 388–99.

—— (1859) *Essay on Classification*, London: Longman, Brown, Green, Longmans, and Roberts and Trubner.

Alexander, R. D. (1979) *Darwinism and Human Affairs*, Seattle: University of Washington Press.

—— (1987) *The Biology of Moral Systems*, New York: Aldine de Gruyter.

Allen, E. *et al.* (1975) 'Letter to the editor', *New York Review of Books*, 22, 18: 43–4.

—— (1976) 'Sociobiology: A new biological determinism', *BioScience* 26: 182–6.

Almond, G., M. Chodorow and R. H. Pearce (eds) (1982) *Progress and its Discontents*, Berkeley: University of California Press.

Appel, T. A. (1987) *The Cuvier-Geoffroy Debate: French Biology in the Decades Before Darwin*, New York: Oxford University Press.

Axelrod, R. (1984) *The Evolution of Cooperation*, New York: Basic Books.

Ayala, F. J. (1974) 'The concept of biological progress', in *Studies in the Philosophy of Biology*, ed. F. J. Ayala and T. Dobzhansky, London: Macmillan, 339–54.

—— (1982) 'The evolutionary concept of progress', in *Progress and Its Discontents*, ed. G. Almond, M. Chodorow and R. H. Pearce, Berkeley: University of California Press, 106–24.

—— (1985) 'Reduction in biology: A recent challenge', in *Evolution at a Crossroads*, ed. D. J. Depew and B. Weber, Cambridge, Mass.: MIT Press, 65–80.

292

—— (1987) 'The biological roots of morality', *Biology and Philosophy* 2: 235–52.

—— (1988) 'Can "progress" be defined as a biological concept?', in *Evolutionary Progress*, ed. M. Nitecki, Chicago: University of Chicago Press, 75–96.

Ayer, A. J. (1946) *Language, Truth and Logic*, 2nd edn, London: Gollancz.

Baker, R. and F. Elliston (1984) *Readings in the Philosophy of Sex*, Buffalo: Prometheus.

Bakshtanovsky, V. I. (1989) *Ethics*, Moscow: Progress Publishers.

Ball, S. W. (1988) 'Evolution, explanation, and the fact/value distinction', *Biology and Philosophy* 3: 317–48.

Barnes, B. (1977) *Interests and the Growth of Knowledge*, London: Routledge.

Barrett, J. (1991) 'Really taking Darwin and the naturalistic fallacy seriously: An objection to Rottschaefer and Martinsen', *Biology and Philosophy* 6: 433–7.

Barrett, P. H., P. J. Gautrey, S. Herbert, D. Kohn and S. Smith (eds) (1987) *Charles Darwin's Notebooks 1836–1844*, Ithaca, NY: Cornell University Press.

Bateson, P. (1986) 'Sociobiology and human politics', in *Science and Beyond*, ed. S. Rose and L. Appignanesi, 79–99. Oxford: Blackwell.

—— (1989) 'Does evolutionary biology contribute to ethics?' *Biology and Philosophy* 4: 287–301.

Bechtel, W. (1984) 'The evolution of our understanding of the cell: A study in the dynamics of scientific progress', *Studies in History and Philosophy of Science* 15: 309–56.

Bellamy, E. (1951) *Looking Backward, 2000–1898*, New York: Modern Library (first published 1889).

Bergson, H. (1907) *L'évolution créatrice*, Paris: Alcan.

Berlin, B. and P. Kay (1969) *Basic Color Terms: Their Universality and Evolution*, Berkeley: University of California Press.

Betzig, L. L., M. Borgerhoff Mulder and P. W. Turke (1987) *Human Reproductive Behaviour*, Cambridge: Cambridge University Press.

Black, M. (1962) *Models and Metaphors*, Ithaca, NY: Cornell University Press.

Bonner, J. T. (1987) *The Evolution of Complexity*, Princeton, NJ: Princeton University Press.

Bowler, P. (1975) 'The changing meaning of "Evolution" ', *Journal of the History of Ideas* 36: 95–114.

—— (1976) *Fossils and Progress*, New York: Science History Publications.

—— (1983) *The Eclipse of Darwinism: Anti-Darwinism Evolution Theories in the Decades around 1900*, Baltimore: Johns Hopkins University Press.

—— (1984) *Evolution: The History of an Idea*, Berkeley: University of California Press.

—— (1986) *Theories of Human Evolution*, Baltimore: Johns Hopkins University Press.

Boyd, R. and P. J. Richerson (1985) *Culture and the Evolutionary Process*, Chicago: University of Chicago Press.

Bradie, M. (1986) 'Assessing evolutionary epistemology', *Biology and Philosophy* 1: 401–60.

Braithwaite, R. (1953) *Scientific Explanation*, Cambridge: Cambridge University Press.

Brewster, D. (1838) 'Review of Comte's "Cours de Philosophie Positive" ' *Edinburgh Review* 67: 271–308.

Bunge, M. (1968) 'Analogy in quantum theory: From insight to nonsense', *British Journal for the Philosophy of Science* 18: 265–86.

Burian, R. M. (1981) 'Human sociobiology and genetic determinism', *Philosophical Forum* 13 (2–3): 43–66.

Burkhardt, R. W. (1977) *The Spirit of System: Lamarck and Evolutionary Biology*, Cambridge, Mass.: Harvard University Press.

Bury, J. W. (1920) *The Idea of Progress: An Inquiry into its Origin and Growth*, London.

Butts, R. (1965) 'Necessary truth in Whewell's theory of science', *American Philosophical Quarterly* 2: 1–21.

Cain, J. A. (1993) 'Common problems and cooperative solutions: organizational activity in evolutionary studies 1936–1947', *Isis* 84: 1–25.

Campbell, B. (1972) *Sexual Selection and the Descent of Man*, Chicago: Aldine.

Campbell, D. T. (1974) 'Evolutionary epistemology', in *The Philosophy of Karl Popper*, ed. P. A. Schilpp, La Salle, Ill.: Open Court, (1) 413–63.

—— (1977) 'Descriptive epistemology', Unpublished William James Lectures, given at Harvard University.

Campbell, D. T., C. M. Heyes and W. Callebaut (1986) 'Evolutionary epistemology bibliography', in *Evolutionary Epistemology: A Multiparadigm Program*, ed. W. Callebaut and R. Pinxten, Dordrecht: Reidel, 405–31.

Caplan, A. (ed.) (1978) *The Sociobiology Debate*, New York: Harper & Row.

Caplan, A. and B. Jennings (eds) (1984) *Darwin, Marx, and Freud: Their Influence on Moral Theory*, New York: Plenum.

Carlyle, T. (1896) 'Characteristics', in *Critical and Miscellaneous Essays of Thomas Carlyle*, ed. H. D. Traill, New York: Chapman & Hall, 1–43.

Cela-Conde, C. (1986) 'The challenge of evolutionary ethics', *Biology and Philosophy* 1: 293–7.

Chambers, C. (1958) 'The belief in progress in twentieth-century America', *Journal of the History of Ideas* 19: 197–224.

Chambers, R. (1846) (fifth edn) *Vestiges of the Natural History of Creation*, London: Churchill (first published 1844).

Charlesworth, B., R. Lande and M. Slatkin (1982) 'A Neo-Darwinian commentary on macroevolution', *Evolution* 36: 474–98.

Chomsky, N. (1957) *Syntactic Structures*, The Hague: Mouton.

—— (1966) *Cartesian Linguistics*, New York: Harper & Row.

Churchland, P. M. (1984) *Matter and Consciousness*, Cambridge, Mass.: MIT Press.

Churchland, P. S. (1986) *Neurophilosophy: Towards a Unified Science of the Mind and Brain*, Cambridge, Mass.: MIT Press.

Clark, A. J. (1986) 'Evolutionary epistemology and the scientific method', *Philosophica* 37: 151–62.

Clark, J. W. and T. M. Hughes (eds) (1890) *Life and Letters of the Reverend Adam Sedgwick*, Cambridge: Cambridge University Press.

Cohen, L. J. (1973) 'Is the progress of science evolutionary?', *British Journal for the Philosophy of Science* 24: 41–61.

Cole, J. R. and S. Cole (1973) *Social Stratification in Science*, Chicago: University of Chicago Press.

Coleman, W. (1964) *Georges Cuvier Zoologist: A Study in the History of Evolutionary Theory*, Cambridge, Mass.: Harvard University Press.

Collier, J. and M. Stingl, (1993) 'Evolutionary naturalism and the objectivity of morality', *Biology and Philosophy* 8: 47–60.

Collins, H. (1985) *Changing Order*, London: Sage.

Condorcet, A. N. (1956) *Sketch for a Historical Picture of the Progress of the Human Mind*, New York: The Noonday Press (first published 1795).

Corsi, P. (1988) *The Age of Lamarck*, Berkeley: University of California Press.

Cosmides, L. (1989) 'The logic of social exchange: Has natural selection shaped how humans reason? Studies with the Wason selection task', *Cognition* 31: 187–276.

Cott, H. (1940) *Adaptive Coloration in Animals*, London: Methuen.

Cronin, H. (1991) *The Ant and the Peacock*, Cambridge: Cambridge University Press.

Daly, M. and M. Wilson (1988) *Homicide*, New York: Aldine.

Dancy, K. (1986) *Contemporary Epistemology*, Oxford: Blackwell.

Darnell, J. H. Lodish and D. Baltimore (1990) *Molecular Cell Biology*, New York: W. H. Freeman.

Darwin, C. (1859) *On The Origin of Species by Means of Natural Selection*, London: John Murray.

—— (1871) *The Descent of Man*, London: John Murray.

—— (1960) 'Darwin's notebooks on transmutation of species, Part III', (Notebook 'D' ed. D. de Beer, *Bulletin of the British Museum (Natural History) Hist. Ser.* 2: 121–50.

—— (1969) *Autobiography*, Editor N. Barlow, New York: Norton.

Darwin, C. and A. R. Wallace (1858) 'On the tendency of species to form varieties; and on the perpetuation of varieties and species by natural means of selection', *Proceedings of the Linnean Society, Zoological Journal* 3: 46–62. Reprinted in C. Darwin and A. R. Wallace (1958) *Evolution by Natural Selection*, Cambridge: Cambridge University Press.

Darwin, E. (1803) *The Temple of Nature*, London: J. Johnson.

Darwin, F. and A. C. Seward (1903) *More Letters of Charles Darwin*, London: John Murray.

Davidson, D. (1974) 'On the very idea of a conceptual scheme', *Proceedings of the American Philosophical Association* 47: 5–20.

Davies, B. (1986) *Storm Over Biology: Essays on Science, Sentiment, and Public Policy*, Buffalo, NY: Prometheus.

Dawkins, R. (1976) *The Selfish Gene*, Oxford: Oxford University Press.

—— (1982) *The Extended Phenotype: The Gene as the Unit of Selection*, Oxford: W. H. Freeman.

—— (1986) *The Blind Watchmaker*, New York: Norton.

Dawkins, R. and J. R. Krebs (1979) 'Arms races between and within species', *Proceedings of the Royal Society of London, B* 205: 489–511.

De Waal, F. (1982) *Chimpanzee Politics: Power and Sex Among Apes*, London: Cape.

Desmond, A. (1989) *The Politics of Evolution*, Chicago: University of Chicago Press.

Desmond, A. and J. Moore (1992) *Darwin: The Life of a Tormented Evolutionist*, New York: Warner.

Dobzhansky, T. (1937) *Genetics and the Origin of Species*, New York: Columbia University Press.

—— (1951) *Genetics and the Origin of Species* (third edn), New York: Columbia University Press.

—— (1967) *The Biology of Ultimate Concern*, New York: New American Library.

—— (1970) *Genetics of the Evolutionary Process*, New York: Columbia University Press.

Dobzhansky, T., F. J. Ayala, G. L. Stebbins and J. W. Valentine (1977) *Evolution*, San Francisco: Freeman.

Duhem, P. (1914) *The Aim and Structure of Physical Theory*, Princeton: Princeton University Press.

Dummett, M. (1978) 'The philosophical basis of intuitionist logic', in *Truth and Other Enigmas*, London: Duckworth, 215–47.

Duncan, D. (ed.) (1908) *Life and Letters of Herbert Spencer*, London: Williams & Norgate.

Durant, J. (1985) *Darwinism and Divinity*, Oxford: Blackwell.

Eldredge, N. (1968) 'Convergence between two Pennsylvanian gastropod species: a multivariate mathematical approach', *Journal of Paleontology* 42: 186–96.

—— (1971) 'The allopatric model and phylogeny in paleozoic invertebrates', *Evolution* 25: 156–67.

—— (1972) 'Systematics and evolution of "Phacops rana" (Green, 1832) and "Phacops iownesis" Delo, 1935 (Trilobita) in the Middle Devonian of North America', *Bulletin of the American Museum of Natural History* 47: 45–114.

—— (1980) *Phylogenetic Patterns and the Evolutionary Process: Method and Theory in Comparative Biology*, New York: Columbia University Press.

—— (1982) *The Monkey Business: A Scientist Looks at Creationism*, New York: Washington Square Press (Pocket Books).

—— (1985a) *Unfinished Synthesis: Biological Hierarchies and Modern Evolutionary Thought*, New York: Oxford University Press.

—— (1985b) *Time Frames*, New York: Simon & Schuster.

—— (1989) *Macroevolutionary Dynamics: Species, Niches, and Adaptive Peaks*, New York: McGraw-Hill.

Eldredge, N. and J. Cracraft (1980) *Phylogenetic Patterns and the Evolutionary Process*, New York: Columbia University Press.

Eldredge, N. and S. J. Gould (1972) 'Punctuated equilibria: an alternative to phyletic gradualism', in *Models in Paleobiology*, ed. T. J. M. Schopf, 82–115, San Francisco: Freeman, Cooper.

Eldredge, N. and M. Grene (1992) *Interactions: The Biological Context of Social Systems*, New York: Columbia University Press.

Eldredge, N. and S. N. Salthe (1984) 'Hierarchy and evolution', *Oxford Surveys in Evolutionary Biology* 1: 182–206.

Eldredge, N. and I. Tattersall (1982) *The Myths of Human Evolution*, New York: Columbia University Press.

Endler, J. (1986) *Natural Selection in the Wild*, Princeton: Princeton University Press.

Fausto-Sterling, A. (1985) *Myths of Gender*, New York: Basic Books.

Fisher, R. A. (1930) *The Genetical Theory of Natural Selection*, Oxford: Oxford University Press.

Flew, A. (1967) *Evolution and Ethics*, London: Macmillan.

Gale, B. (1972) 'Darwin and the concept of a struggle for existence', *Isis* 63: 321–44.

Gasman, D. (1971) *The Scientific Origins of National Socialism: Social Darwinism in Ernst Haeckel and the Monist League*, New York: Elsevier.

Gayon, J. (1990) 'Critics and criticisms of the modern synthesis: The viewpoint of a philosopher', *Evolutionary Biology* 24: 1–49.

Geiger, G. (1992) 'Why there are no objective values: A critique of ethical intuitionism from an evolutionary point of view', *Biology and Philosophy* 7: 315–30.

—— (1993) 'Evolutionary anthropology and the non-cognitive foundation of moral validity', *Biology and Philosophy* 8: 133–51.

George, H. (1926) *Progress and Poverty*, Garden City, NY: Doubleday, Page (first published 1879).

George, K. P. (1992) 'Moral and nonmoral innate constraints', *Biology and Philosophy* 7: 189–202.

Gewirth, A. (1986) 'The problem of specificity in ethics', *Biology and Philosophy* 1: 297–305.

Ghiselin, M. (1969) *The Triumph of the Darwinian Method*, Berkeley: University of California Press.

Gibbard, A. (1982) 'Human evolution and the sense of justice', in *Midwest Studies in Philosophy*, ed. P. French, Minneapolis: University of Minnesota Press, 31–46.

—— (1990) *Wise Choices, Apt Feelings: A Theory of Normative Judgment*, Cambridge, Mass.: Harvard University Press.

Gillan, D. J. (1981) 'Reasoning in the chimpanzee: 2. Transitive inference', *Journal of Experimental Psychology: Animal Behavior Processes* 7: 150–64.

Gillan, D. J., D. Premack and G. Woodruff (1981) 'Reasoning in the chimpanzee: 1. Analogical reasoning', *Journal of Experimental Psychology: Animal Behavior Processes* 7: 1–17.

Gingerich, P. D. (1976) 'Paleontology and phylogeny: patterns of evolution at the species level in early tertiary mammals', *American Journal of Science* 276: 1–28.

—— (1977) 'Patterns of evolution in the mammalian fossil record', in *Patterns of Evolution, as Illustrated by the Fossil Record*, ed. A. Hallam, Amsterdam: Elsevier, 469–500.

—— (1984) 'Punctuated equilibria – where is the evidence?', *Systematic Zoology* 33: 335–8.

—— (1985) 'Species in the fossil record: concepts, trends, and transitions', *Paleobiology* 11: 27–41.

Goldschimdt, R. (1940) *The Material Basis of Evolution*, New Haven: Yale University Press.

Goodall, J. (1986) *The Chimpanzees of Gombe: Patterns of Behavior*, Cambridge, Mass.: Belknap.

Gould, S. J. (1966) 'Allometry and size in ontogeny and phylogeny', *Biological Reviews of the Cambridge Philosophical Society* 41: 587–640.

—— (1969) 'An evolutionary microcosm: Pleistocene and recent history of the land snail "P. (Poecilozonites)" in Bermuda', *Bulletin of the Museum of Comparative Zoology* 138: 407–532.

—— (1971) 'D'Arcy Thompson and the science of form', *New Literary History* 2: 229–58.

—— (1977a) *Ever Since Darwin*, New York: Norton.

—— (1977b) *Ontogeny and Phylogeny*, Cambridge, Mass.: Belknap Press.

—— (1979) 'Episodic change versus gradualist dogma', *Science and Nature* 2: 5–12.

—— (1980a) 'Sociobiology and the theory of natural selection', in *Sociobiology: Beyond Nature/Nurture?*, ed. G. Barlow and J. Silverberg, Boulder, Col.: Westview, 257–69.

—— (1980b) 'The promise of paleobiology as a nomothetic, evolutionary discipline', *Paleobiology* 6: 96–118.

—— (1980c) 'Is a new and general theory of evolution emerging?', *Paleobiology* 6: 119–30.

—— (1981) *The Mismeasure of Man*, New York: Norton.

—— (1982) 'Darwinism and the expansion of evolutionary theory', *Science* 216: 380–7.

—— (1983) 'Irrelevance, submission and partnership: The changing role of paleontology in Darwin's three centennials, and a modest proposal for macroevolution', *Evolution from Molecules to Men*, ed. D. S. Bendall, Cambridge: Cambridge University Press, 347–66.

—— (1985) 'The paradox of the first tier: an agenda for paleobiology', *Paleobiology* 11: 2–12.

—— (1986) 'Allometry and size in ontogeny and phylogeny', *Biological Reviews of the Cambridge Philosophical Society* 41: 587–640.

—— (1989) *Wonderful Life*, New York: Norton.

—— (1990) 'Speciation and sorting as the source of evolutionary trends, or "Things are seldom what they seem" ', in *Evolutionary Trends*, ed. K. J. McNamara, London: Belhaven, 3–27.

Gould, S. J. and N. Eldredge (1993) 'Punctuated equilibrium comes of age', *Nature* 366: 223–7.

Gould, S. J. and N. Eldredge (1977) 'Punctuated equilibria: The tempo and mode of evolution reconsidered', *Paleobiology* 3: 115–51.

Gould, S. J. and R. C. Lewontin (1979) 'The spandrels of San Marco and the Panglossian paradigm: A critique of the adaptationist program', *Proceedings of the Royal Society of London, Series B: Biological Sciences* 205: 581–98.

Gould, S. J. and E. S. Vrba (1982) 'Exaptation – a missing term in the science of form', *Paleobiology* 8: 4–15.

Graham, L. (1981) *Between Science and Values*, New York: Columbia University Press.

Greene, J. (1959) *The Death of Adam*, Iowa City: University of Iowa Press.

—— (1977) 'Darwin as a social evolutionist', *Journal of the History of Biology* 10: 1–27.

Haeckel, E. (1866) *Generelle Morphologie der Organismen*, Berlin: Reimer.

—— (1868) *The History of Creation*, London: Kegan Paul, Trench.

Haji, I. (1992) 'Evolution, altruism, and the prisoner's dilemma', *Biology and Philosophy* 7: 161–76.

Haldane, J. B. S. (1932) *The Causes of Evolution*, London: Longmans.

Hamilton, W. D. (1964a) 'The genetical evolution of social behaviour I', *Journal of Theoretical Biology* 7: 1–16.

—— (1964b) 'The genetical evolution of social behaviour II', *Journal of Theoretical Biology* 7: 17–32.

Hanson, N. R. (1958) *Patterns of Discovery*, Cambridge: Cambridge University Press.

Haraway, R. (1989) *Primate Visions*, New York: Routledge.

Harvey, P. and R. May (1989) 'Out for the sperm count', *Nature* 337: 508–9.

Hegel, G. F. W. (1970) *Philosophy of Nature*, Oxford: Oxford University Press.

Hempel, C. G. (1965) *Aspects of Scientific Explanation*, New York: Free Press.

—— (1966) *Philosophy of Natural Science*, Englewood Cliffs, NJ: Prentice Hall.

Henderson, L. J. (1913) *The Fitness of the Environment*, New York: Macmillan.

Herbert, S. (1971) 'Darwin, Malthus, and selection', *Journal of the History of Biology* 4: 209–17.

Hesse, M. (1966) *Models and Analogies in Science*, Indiana: University of Notre Dame Press.

Hesse, M. and M. Arbib (1986) *The Construction of Reality*, Cambridge: Cambridge University Press.

Hicks, D. and J. Potter (1991) 'Sociology of scientific knowledge: A reflexive citation analysis', *Social Studies of Science* 21: 459–501.

Hoffman, A. (1992) 'Twenty years later: Punctuated equilibrium in retrospect', in *The Dynamics of Evolution: The Punctuated Equilibrium Debate in the Natural and Social Sciences*, ed. A. Somit and S. A. Peterson, Ithaca, NY: Cornell University Press, 121–38.

Hofstadter, R. (1959) *Social Darwinism in American Thought*, New York: Braziller.

Hölldobler, B. and E. O. Wilson (1990) *The Ants*, Cambridge, Mass.: Harvard University Press.

299

Hrdy, S. B. (1981) *The Woman that Never Evolved*, Cambridge, Mass.: Harvard University Press.

Hubbard, R. (1983) 'Have only men evolved?' in *Discovering Reality*, eds. S. Harding and M. B. Hintikka, Dordrecht, Holland: Reidel, 45–69.

Hubby, J. L. and R. C. Lewontin (1966) 'A molecular approach to the study of genic heterozygosity in natural populations I: The number of alleles at different loci in *Drosophila pseudoobscura*', *Genetics* 54: 577–94.

Hudson, W. D. (1983) *Modern Moral Philosophy* (second edn), London: Macmillan.

Hughes, W. (1986) 'Richards' defense of evolutionary ethics', *Biology and Philosophy* 1: 306–15.

Hull, D. (1973) *Darwin and His Critics*, Cambridge, Mass.: Harvard University Press.

—— (1982) 'The naked meme', in *Learning, Development and Culture: Essays in Evolutionary Epistemology*, ed. H. C. Plotkin, Chichester: Wiley, 273–327.

—— (1988a) 'A mechanism and its metaphysics: An evolutionary account of the social and conceptual development of science', *Biology and Philosophy* 3: 123–55.

—— (1988b) *Science as a Process*, Chicago: University of Chicago Press.

—— (1989) *The Metaphysics of Evolution*, Albany, NY: SUNY Press.

Hume, D. (1978) *A Treatise of Human Nature*, Oxford: Oxford University Press.

Huxley, J. S. (1912) *The Individual in the Animal Kingdom*, Cambridge: Cambridge University Press.

—— (1932) *Problems of Relative Growth*, London Methuen.

—— (1942) *Evolution: The Modern Synthesis*, London: Allen & Unwin.

—— (1948) *UNESCO: Its Purpose and its Philosophy*, Washington, DC: Public Affairs Press.

Huxley, J. S. and J. B. S. Haldane (1927) *Animal Biology*, Oxford: Oxford University Press.

Huxley, L. (1902) *Life and Letters of Thomas Henry Huxley*, New York: Appleton.

Huxley, T. H. (1863) *Evidence as to Man's Place in Nature*, London: Williams & Norgate.

—— (1888) 'The struggle for existence in human society', *Nineteenth Century* 23: 132, 161–80.

—— (1893) 'The coming of age of the origin of species', *Collected Essays: Darwiniana*, London: Macmillan, 227–43.

—— (1989) *Evolution and Ethics*, ed. J. Paradis and G. C. Williams, Princeton: Princeton University Press (first published 1894).

Hyatt, A. (1893) 'Phylogeny of an acquired characteristic', *Proceedings of the American Philosophical Society* 32: 349–647.

Isaac, G. (1983) 'Aspects of human evolution', in *Evolution from Molecules to Men*, ed. D. S. Bendall, Cambridge: Cambridge University Press, 509–43.

Jacob, F. and J. Monod (1961a) 'Genetic regulatory mechanisms in the synthesis of proteins', *Journal of Molecular Biology* 3: 318–56.

—— (1961b) 'On the regulation of gene activity', *Cold Spring Harbor Symposia on Quantitative Biology* 26: 193–211.

Johnson, M. (1987) *The Body in the Mind: The Bodily Basis of Meaning, Imagination, and Reason*, Chicago: University of Chicago Press.

Jones, G. (1980) *Social Darwinism and English Thought*, Brighton: Harvester.

Kant, I. (1949) *Critique of Practical Reason*, trans. L. W. Beck, Chicago, University of Chicago Press.

—— (1959) *Foundations of the Metaphysics of Morals*, trans. L. W. Beck, Indianapolis: Bobbs-Merrill.

Kelley, A. (1981) *The Descent of Darwin: The Popularization of Darwinism in Germany, 1860–1914*, Chapel Hill: University of North Carolina Press.

Kitcher, P. (1962) *Abusing Science: The Case Against Creationism*, Cambridge, Mass.: MIT Press.

—— (1985) *Vaulting Ambition*, Cambridge, Mass.: MIT Press.

—— (1992) 'The naturalists return', *Philosophical Review* 101: 53–114.

—— (1993) 'Four ways to "biologicize" ethics', in *Evolution und Ethik*, ed. K. Bayertz, Reclam.

Kohn, D. (ed.) (1985) *The Darwinian Heritage*, Princeton: Princeton University Press.

Körner, S. (1960) *Philosophy of Mathematics*, London: Hutchinson.

Krebs, J. R. and N. B. Davies (eds) (1991) *Behavioural Ecology: An Evolutionary Approach* (third edn) Oxford: Blackwell Scientific Publications.

Kropotkin, P. (1955) *Mutual Aid*, ed. A. Montague, Boston: Extending Horizons Books (first published 1902).

Kruger, L. (ed.) (1987) *The Probabilistic Revolution*, Cambridge, Mass.: Massachusetts Institute of Technology Press.

Kuhn, T. (1957) *The Copernican Revolution*, Cambridge, Mass.: Harvard University Press.

—— (1962) *The Structure of Scientific Revolutions*, Chicago: University of Chicago Press.

Lakatos, I. (1970) 'Falsification and the methodology of scientific research programmes', in *Criticism and the Growth of Knowledge*, ed. I. Lakatos and A. Musgrave, Cambridge: Cambridge University Press, 91–5.

Lakatos, I., and A. Musgrave (eds) (1970) *Criticism and the Growth of Knowledge*, Cambridge: Cambridge University Press.

Lakoff, G. (1986) *Women, Fire, and Dangerous Things: What Categories Reveal about the Mind*, Chicago: University of Chicago Press.

Lakoff, G. and M. Johnson (1980) *Metaphors We Live By*, Chicago: University of Chicago Press.

Lamarck, J. B. (1963) *Zoological Philosophy*, New York: Hafner (first published 1809).

Lande, R. (1980) 'Macroevolution by Steven M. Stanley', *Paleobiology* 6: 233–8.

Lankester, E. R. (1880) *Degeneration: A Chapter in Darwinism*, London: Macmillan.

Laudan, L. (1977) *Progress and its Problems: Towards a Theory of Scientific Growth*, Berkeley: University of California Press.

Lerner, I. M. (1954) *Genetic Homeostasis*, New York: John Wiley.

Levins, R. and R. Lewontin (1985) *The Dialectical Biologist*, Cambridge, Mass.: Harvard University Press.

Lewin, R. (1980) 'Evolutionary theory under fire', *Science* 210: 883–7.

Lewontin, R. C. (1974) *The Genetic Basis of Evolutionary Change*, New York: Columbia University Press.

Lewontin, R. C. and J. L. Hubby (1966) 'A molecular approach to the study of genic heterozygosity in natural populations. II. Amount of variation and degree of heterozygosity in natural populations of *Drosophila pseudoobscura*', *Genetics* 54: 595–609.

Lewontin, R. C., J. A. Moore, B. Wallace and W. B. Provine (eds) (1981) *Dobzhansky's Genetics of Natural Populations*, New York: Columbia University Press.

Lieberman, P. (1984) *The Biology and Evolution of Language*, Cambridge, Mass.: Harvard University Press.

Limoges, C. (1979) *La sélection naturelle*, Paris: Presses Universitaires de France.

Locke, J. (1975) *An Essay Concerning Human Understanding*, ed. P. H. Nidditch, New York: Oxford University Press.

Longino, H. (1990) *Science as Social Knowledge*, Princeton: Princeton University Press.

Lorenz, K. (1982) 'Kant's Lehre vom a priorischen im Lichte, geganwartiger Biologie. "Blatter fur Deutsche Philosophie" ' 15: 94–125. Translated and reprinted as 'Kant's doctrine of the "a priori" in the light of contemporary biology', in *Learning, Development, and Culture; Essays in Evolutionary Epistemology*, ed. H. C. Plotkin, Chichester: Wiley (first published 1941), 121–43.

Losee, J. (1972) *A Historical Introduction to the Philosophy of Science*, London: Oxford University Press.

Lovejoy, A. O. (1936) *The Great Chain of Being*, Cambridge, Mass.: Harvard University Press.

Lumsden, C. J. and E. O. Wilson (1981) *Genes, Mind, and Culture*, Cambridge, Mass.: Harvard University Press.

—— (1983) *Promethean Fire: Reflections on the Origin of Mind*, Cambridge, Mass.: Harvard University Press.

Lyell, C. (1830) *Principles of Geology*, London: John Murray.

Lynne, J. and H. F. Howe. (1986) ' "Punctuated equilibria": rhetorical dynamics of a scientific controversy', *Quarterly Journal of Speech* 72: 132–47.

MacArthur, R. W. and E. O. Wilson (1967) *The Theory of Island Biogeography*, Princeton: Princeton University Press.

Mackie, J. (1977) *Ethics*, Harmondsworth: Penguin.

—— (1978), 'The law of the jungle', *Philosophy* 53: 553–73.

—— (1979) *Hume's Moral Theory*, London: Routledge & Kegan Paul.

MacRoberts, M. and B. MacRoberts (1986) 'Quantitative measures of communication in science: A study of the formal level' *Social Studies of Science* 16: 151–72.

Malthus, T. R. (1914) *An Essay on the Principle of Population* (sixth ed), London: Everyman (first published 1826).

Maynard Smith, J. (1958) *The Theory of Evolution*, Harmondsworth, Penguin.

—— (1981) 'Did Darwin get it right?', *London Review of Books* 3 (11): 10–11.

—— (1983) 'The genetics of stasis and punctuation', *Annual Reviews of Genetics* 17: 11–25.

Mayr, E. (1942) *Systematics and the Origin of Species*, New York: Columbia University Press.

—— (1954) 'Change of genetic environment and evolution', in *Evolution as a Process*, ed. J. Huxley, A. C. Hardy and E. B. Ford, London: Allen & Unwin, 157–80.

—— (1959) 'Where are we?' *Cold Spring Harbor Symposia on Quantitative Biology* 24: 1–14.

—— (1963) *Animal Species and Evolution*, Cambridge, Mass.: Harvard University Press.

—— (1988) *Towards a New Philosophy of Biology: Observations of an Evolutionist*, Cambridge, Mass.: Belknap.

Mayr, E. and W. Provine (ed) (1980) *The Evolutionary Synthesis: Perspectives on the Unification of Biology*, Cambridge, Mass.: Harvard University Press.

McMullin, E. (1983) 'Values in science', *PSA 1982*, ed. P. D. Asquith and T. Nickles, East Lansing, Mich.: Philosophy of Science Association, 3–28.

McNeill, M. (1987) *Under the Banner of Science: Erasmus Darwin and His Age*, Manchester: Manchester University Press.

Midgley, M. (1979) 'Gene-juggling', *Philosophy* 54: 439–58.

—— (1985) *Evolution as Religion: Strange Hopes and Stranger Fears*, London: Methuen.

—— (1992) *Science as Salvation: A Modern Myth and its Meaning*, London: Routledge.

Mitman, G. (1992) *The State of Nature: Ecology, Community, and American Social Thought, 1900–1950*, Chicago: University of Chicago Press.

Moore, G. E. (1903) *Principia Ethica*, Cambridge: Cambridge University Press.

Moore, J. (1979) *The Post-Darwinian Controversies*, Cambridge: Cambridge University Press.

Morgan, E. (1972) *The Descent of Woman*, London: Souvenir.

Murphy, J. (1982) *Evolution, Morality, and the Meaning of Life*, Totowa, NJ: Rowman & Littlefield.

Nagel, E. (1961) *The Structure of Science*, London: Routledge & Kegan Paul.

Nagel, T. (1986) *The View from Nowhere*, New York: Oxford University Press.

Nitecki, M. (ed.) (1988) *Evolutionary Progress*, Chicago: University of Chicago Press.

Nozick, R. (1981) *Philosophical Explanations*, Cambridge, Mass.: Harvard University Press.

Ospovat, D. (1981) *The Development of Darwin's Theory*, Cambridge: Cambridge University Press.

Oster, G. and E. O. Wilson (1978) *Caste and Ecology in the Social Insects*, Princeton: Princeton University Press.

Outram, D. (1984) *Georges Cuvier: Vocation, Science and Authority in Post Revolutionary France*, Manchester: Manchester University Press.

Owen, R. (1834) 'On the generation of the marsupial animals, with a description of the impregnated uterus of the kangaroo', *Philosophical Transactions* 333–64.

Parker, G. (1978) 'Searching for mates', in *Behavioural Ecology: An Evolutionary Approach*, ed. J. Krebs and N. Davies, Sunderland, Mass.: Sinauer.

Peckham, M. (ed.) (1959) *The 'Origin of Species' by Charles Darwin: A Variorum Text*, Philadelphia: University of Pennsylvania Press.

Peel, J. D. Y. (1971) *Herbert Spencer: The Evolution of a Sociologist*, London: Heinemann.

Pilbeam, D. (1984) 'The descent of Hominoids and Hominids', *Scientific American* 250 (3): 84–97.

Pittenger, M. (1994) *American Socialists and Evolutionary Thought, 1870–1920*, Madison, Wisconsin: University of Wisconsin Press.

Plantinga, A. (1991) 'An evolutionary argument against naturalism', *Logos* 12: 27–49.

Pollard, S. (1968) *The Idea of Progress*, London: Watts.

Popper, K. R. (1959) *The Logic of Scientific Discovery*, London: Hutchinson.

—— (1963) *Conjectures and Refutations*, London: Routledge & Kegan Paul.

—— (1970) 'Normal science and its dangers', in *Criticism and the Growth of Knowledge*, ed. I. Lakatos and A. Musgrave, Cambridge: Cambridge University Press, 51–8.

—— (1972) *Objective Knowledge*, Oxford: Oxford University Press.

—— (1974) 'Intellectual autobiography', *The Philosophy of Karl Popper*, ed. P. A. Schilpp, La Salle, Ill.: Open Court, 3–18.

—— (1976) *Unended Quest: An Intellectual Autobiography*, La Salle, Ill.: Open Court.

Provine, W. (1986) *Sewall Wright and Evolutionary Biology*, Chicago: University of Chicago Press.

Pusey, J. R. (1983) *China and Charles Darwin*, Cambridge, Mass.: Harvard University Press.

Putnam, H. (1981) *Reason, Truth, and History*, Cambridge: Cambridge University Press.

—— (1982) 'Why reason can't be naturalized', *Synthese* 52: 3–23.

Rainger, R. (1991) *An Agenda for Antiquity: Henry Fairfield Osborn and Vertebrate Paleontology at the American Museum of Natural History 1890–1935*, Tuscaloosa: University of Alabama Press.

Raphael, D. D. (1958) 'Darwinism and ethics', in *A Century of Darwin*, ed. S. A. Barnet, London: Heinemann, 334–59.

Raup, D. and S. M. Stanley (1971), *Principles of Paleontology*, San Francisco: W. H. Freeman.

Rawls, J. (1971) *A Theory of Justice*, Cambridge, Mass.: Harvard University Press.

—— (1980) 'Kantian constructivism in moral theory', *Journal of Philosophy* 77: 515–72.

Reidl, R. (1984) *Biology of Knowledge: The Evolutionary Basis of Reason*, Chichester: Wiley.

Reynolds, V. and R. Tanner (1983) *The Biology of Religion*, London: Longman.

Richards, R. J. (1986a) 'A defense of evolutionary ethics', *Biology and Philosophy* 1: 265–93.

—— (1986b) 'Justification through scientific faith: a rejoinder', *Biology and Philosophy* 1: 337–54.

—— (1987) *Darwin and the Emergence of Evolutionary Theories of Mind and Behavior*, Chicago: University of Chicago Press.

—— (1989) 'Dutch objections to evolutionary ethics', *Biology and Philosophy* 4: 331–43.

—— (1992) *The Meaning of Evolution: The Morphological Construction and Ideological Reconstruction of Darwin's Theory*, Chicago: University of Chicago Press.

Rifkin, J. (1984) *Algeny: A New Word – A New World*, New York: Penguin.

Rorty, R. (1979) *Philosophy and the Mirror of Nature*, Princeton: Princeton University Press.

Rose, S. (1982) *Against Biological Determinism*, London: Allison & Busby.

Rottschaeffer, W. A. and D. Martinsen (1990) 'Really taking Darwin seriously: An alternative to Michael Ruse's Darwinian metaethics', *Biology and Philosophy* 5: 149–73.

—— (1991) 'The insufficiency of supervenient explanations of moral actions: Really taking Darwin and the naturalistic fallacy seriously', *Biology and Philosophy* 6: 439–45.

Rudwick, M. J. S. (1972) *The Meaning of Fossils*, New York: Science History Publications.

Ruse, M. (1969) 'Definitions of species in biology', *British Journal for the Philosophy of Science* 20: 97–119.

—— (1973a) *The Philosophy of Biology*, London: Hutchinson.

—— (1973b) 'The value of analogical models in science', *Dialogue* 12: 246–53.

—— (1975a) 'Charles Darwin and artificial selection', *Journal of the History of Ideas* 36: 339–50.

—— (1975b) 'Charles Darwin's theory of evolution: An analysis', *Journal of the History of Biology* 8: 219–41.

—— (1975c) 'Darwin's debt to philosophy: an examination of the influence of the philosophical ideas of John F. W. Herschel and William Whewell, on the development of Charles Darwin's theory of evolution', *Studies in History and Philosophy of Science* 6: 159–81.

—— (1975d) 'The relationship between science and religion in Britain, 1830–1870', *Church History* 44: 505–22.

—— (1976) 'The scientific methodology of William Whewell', *Centaurus* 20: 227–57.

—— (1977) 'Is biology different from physics?' in *Laws, Logic, and Life*, ed. R. Colodny, 89–127, Pittsburgh: University of Pittsburgh Press.

—— (1979a) 'Philosophical factors in the Darwinian Revolution', in *Pragmatism and Purpose*, ed. F. Wilson, Toronto: University of Toronto Press, 220–35.

—— (1979b) *Sociobiology: Sense or Nonsense?*, Dordrecht, Holland: Reidel.

—— (1979c) *The Darwinian Revolution: Science Red in Tooth and Claw*, Chicago: University of Chicago Press.

—— (1980) 'Charles Darwin and group selection', *Annals of Science* 37: 615–30.

—— (1981) 'What kind of revolution occurred in geology?', *PSA 1978*, ed. P. Asquith and I. Hacking, East Lansing, Mich.: Philosophy of Science Association, 240–73. Reprinted in M. Ruse (1989a), *The Darwinian Paradigm: Essays on its History, Philosophy and Religious Implication*, London: Routledge, 55–89.

—— (1982) *Darwinism Defended: A Guide to the Evolution Controversies*, Reading, Mass.: Addison-Wesley.

—— (1985) 'Is rape wrong on Andromeda? An introduction to extraterrestrial evolution, science, and morality', in *Extraterrestrials: Science and Alien Intelligence*, ed. E. Regis, Cambridge: Cambridge University Press, 43–78.

—— (1986) *Taking Darwin Seriously: A Naturalistic Approach to Philosophy*, Oxford: Blackwell.

—— (1988a) *Homosexuality: A Philosophical Inquiry*, Oxford: Blackwell.

—— (1988b) 'Molecules to men: the concept of progress in evolutionary biology', in *Evolutionary Progress*, ed. M. Nitecki, Chicago: University of Chicago Press, 97–128.

—— (ed.) (1988c) *But is it Science? The Philosophical Question in the Creation/Evolution Controversy*, Buffalo, NY: Prometheus.

—— (1989a) *The Darwinian Paradigm: Essays on its History, Philosophy and Religious Implications*, London: Routledge.

—— (1989b) 'Great expectations', *Quarterly Review of Biology* 64: 463–8.

—— (1989c) 'Is the theory of punctuated equilibria a new paradigm?' *Journal of Social and Biological Structures* 12: 195–212.

—— (1990) 'Evolutionary ethics and the search for predecessors: Kant, Hume, and all the way back to Aristotle?', *Social Philosophy and Policy* 8 (1): 59–87.

—— (1993) 'Evolution and progress', *Trends in Ecology and Evolution* 8(2): 55–9.

—— (1994) 'From belief to unbelief – and halfway back', *Zygon* 29: 25–35.

—— (1995) *Monad to Man: The Concept of Progress in Evolutionary Biology*, Cambridge, Mass.: Harvard University Press.

Ruse, M. and E. O. Wilson. (1985), 'The evolution of morality', *New Scientist* 1478: 108–28.

—— (1986) 'Moral philosophy as applied science', *Philosophy* 61: 173–92.

Russell, E. S. (1916) *Form and Function: A Contribution to the History of Animal Morphology*, London: John Murray.

Russett, C. E. (1966) *The Concept of Equilibrium in American Social Thought*, New Haven: Yale University Press.

—— (1976) *Darwin in America: The Intellectual Response, 1865–1912*, San Francisco: Freeman.

—— (1989) *Sexual Science*, Cambridge, Mass.: Harvard University Press.

Salmon, W. (1973) *Logic* (second edn), Englewood Cliffs: Prentice Hall.

Sebright, J. (1809) 'The art of improving the breeds of domestic animals in a letter addressed to the Right Hon. Sir Joseph Banks, K.B.' London: privately printed.

Secord, J. A. (1989) 'Behind the veil: Robert Chambers and "Vestiges"', in *History, Humanity and Evolution: Essays for John C. Greene*, ed. J. R. Moore, Cambridge: Cambridge University Press, 165–94.

Segerstrale, U. (1985) 'Colleagues in conflict: An "in vitro" analysis of the sociobiology debate', *Biology and Philosophy* 1: 53–88.

Simpson, G. G. (1944) *Tempo and Mode in Evolution*, New York: Columbia University Press.

—— (1950) *The Meaning of Evolution*, New Haven, Conn.: Yale University Press.

—— (1953) *The Major Features of Evolution*, New York: Columbia University Press.

Singer, P. (1981) *The Expanding Circle: Ethics and Sociobiology*, New York: Farrar, Straus, and Giroux.

Skelton, P. (ed.) (1993) *Evolution: A Biological and Palaeontological Approach*, Wokingham, England: Addison-Wesley.

Smith, A. (1937) *The Wealth of Nations*, New York: Modern Library (first published 1776).

—— (1976) *The Theory of Moral Sentiments*, ed. D. D. Raphael and A. L. Macfie, Oxford: Oxford University Press (first published 1759).

Sober, E. (1984) *The Nature of Selection*, Cambridge, Mass.: MIT Press.

—— (1993) 'Did evolution make us psychological egoists?' in *Pittsburgh Studies in the Philosophy of Science*, ed. J. Earman, Pittsburgh: University of Pittsburgh Press.

—— (1994) 'Prospects for an evolutionary ethics', in *From a Biological Point of View*, Cambridge: Cambridge University Press, 93–113.

Sorel, T. (1991) *Scientism: Philosophy and the Infatuation with Science*, London: Routledge.

Spadefora, D. (1990) *The Idea of Progress in Eighteenth Century Britain*, New Haven, Conn.: Yale University Press.

Spencer, H. (1851) *Social Statics: Or, the Conditions Essential to Human Happiness Specified, and the First of them Developed*, London: Chapman.

—— (1857) 'Progress: Its laws and cause', *Westminster Review* 67: 244–67.

—— (1864) *Principles of Biology*, London: Williams & Norgate.

—— (1868) *Essays: Scientific, Political, and Speculative*, London: Williams & Norgate.

—— (1892) *The Principles of Ethics*, London: Williams & Norgate.

—— (1904) *Autobiography*, London: Williams & Norgate.

Stanley, S. M. (1975) 'A theory of evolution above the species level', *Proceedings of the National Academy of Sciences* 72: 646–50.

—— (1979) *Macroevolution, Pattern and Process*, San Francisco: W. H. Freeman.

Stebbins, G. L. (1950) *Variation and Evolution in Plants*, New York: Columbia University Press.

—— (1969) *The Basis of Progressive Evolution*, Chapel Hill, North Carolina: University of North Carolina Press.

Stebbins, G. L. and F. J. Ayala (1981), 'Is a new evolutionary synthesis necessary?' *Science* 213: 967–71.

Stich, S. (1985) 'Could man be an irrational animal?' *Synthese* 64: 115–35.

Stroud, B. (1981) 'Evolution and the necessities of thought', *Pragmatism and Purpose*, ed. L. W. Sumner, F. Wilson and J. Slater, Toronto: University of Toronto Press, 236–47.

—— (1984) *Scepticism*, Oxford: Oxford University Press.

Suppe, F. (1974) *The Structure of Scientific Theories*, Urbana: University of Illinois Press.

Taylor, P. J. and A. S. Blum (1991) 'Ecosystems as circuits: diagrams and the limits of physical analogies', *Biology and Philosophy* 6: 255–74.

Taylor, P. W. (ed.) (1978) *Problems of Moral Philosophy*, Belmont, Calif.: Wadsworth.

Teilhard de Chardin, P. (1955) *The Phenomenon of Man*, New York: Harper.

Templeton, A. R. (1980), 'Macroevolution', *Evolution* 34: 1224–7.

Thagard, P. (1980) 'Against evolutionary epistemology', in *PSA 1980*, ed. P. Asquith and R. N. Giere, East Lansing, Mich.: Philosophy of Science Association, 187–96.

Thomas, L. (1986) 'Biological moralism', *Biology and Philosophy* 1: 316–25.

Thompson, D. W. (1917) *On Growth and Form*, Cambridge: Cambridge University Press.

Thornhill, R. and N. Thornhill (1983) 'Human rape: An evolutionary analysis', *Ethology and Sociobiology* 4: 37–73.

Todes, D. (1989) *Darwin Without Malthus: The Struggle for Existence in Russian Evolutionary Thought*, New York: Oxford University Press.

Toulmin, S. (1967) 'The evolutionary development of science', *American Scientist* 57: 456–71.

—— (1972) *Human Understanding*, Oxford: Clarendon Press.

Trigg, R. (1986) 'Evolutionary ethics', *Biology and Philosophy* 1: 325–35.

Trivers, R. (1971) 'The evolution of reciprocal altruism', *Quarterly Review of Biology* 46: 35–57.

Turner, J. R. G. (1985) 'Fisher's evolutionary faith and the challenge of mimicry', in *Oxford Surveys in Evolutionary Biology*, ed. R. Dawkins and M. Ridley, Oxford University Press: Oxford, 159–96.

Van den Berghe, P. (1979) *Human Family Systems*, New York: Elsevier.

—— (1983) 'Human inbreeding avoidance: Culture in nature', *Behavioral and Brain Sciences* 6: 91–124.

Vermeij, G. J. (1987) *Evolution and Escalation*, Princeton, NJ: Princeton University Press.

Vine, F. J. (1966) 'Spreading on the ocean floor: New evidence', *Science* 154: 1405–15.

Vine, F. J. and D. H. Matthews (1963) 'Magnetic anomalies over oceanic ridges', *Nature* 199: 947–9.

Vollmer, G. (1987) 'On supposed circularities in an empirically oriented epistemology', in *Evolutionary Epistemology, Theory of Rationality, and the Sociology of Knowledge*, ed. G. Radnitzky and W. W. Bartley, La Salle, Ill.: Open Court, 163–200.

Voorzanger, B. (1987) 'No norms and no nature – the moral relevance of evolutionary biology', *Biology and Philosophy* 2: 253–70.

Vorzimmer, P. (1970) *Charles Darwin: The Years of Controversy*, Philadelphia: Temple University Press.

Vrba, E. S. and S. J. Gould (1986) 'The hierarchical expansion of sorting, and selection: sorting and selection cannot be equated', *Paleobiology* 12: 217–28.

Vucinich, A. (1988) *Darwin in Russian Thought*, Berkeley: University of California Press.

Waddington, C. H. (1956) *The Strategy of the Genes*, London, Allen & Unwin.

—— (1960) *The Ethical Animal*, London: Allen & Unwin.

—— (1966) *Principles of Embryology*, New York: Macmillan.

Wade, M. J. (1978) 'A critical view of the models of group selection', *Quarterly Review of Biology* 53: 101–14.

Wagar, W. (1972) *Good Tidings: The Belief in Progress from Darwin to Marcuse*, Bloomington, Ind.: Indiana University Press.

Wallace, A. R. (1870a) *Contributions to the Theory of Natural Selection*, London: Macmillan.

—— (1870b) 'The limits of natural selection as applied to man', *Contributions to the Theory of Natural Selection*, London: Macmillan, 332–715.

—— (1905) *My Life*. London: Chapman & Hall.

Wallwork, E. (1982) 'Thou shalt love thy neighbour as thyself: The Freudian critique', *Journal of Religious Ethics* 10: 264–319.

Wason, P. C. and P. N. Johnson-Laird (1972) *The Psychology of Reasoning: Structure and Content*, London: Batsford.

Weber, M. (1972) *Wirtschaft und Gesellschaft* (fifth edn), Mohr-Siebeck, Tübingen (English trans. (1968), *Economy and Society*, Bedminster NY).

West Eberhard, M. J. (1975) 'The evolution of social behavior by kin selection', *Quarterly Review of Biology* 50: 1–33.

Whewell, W. (1837) *History of the Inductive Sciences*, London: Parker.

—— (1840) *The Philosophy of the Inductive Sciences*, London: Parker.

White, J. F. and S. J. Gould (1965) 'The interpretation of the coefficient in the allometric equation', *American Naturalist* 99: 5–18.

Williams, G. C. (1966) *Adaptation and Natural Selection*, Princeton: Princeton University Press.

—— (1975) *Sex and Evolution*, Princeton: Princeton University Press.

—— (1988) 'Huxley's evolution and ethics in sociobiological perspective', *Zygon* 23: 383–407.

—— (1989) 'A sociobiological expansion of "Evolution and Ethics" ', in

'Evolution and Ethics': T. H. Huxley's 'Evolution and Ethics' with New Essays on Its Victorian and Sociobiological Context, ed. J. Paradis and G. C. Williams, Princeton: Princeton University Press, 179–219.

Williams, P. (1990) 'Evolved ethics re-examined: The theory of Robert J. Richards', Biology and Philosophy 5: 451–7.

Williamson, P. G. (1981) 'Paleontological documentation of speciation in Cenozoic molluscs from Turkana basin', Nature 293: 437–43.

—— (1985) 'Punctuated equilibrium, morphological stasis and the paleontological documentation of speciation', Biological Journal of the Linnaean Society of London 26: 307–24.

Wilson, D. S. (1992) 'On the relationship between evolutionary and psychological definitions of altruism and selfishness', Biology and Philosophy 7: 61–8.

Wilson, E. O. (1971) The Insect Societies, Cambridge, Mass.: Belknap Press.

—— (1975) Sociobiology: The New Synthesis, Cambridge, Mass.: Harvard University Press.

—— (1978) On Human Nature, Cambridge, Mass.: Cambridge University Press.

—— (1984) Biophilia, Cambridge, Mass.: Harvard University Press.

Wilson, E. O. and F. M. Peter (eds) (1988) Biodiversity, Washington, DC: National Academy Press.

Wiltshire, D. (1978) The Social and Political Thought of Herbert Spencer, Oxford: Oxford University Press.

Wimsatt, W. (1986) 'Developmental constraints, generative entrenchment and the innate-acquired distinction', in Integrating Scientific Disciplines, ed. W. Bechtel, Dordrecht: Nijhoff, 185–208.

—— (1987) 'False models as means to truer theories', in Neutral Models in Biology, ed. M. Nitecki and A. Hoffman, Oxford: Oxford University Press, 23–55.

Winsor, M. P. (1991) Reading the Shape of Nature: Comparative Zoology at the Agassiz Museum, Chicago: University of Chicago Press.

Wolff, R. P. (1960) 'Hume's theory of mental activity', Philosophical Review 49: 289–310.

Woodruff, D. S. (1980) 'Evolution: The paleobiological view', Science 208: 716–17.

Woolcock, P. (1993) 'Ruse's Darwinian meta-ethics: A critique', Biology and Philosophy 8: 423–39.

Wright, S. (1931) 'Evolution in Mendelian populations', Genetics 16: 97–159.

—— (1932) 'The roles of mutation, inbreeding, crossbreeding and selection in evolution', Proceedings of the Sixth International Congress of Genetics 1: 356–66.

Young, R. (1985) Darwin's Metaphor, Cambridge: Cambridge University Press.

INDEX